ARMS
CANADA

ARMS

The Deadly Business of Military Exports

CANADA

ERNIE REGEHR

James Lorimer & Company, Publishers
Toronto, 1987

Cover design: Brant Cowie/Artplus Ltd.
Cover illustration: Peter Mossman/Graphcomm Group
Figure illustrations: Dave Hunter

Canadian Cataloguing in Publication Data
   Regehr, Ernie, 1941—
      Arms Canada
   Includes index.
   ISBN 0-88862-960-5 (bound) ISBN 0-88862-959-1 (pbk.)
   1. Munitions - Canada. 2. Munitions - Political
   aspects - Canada. I Title.

HD9743.C32R44 1987   338.4'76234'0971
                                       C86-094534-0

James Lorimer & Company, Publishers
Egerton Ryerson Memorial Building
35 Britain Street
Toronto, Ontario M5A 1R7

Printed and bound in Canada
6 5 4 3 2 1 87 88 89 90 91 92

to Matthew, Joel and Stefan

Contents

Acknowledgements

In the course of producing this volume I have become indebted to many people. I would like to express my thanks to my colleagues on the board and staff of Project Ploughshares, all of whom were more than patient while my primary attention was devoted to this project. I am especially indebted to several of my staff colleagues. Kathy Sage typed and corrected large sections of the manuscript and was an important help in various stages of preparing drafts. Carolyn Musselman-Wigboldus assisted in the research, especially by maintaining an efficient library and by helping to track down a variety of sources and references. Ken Epps also assisted in the research, primarily through his management of the Ploughshares Military Industry Database. In particular, Ken prepared appendix 1 on indirect Canadian military exports and provided notes on several of the companies discussed. Bill Robinson assisted Ken Epps in the preparation of appendix 2 on Canadian military components for nuclear systems. Simon Rosenblum, as always, was more than generous with advice, commentary and criticism on a variety of the issues addressed. I am grateful to all of these friends and colleagues.

I would also like to thank Ted Mumford for his initial encouragement and guidance on this project. I especially want to thank Robert Chodos for his sensitivity and his many comments and suggestions in the course of editing the manuscript.

I am the most indebted and grateful to Nancy Regehr. Through this project, as in all other endeavours, I have been sustained professionally and personally by her discerning criticism and her constant support.

Ernie Regehr

Introduction

Making War for All the Right Reasons

Canadians were surprised, and many were angered, when they learned in late 1986 that Canadian-built helicopter engine parts were going to Iran. The anger stemmed from the very real possibility that these engine parts might find their way into the Iran-Iraq War and thus help, in a small way, to sustain a steady, murderous conflict that has claimed more than 500,000 combat victims in six years — an average of 250 a day.

The fear that equipment with military applications might end up in the war was well-founded. While the engine parts were apparently intended for civilian helicopters, the Iranian armed forces use the same model of helicopter in a military version and the parts, with some modification, are interchangeable. Furthermore, all of Iranian society is mobilized for war. About a third of the national budget is devoted to war-related expenditures, but even that figure substantially understates the war's real impact.[1] Reports from Iran indicate that the government has shifted much of the burden of the war to the voluntary sector, relying not only on donated time but also on gifts from the public of everything from cash and food to major equipment such as trucks. In such an environment, transport helicopters, whether designated as military or as civilian, stand a rather good chance of participating in mobilization for war somewhere along the way.

So the anger of Canadians was understandable. It is a little more difficult, however, to explain the surprise. Iran has been a preferred military customer of Canada's for more than two decades. When the Shah was still on his throne, kept there through a combination of American military patronage and his own notorious secret police, SAVAK, the Canadian government's military trade bureau had a representative in Tehran. Iran under the Shah represented a windfall market, and while Canada never got in on the windfall, it certainly tried. Canada sold about $60 million worth of military commodities to Iran during the 1970s, and six times during the decade Iran made the annual list of the top twenty non-U.S. recipients of Canadian military commodities.

This was a period during which Amnesty International reported that "no country in the world has a worse record in human rights than Iran."[2] For Canada, this does not seem to have been a relevant factor, guidelines limiting arms sales to human rights violators notwithstanding. More to the point was the fact that the Shah was buying all the arms he could manage — in fact quite a lot more than he could manage — from the United States. This created a special opportunity for Canada, deriving from the particular orientation of the Canadian arms industry towards supplying components for U.S. weapons. In most situations, this orientation made sales to the Third World hard for Canada to get, but the concentration of American major weapons systems in Iran promised a Third World haven for Canadian spare parts.

Then came the 1980s, the Ayatollah Khomeini, and the war with Iraq, and we are obviously still at it. Some things have changed, however — notably secrecy. Ottawa has never been fully forthcoming about Canadian arms sales, but in the 1980s official information about Canada's military exports has dried up completely. This means that one cannot be entirely certain about direct military sales to Iran during the 1980s, but the evidence points to business as usual. There is no longer a military trade representative in Tehran, but Canadian military commodities have been going to both sides of the Iran-Iraq war. Both countries have received military helicopters and fixed-wing aircraft with Canadian engines through third parties since the war began. Brazilian military trainer aircraft with Canadian engines have gone to Iraq via Egypt. Similar Swiss military trainers, with the same model of Canadian engine, have been sold to Iran. And Italian helicopters built under licence from the United States, again with Canadian engines, have gone to Iraq.

Military exports are obviously an expression of an entrepreneurial spirit. If the inalienable right to national defence, or even the exporting country's strategic interests, were the motive for arms sales, that country would not be likely to sell to both sides in a war (except perhaps to debilitate the two sides and make them more amenable to manipulation in the postwar environment). And while Adnan Khashoggi and his Canadian associates may be the most flamboyant expression of the weapons-for-profit spirit, in the international arms market they and their kind are the bit players. Jet-set billionaires become useful agents when misguided politicians try to pull deals like the arms-for-Iran-and-profits-for-the-contras caper that by early 1987 had become the subject of multiple investigations in Washington, but that is not where the real arms trade action takes place. The really high-flying arms dealers are not sheiks and soldiers of fortune, but middle-level bureaucrats in drab government offices. It is these institutional arms dealers who are the primary subject of this book.

It is in such government offices that the entrepreneurial spirit awakened by the Iran-Iraq War has been most in evidence. According to the Stockholm International Peace Research Institute (SIPRI), the number of governments which have become above-the-table, "legitimate" military suppliers for each side has increased dramatically during the war: in the case of Iraq, from three regular suppliers in 1980 to eighteen in 1984, and in the case of Iran, from five to seventeen.[3] The SIPRI study further showed that the United States, the Soviet Union, China, France, Italy, East Germany, Switzerland, North Korea and Brazil all have supplied major weapons to both sides during the war. The Iran-Iraq War is frequently portrayed as an irrational conflict. To portray the suppliers of the instruments of war, our choice of adjectives would be between irrational and diabolical.

Canada is not among the countries that have supplied major weapons to this war. It is not clear, however, whether this is a matter of principle, or whether it is simply a consequence of the fact that Canada has few major weapons to sell. What is clear is that Canada makes no effort to control the sale of weapons with Canadian components — even when these are major components, such as engines, which can account for as much as one-fifth of the total system price.

The Iran-Iraq War illustrates the fact that the arms industry is no longer the monopoly of a few. Military production capabilities for sophisticated weapons systems now exist throughout the world. But few countries need a fully integrated weapons industry because weapons are increasingly built by international consortia: for example, Iraq buys fixed-wing aircraft with Canadian engines from Egypt, which builds them under licence from Brazil. This business is obviously strictly business.

The international arms trade that currently sustains and extends the Iran-Iraq War, and has sustained more than a hundred other wars since 1945, is an accumulation of good business decisions. Arms, in other words, are sold for all the right reasons. James Kelleher, at the time Canada's trade minister, had not hit upon a new idea when he told Canadian trade commissioners and military producers in 1986 that their "success in expanding defence and high technology exports is one of the keys to some of the things this country needs most — more research and development, more high-quality jobs, and more prosperity for all Canadians."[4] The $50 billion annual arms trade is a tribute to the fact that Canada is not alone in looking to arms exports for a route to easy prosperity.

Nor was External Affairs Minister Joe Clark on to a new thing when he went to Saudi Arabia in the spring of 1986 to sell the Saudi royal family a fleet of armoured vehicles, and defended the proposed deal as part of Canada's special contribution to peace and security in the region. External Affairs officials were said to be concerned about the threat posed to Saudi Arabia by Iran, and selling the Saudis some armoured vehicles was, it seemed, the least we could do. Clark and his Saudi counterpart, Prince Saud, were apparently in agreement that these weapons, should the sale go through, would aid peace and would be used "only for self-defence."

To be sure, some members of the Canada-Israel Committee didn't see it quite that way, while other observers, aware that Saudi Arabia is a prominent supplier of weapons to Iraq, permitted themselves at least to wonder about the ultimate destination of the Canadian vehicles. For Clark and Prince Saud, however, the issue was clear. While both were no doubt aware that a runaway worldwide arms trade sustains wars that collectively have produced twenty million combat deaths since 1945, with the Iran-Iraq War still claiming several thousand each month, they were confident that this sale would be different. The prince had said, had he not, that these armoured vehicles would help to make Saudi Arabia "strong and respected" in the region, a condition that could not but advance the cause of peace.[5]

A decade earlier, another Canadian cabinet minister, Mitchell Sharp, had claimed a similar and special virtue for Canadian military exports. Sharp told the House of Commons that "there are certain types of arms that might be considered arms for warlike purposes and we do not supply those. Many of the things we supply are not intended for the purpose of killing people."[6]

Canadian cabinet ministers may be the last to know, but it turns out that no arms seem to be sold with the intention of killing people — this is not a peculiarly Canadian claim. All weapons, at least from the point of view of the vendor, are strictly in the service of peace. The U.S. Air Force is well aware of this and accordingly designates its fighter aircraft sales programs with the prefix "peace." Thus sales to Israel, Saudi Arabia, Egypt and Japan are code-named "Peace Fox", "Peace Sun", "Peace Farrow", "Peace Marble", and "Peace Eagle."[7]

If President Reagan can, without apparent embarrassment, christen as "Peacekeeper" a missile that could destroy ten cities the size of Winnipeg within thirty minutes of the command to launch, then perhaps

Joe Clark should be entitled to claim his few armoured cars as servants of peace. It may, therefore, seem somewhat indelicate to describe Canada's exports of military trucks, microcircuits, aircraft shock absorbers, sonobuoys and the like as expanding the world's capacity to make war. After all, if military forces "deter" attack, "defend" the weak, "advance" the national interest, "preserve" order and "maintain" the peace — just about anything, it seems, but fight wars — then military production, far from making war, must, in the words of the U.S. Air Force, be the profession of peace. And if others can call multibillion-dollar, weapons-induced deficits "economic recovery," why can't James Kelleher expect Canadian arms sales to produce a new age of prosperity for this country?

Some people in government and industry see a new arms sales push as an attractive option. The pressure is on to "liberalize" Canada's arms export policy and to find new markets for Canadian military technology. Col. W.N. Russell, now retired from the Canadian Forces and a frequent writer on Canadian defence industry issues, speaks for others when he calls on Canada to emulate France in military exports:

> The French policy regarding the export of military equipment should be considered, at least in passing. The French policy is, of course, very liberal, encouraging defence exports because of their contribution to the economy and because such exports are necessary to help foster the self-supporting armament industry. It is doubted whether Canada would or should adopt an equally liberal export policy. But, if emphasis is to be given to creating work in Canada, and if we too wish to become more self-supporting in our capability to manufacture defence products, then a more broadminded and aggressive export policy should be considered.[8]

Thus, the international traffic in arms is not so much a problem to be solved as an expression of broadmindedness that should presumably be the pursuit of all freethinking people. Of course, military producers and their government sponsors do sometimes acknowledge that there is indeed a deadly and destructive arms race and that, overall, too much is spent on weapons of war. Invariably, however, they are convinced that their particular production is either incidental to the problem or else part of the solution.

These claims are part of official Canadian rationales for the export of military commodities, which emphasize either solemn responsibility or irrelevance. The responsibility approach appeals to the right of all states, notably those that have no indigenous military production capability, to acquire military equipment sufficient to meet their and control social and political developments in regions where these powers deem their national interests to be threatened represent social engineering on a frightening scale. The major powers' armed forces are trained and equipped not to preserve national institutions and to defend borders but to transcend and violate borders and to intervene in the affairs of other nation-states, and they are deployed not for the maintenance of global peace but for the protection and aggrandizement of the interests of their sponsors.

But despite the world's extraordinary capacity to destroy, and despite the ordinary human needs that go unmet, the world continues to add to its destructive capacity at a ferocious rate. Canada's production of military commodities for export has tripled within the past six years. This is not at all to say that Canada is a leader in military destructive capacity, but only that global war-making is growing exponentially and Canada is not averse to taking advantage of it. The acceleration of the arms race, from the development of nuclear first-strike and war-fighting weapons to the global marketing of the tools of torture and other repression technology, all in the face of growing military domination, famine and gross and systematic violation of human rights, is tragic proof that something has gone terribly awry in global decision-making processes.

Though weapons have come to undermine our military security and frustrate our social and economic security, they continue to get priority treatment. Vast propaganda machines are employed to justify the devotion of the globe's best scientific and engineering minds to the development of yet more destructive capacity. So effective is this propaganda that we come to accept the rationality of assertions that new weapons systems are needed the better to negotiate their removal, that we build weapons only so that we won't have to use them, and that villages sometimes do unfortunately have to be destroyed in order to save them.

To charge that making weapons is making war is neither a rhetorical excess nor a blanket rejection of all state force. Rather, it is an acknowledgement that, given the obscene level of destructiveness already available, the burden of proof is now on any nation or producer that proposes to add to this extraordinary level of destructive power. If you plan to produce still more weapons, it is up to you to prove that you are not simply adding to the obscenity. And if we recapture a capacity for rational judgement, it will not be an easy case to make.

The American disarmament activist and engineer-economist Seymour Melman says that "disarmament means diminishing the decision-power of the war-making machine."[12] Within the United States, as he has shown in his classic study of the "permanent war economy" and other writings, the war-making machine casts a long shadow. Melman notes in particular the collusion between the Department of Defense, the administration and the military industry. The United States boasts a wide literature on the military-industrial complex (the bureaucracy can appropriately be added to the complex, in both the United States and the Soviet Union). This literature reflects a broad consensus within American society that the military industry has acquired extraordinary influence over defence and foreign policy decision-making — what Melman calls "decision-power." In other words, little progress will be made towards disarmament until the decision-power of this war-making machine is brought under control.

In the following pages, the question of the nature and extent of Canada's place in the international war-making machine is addressed, and the degree of the war-making machine's "decision-power" within this country is explored.

While popular mythology portrays Canada's military industry and military forces as small, weak and irrelevant, a second look shows that this picture is deceptive. This does not mean that the Canadian military industry and armed forces are large, strong and of key global importance. Rather, the point is that in Canada too, the military production industry and its supporters in government represent decision-power. The question that should occupy the attention of Canadians is the extent to which this decision-power — which in the case of Canada is fully integrated into an international war-making machine — contributes to or undermines constructive Canadian policies for peace and justice. John M. Treddenick, an economist at the Royal Military College of Canada who has documented the Canadian government's use of military procurement as an instrument of economic policy, warns: "The danger is that neither Canada's security interests nor its economic interests will be effectively addressed. But more importantly, the intermingling of military and economic considerations may blunt the nation's sensitivity to the dangers of the arms race with the result that incentives to search for ways to reduce armament expenditures may be submerged."[13]

Canada's current approach to military production, which is primarily military production for export, undermines constructive policies for three reasons:

- Canadian military production involves Canada uncritically in military doctrines and programs that are a threat to peace;

- the structure of the military industry leaves Canada unduly vulnerable to political pressures from our primary customer, the United States, and thereby undermines Canada's capacity to assess and pursue independent and innovative foreign policy and defence options;
- Canadian military production does not deliver the economic benefits it promises.

The conclusion to be drawn from this, however, is not that Canada should eliminate military production in a grand gesture towards Canadian purity. Rather, it is that military production in Canada should be restructured to support a permanent Canadian peace initiative. For a country such as Canada, which enjoys secure and mature political and social institutions and an absence of direct military threats, the fundamental and inescapable requirement is to employ its resources in the urgent pursuit of alternative policies and technologies for the management of international conflict.

The nine chapters of this book attempt to fill in some details of Canadian military production and exports, consider their political consequences for Canada, and outline possible options. Chapter 1 provides an overview of the international arms trade and Canada's participation in it. In chapters 2 and 3, the origins of current Canadian military production arrangements are examined. The fourth chapter presents a profile of Canada's military industry today, and chapter 5 examines the federal government's efforts to promote military exports. Chapter 6 looks at the current Canadian military production relationship with the United States and Europe, while the sale of Canadian military commodities to the Third World and the system that is intended to control such exports are explored in chapter 7. Chapter 8 considers the impact of military production and exports on Canadian economic and political life. The concluding chapter explores alternative means of providing the Canadian Armed Forces with equipment appropriate to this country's security needs and obligations — including the obligation to make a sustained contribution to building international peace and controlling the international war-making machine.

1

Canada at the Global Arms Bazaar

In the early dawn of October 25, 1983, U.S. Marines staged amphibious landings at St. George's, the capital of Grenada, beginning Operation Urgent Fury, the U.S./Caribbean intervention in the tiny West Indian nation. That afternoon, in Ottawa, politcians argued over whether the Canadian government had been misled, or merely ignored, in the operation. In fact, however, Canada had already been busy at the invasion.[1]

The Marines had acted under the protection of air cover from F-15 jet fighters, whose attacks on the positions of the island's resisting forces were guided with the aid of sophisticated microcircuitry from Garrett Manufacturing Limited of Rexdale, Ontario. Pilots in the cockpits of the F-15s enjoyed a precisely controlled climate by virtue of Garrett's world-renowned electronic environmental control system, while, closer to the beach below, two UH-60A "Black Hawk" helicopters swept in on rotor blade assemblies from the St. Catharines, Ontario, plant of Fleet Aerospace Corporation. The two helicopters' Doppler navigation systems from Canadian Marconi Co. of Montreal did not, however, prevent them from being shot down by the unexpectedly heavy resistance which the invading forces encountered.

Across the island to the north, 400 U.S. Marines were arriving at Pearls Airport aboard CH-46 "Sea Knight" helicopters with hydraulic systems, engine parts and rotor assemblies supplied through the Canadian Commercial Corporation (a federal crown corporation). On return to their mother ship, the helicopter carrier *Guam*, the CH-46 were safely hauled down onto the pitching deck by an innovative recovery, assist, securing and traversing (RAST) system developed and supplied by Indal Technologies Inc. of Mississauga, Ontario.

At about the same time, C-130 "Hercules" transport aircraft, with navigational and landing gear components supplied through the Canadian Commercial Corporation, began releasing U.S. Army Ranger paratroopers 150 metres above the runway of the airport under construction at Point Salines at the southern tip of the island state.

Later in the day C-5A "Galaxy" transport aircraft began transporting additional troops and equipment, disgorging large quantities of jeeps, armoured vehicles, communications systems and other support equipment through the aft cargo doors provided by Canadair Limited of Montreal (then owned by the federal government, but now controlled by Bombardier Inc. of Montreal). Ailerons and leading wing edges on the C-5A were also provided by Canadair.

When ground troops called for air strikes, A-7 "Corsair" attack planes, with components from de Havilland Aircraft of Canada Ltd. of Downsview, Ontario (also then crown-owned, but since purchased by the Boeing aircraft company of Seattle, Washington), left the aircraft carrier USS *Independence*. Aided also by navigational components from Bristol Aerospace Limited of Winnipeg, one of the aircraft strafed and killed a U.S. Army radio operator as the result of incorrect coordinates supplied by a marine officer on the ground.

Canadian military products, not suprisingly, go where the military action is. Canada's military export guidelines include the somewhat ingenuous principle that Canadian military commodities "should not be supplied to countries involved in hostilities or where there is an imminent threat of hostilities"[2], but weapons seem to have an uncanny way of ending up on battlefields. When Israeli-built aircraft fly counter-insurgency excursions for the Salvadoran Armed Forces, Canadian industry is there. When a U.S.-built M-60 main battle tank or M-48 armoured vehicle moves through the streets of Beirut, Canadian industry is there. When U.S. F-14 fighter aircraft intercept an Egyptian airliner over the Mediterranean, or when F-111 bombers attack Tripoli, Canadian avionics are there. Canadian technology is there when Iranians fire South African-built 155-MM guns on Iraqi forces, but that doesn't stop Iraqi pilots from being trained in Swiss-built aircraft powered by Canadian engines. And when U.S. strategic nuclear missiles sit poised in their silos, each ready to destroy several Soviet cities simultaneously, Canadian aluminum supplies the fuel. With Canada supplying components to military aircraft, missiles, helicopters, submarines, surface ships, tanks, armoured vehicles and an assortment of other weapons systems, there is not much chance that Canadian military commodities will respect the government's guideline prohibiting involvement in hostilities.

Canadians are reluctant to include the role of weapons merchant in their self-definition. When it was revealed in the spring of 1986 that the

West German tank and armoured vehicle manufacturer, Thyssen Henschel, was considering establishing a plant in Cape Breton, the Ottawa *Citizen* called on the government to reject the proposal on the grounds that this was not true to "Canadians' sense of their place in the world. We are peacemakers, not arms dealers."[3] While admirably indignant, the *Citizen* was apparently unaware that, in the heart of Loyalist, Protestant southwestern Ontario, just such a plant was already building armoured vehicles for the U.S. Marines and was mounting an aggressive promotional strategy, with government support, to expand sales to the Third World.

Canadian military production, in fact, is part of a Western, transnational armaments industry, led by the major industrial powers, most notably the United States. That industry, joined by its Eastern counterparts, led by the Soviet Union, and by increasing numbers of Third World countries, supplies an international arms trade valued at $35 to $50 billion annually (dollar figures where not otherwise specified refer to Canadian dollars). Through this international "war machine," Canadian military components have in recent years been supplied for weapons systems, built mainly in the United States, that went to almost all of the world's current war zones and prominent trouble spots: Zimbabwe and Angola in southern Africa; Chad, Libya and Morocco in northern Africa; Sudan in the Horn of Africa; Egypt, Israel, Jordan, Syria, Lebanon and Saudi Arabia in the Middle East; Iran and Iraq in the Persian Gulf region; Indonesia and the Philippines in the Pacific; Pakistan, Thailand and South Korea in Asia; El Salvador and Honduras in Central America; and Chile and Argentina in South America (see appendix 1).[4]

The Worldwide Arms Trade

The global arms trade is about as hard to tabulate as it is to control.[5] But for all the obstacles to a precise accounting, virtually all sources agree on two things: the demand for weapons has increased at least tenfold in the past twenty years; and, while the market remains buoyant, the competition is getting a lot tougher. According to the United States Arms Control and Disarmament Agency (ACDA), world arms transfers (tabulated in current U.S. dollars) rose from between $3 and $4 billion per year in the early 1960s to between $30 and $35 billion per year in the early 1980s, while sales to Third World countries rose from between $1 and $2 billion to between $25 and $30 billion in the same period.[6]

In the twenty years ending in 1983, the United States and the Soviet Union supplied two thirds of all military commodities going to the Third World, but the dominance of the major powers is now challenged by the entry of a wide range of new producers into the arms-for-export competition. As recently as the period 1976 – 79, the United States and the Soviet Union jointly accounted for 65 per cent of all sales to the Third World, while the next most significant suppliers — France, Britain, West Germany and Italy — accounted for another 24 per cent. All other suppliers were left to divide the remaining 11 per cent. In 1980 – 83, however, the pattern changed, with the U.S./Soviet share dropping to 53 per cent while that of the European Big Four fell to 14.5 per cent. It was the "others" who came on strong, increasing their share to 30 per cent.[7] (A 1986 U.S. congressional study indicates, however, that in 1985 western European arms sales to the Third World accounted for 31.3 per cent of all weapons sold to the area. According to the report, western European nations have now overtaken both the United States and the Soviet Union in arms sales to the Third World.[8])

The sharp increase in the "other" category suggests the development of a much more competitive arms export environment. While it indicates the continued assertion of various smaller western and eastern European producers, and even countries such as Canada, it primarily reflects the entry of Third World producers as arms merchants in their own right. The largest Third World military producers are India and Israel, which between them represent half of all Third World production. Others include South Africa, Brazil, Taiwan, the two Koreas, and Argentina. Ninety per cent of all Third World production is accounted for by these eight leading producers.[9]

The tendency of military commodities to follow the military action is most dramatically illustrated by the Middle East, which receives half of all Third World military imports. This war-torn region has dominated the market throughout the post – World War II period, with the prominence of the other major Third World regions (Africa, Latin America, South Asia and the Far East) fluctuating according to political and military conditions. In the first half of the 1980s, Africa dominated with about 16 per cent of all imports, followed by Latin America with 13 per cent and South Asia and the Far East each with about 10 per cent (see table 1 for the top twenty Third World military importers during 1980 – 84).[10]

While the arms trade has been steadily expanding, its changing patterns reflect changes in international conditions. During the late 1950s and the 1960s, weapons transfers — more through aid than through sales — were based largely on political and military objectives. The

TABLE 1
Top 20 Third World Importers of Major Weapons
1980–84

Country	% of total Third World Imports
Egypt	10.6
Syria	10.5
Iraq	10.3
India	7.5
Libya	6.9
Saudi Arabia	6.7
Israel	4.8
Cuba	3.7
Argentina	3.1
Jordan	2.1
Taiwan	1.8
Pakistan	1.6
South Yemen	1.5
Morocco	1.5
Indonesia	1.5
Nigeria	1.3
Peru	1.3
Algeria	1.2
South Korea	1.2
Venezuela	1.2
Others	19.7
Total	100.0

Source: The Stockholm International Peace Research Institute

superpowers enjoyed a virtual monopoly as arms suppliers and used it to win and work on as many friends as possible, extending and consolidating their respective spheres of influence. Weapons exports increased by an average of 7 per cent a year during that time.

In the 1970s the emphasis was not so much on winning friends as on winning profits. Western Europeans became prominent suppliers, and the United States and the Soviet Union began to emphasize sales over aid. During the 1970s demand increased by an average of 12 per cent per year, but higher volume was not the only sign that the arms trade was burgeoning. There were at least four other measures of its escalation:

- the increased number of Third World importers;

- the proliferation of advanced weapons systems, such as supersonic fighter aircraft and short-range missiles, throughout the Third World;
- the growing number of arms production facilities in semi-industrialized countries in the Third World;
- the increased sale of repression technology — military and para-military equipment that is by design intended to be effective against civilians and dissidents or insurgents, rather than being primarily for national defence against external threats.

During the first half of the 1980s, following the peak year of 1982, there was an overall decline in demand, although current evidence suggests sales are beginning to climb once more. The decrease in demand can be attributed to several factors. First, declining oil revenues have resulted in a sharply reduced cash flow in the high-spending Middle East and Persian Gulf regions. Second, Third World countries' high debt burden has meant that less money has been available for national aggrandizement through the latest in military hardware. Fully one-fifth of the Third World's new borrowing in the past decade was directly or indirectly linked to weapons.[11] Third, the high volumes of arms imports in the late 1970s and early 1980s have produced an at least temporary market saturation. You can only use so much of this stuff short of going to war, and the worldwide supply of weapons is currently so great that even with the combination of war and planned obsolescence it is difficult to consume all that the weapons factories have to offer. And finally, the increase in domestic production capability by some prominent Third World military spenders has meant that their purchase of complete weapons systems in the international market has been reduced.

Ironically, this reduction in demand has been accompanied by much heavier competition on the supply side of the arms trade. Not only the buyers of arms but also the sellers have experienced economic downturns and growing unemployment, and many have looked to the multi-billion dollar arms market as one means of combating recession. For most of the non-superpower suppliers — who, as noted earlier, now supply the majority of weapons internationally — the motives are commercial rather than strategic. Countries like Canada and West Germany and Brazil want jobs out of the arms trade more than they want political influence. This results in aggressive salesmanship and the feeling that if we don't sell it, somebody else will.[12] It is a process that bodes ill for any attempt at genuine control of the arms trade.

One of the consequences of the aggressive salesmanship of the 1980s has been to accelerate important changes in the structure of worldwide military production. In particular, there has been a proliferation of weapons technology. The acquisition of weapons technology by more countries has immense, though often contradictory, implications. The ability to build weapons domestically creates independence from suppliers, but few emerging or semi-industrialized countries have the indigenous capital or technology to be able to develop home-grown designs.

The surplus of suppliers has meant fewer off-the-shelf orders. Buyers have acquired greater leverage and, by playing one supplier off against another, are able to insert new demands into arms trade deals. One prominent demand is the requirement that the supplier country enter into a joint production arrangement with the recipient, involving a permanent transfer of some element of the technology involved. For countries with an insufficient industrial base to enter joint production arrangements, conditions of sales may include offset purchases of commodities which the recipient country can provide. In some cases, this condition may be in the form of a barter agreement such as oil for arms. Other deals include licensed production, which may include rights to independent export marketing of the commodity (thus, Canada's production of light armoured vehicles under licence from a Swiss firm includes the right to market these vehicles to certain parts of the world). Economic recession and growing debt burdens have also meant a greater interest in extending the life of existing weapons, which in turn has created a prominent market for modernization kits (Pratt and Whitney produces engine conversion kits for Sikorsky helicopters, and Levy Auto Parts Company makes engine and drive-train modernization kits for tanks and armoured vehicles).

The Search for a Militarized Prosperity

The international arms trade derives its buoyancy from the political and economic interests it advances. Greed and lust for power are not irrelevant in a review of the political economy of the arms trade, but in most cases the motives tend to be rather more nuanced, or at least more delicately articulated. Military exports are defended and promoted as opportunities to advance a variety of widely supported and legitimate national objectives.[13] Obviously, not the least of these objectives is national security. Canadian government officials describe the basis of Canada's participation in joint defence production with the United

States and the European NATO allies as being "to provide the armed forces of our countries with the best equipment at the lowest cost, at the right time."[14] For most governments without a superpower's hegemonic ambitions, however, the proverbial bottom line is economic.

Economic incentives to export arms include the predictable interest in improving the supplier's balance of payments, creating employment and seeking technological spinoffs from military technology. A prominent interest of national governments is in compensating for the costs of their own military procurement by exporting military goods. Canadian officials of the Department of National Defence (DND), for example, give direct support to the export of military products for both strategic and economic reasons.

Strategically, they argue that Canada requires an ongoing industrial base to supply Canadian equipment needs but Canadian procurements alone are not sufficient to sustain the long-term viability of that base. Foreign military sales, in other words, are viewed as central to keeping the industry viable and retaining it as a supplier of Canadian defence needs. Without such a military industry, it is argued, Canada would find itself even more dependent than it already is, not only on imported major systems, but also on imported spare parts and replacements. The economic incentive for DND's support of military exports is a reduction in the unit costs of Canadian procurement. In the case of the armoured vehicles produced for the Canadian Armed Forces by General Motors in London, Ontario, for example, the capital costs of the production plant need not all be absorbed by Canada if the equipment can also be exported.

Starting in the mid-1970s, repatriating petrodollars became another prominent concern of weapons suppliers. Countries have a general interest in having arms exports offset the costs of imports, and there is a demonstrated relationship between arms exports and mineral imports. In the case of oil in particular, this relationship is manifested in a tendency for arms exporters to sell their wares to countries from which they import oil. This is, however, less the case for the superpowers, who are more inclined to pursue longer-term strategic interests than immediate economic interests.[15]

For the major powers, arms sales are a tool for advancing the national interest in the international arena. At the most basic level, arms transfers between allies take advantage of economies of scale and promote weapons standardization for the benefit of the common defence. Suppliers also transfer arms to key states or friends within particular regions in order to influence the balance of power in support of their interests there. In addition, they seek political leverage within individual states by encouraging a relationship of dependence between the supplier and the recipient. If you sell a fleet of aircraft to a nonindustrialized or semi-industrialized country, the recipient of the aircraft will be fully dependent on the supplier for the full range of services that attend the operation and maintenance of the fleet — training personnel to fly the aircraft, providing service personnel, supplying replacement parts.

Military equipment transfers frequently also go hand in hand with extensive military training, which includes a generous measure of political "training" or education. Military equipment offers a means of access to the military elites of recipient countries and the opportunity to influence them in favour of policies consistent with the interests of the supplier state.[16] In other instances the supply of military equipment is linked to access to military facilities in the recipient country — such as military bases or ports — and to efforts to have recipient countries share the burden of maintaining a military presence within a particular region.

It is worth noting that there is no guarantee that the economic and strategic objectives of the arms exporter will always be compatible — something Britain discovered when British troops were fired upon by British-built and British-financed weapons during the Falklands/Malvinas war. In less dramatic terms, northern industrialized countries in general are discovering that when competition between suppliers leads to increased technology transfers to the buyer in order to sweeten the deal, such transfers in the long run reduce the buyer's dependence and hence the supplier's political leverage.

Canadian military exports are not premised on extensive strategic objectives, although strategic considerations are not entirely absent. The strategic goal of maintaining a military production capability in support of Canadian military requirements has already been mentioned. Given that Canada is dependent on offshore contracts for virtually all its major military equipment acquisitions, this consideration is a minor one. Strategic considerations, however, do have an impact on the process of granting export permits (see chapter 7). For example, export permits are more likely to be granted to countries with which Canada has a longstanding trade relationship or is interested in developing closer political and economic relations.

The motivations of weapons importers are also a mixture of political, military and economic considerations. Most obvious is the strategic requirement to arm national defence forces against real or potential external adversaries. Perhaps more prominent, though by most standards of national behaviour less legitimate, is the desire of the regime to arm itself against real or perceived internal adversaries — hence the demand for repression technology. Beyond that, considerations such as image and the desire to increase a state's influence or stature within a particular region are also significant. Sometimes, countries import arms with the explicit purpose of giving the exporting nation a stake in the survival of the importing regime. Economic interests include the pursuit of technology and an enhanced industrial capacity through joint production, licensed production or offset orders related to military imports.

Paying the Price

It is not the fabled "merchants of death," whose only interest is in profiting from a base human penchant for violence, who build and sell these weapons. There may not be a shortage of Adnan Khashoggis ready to arrange a private deal, but weapons sales are for the most part promoted and regulated by governments acting out of deep commitment to rational policymaking and human and social wellbeing. These governments are concerned with creating jobs, remaining competitive in the international economy, and maintaining military and political influence abroad. In short, the arms race is the result of an accumulation of decisions each of which, if examined in isolation, seems eminently sensible. But the consequences of this "prudent planning" are there for all to see: an international arms trade that is out of control and serves as the pre-eminent vehicle for the militarization of the planet. The arms trade is a free-for-all that continues to attract new players. Most of these players deplore the waste that is represented by the global arms race and arms trade, but all of them believe that their particular participation is not the problem and, besides, their own citizens are just as entitled to the benefits of arms exports as those of the next country.

Even without ever being used in war, these military commodities produce gross economic and political distortions within the recipient countries. In a world survey of military and social expenditures, Ruth Leger Sivard describes the military usurpation of political power that has accompanied the post – World War II buildup of military power around the globe. In 1960 twenty-two out of seventy-eight independent Third World countries were under military-controlled governments. In the next twenty-five years there were a total of 138 successful coups, and by 1985 fifty-seven out of 114 independent Third World countries were

under military control. All current military governm
eliminated or severely restricted the franchise of their c.
have used various forms of violence to control them. M
thirds resort to torture, brutality, disappearances, and poli   ...ngs
frequently enough to have what Sivard calls "institutionaliz_.. violence
as a matter of policy."[17]

However, these weapons are, of course, also used in war. In fact, this
has by all accounts been an unusually bloody century. In addition to
the 50 million people killed in World Wars I and II, an estimated 28
million people have lost their lives this century in more than 200 other
wars. Most of these wars have occurred since 1945, resulting in about 20
million dead, more than half of them civilians rather than combatants.
These wars have been fought almost exclusively in the Third World using weapons manufactured in the northern industrialized countries.

It should, therefore, not be a surprise that the political and economic
effects of the arms trade are not equally shared between exporters and
importers. Military exports, undertaken by and large by economically
advanced states, are pursued in support of explicit political and economic goals. For the superpower exporters, these goals, as already noted, include a reinforcement of relationships of economic dependence
between the supplier and the recipient. For virtually all exports, the objectives include the transfer of some of the costs of domestic procurement to the arms recipient. These stated objectives are frequently
met, meaning that importing countries experience greater economic dependence and costs, with profound implications for political life in
those countries.

From the perspective of the arms recipient, perhaps the most readily
understood consequence of military expenditures and the arms trade is
the diversion of resources represented by the import of military commodities. Ruth Leger Sivard's annual review illustrates the point each
year with tragic new examples. While one person in four is hungry and
one adult in three cannot read or write, so much attention has been
paid to the buildup of a destructive military capacity that there is
enough nuclear explosive power to kill 58 billion people, providing the
possibility of 12 deaths for each person now living. Governments on average have supplied one soldier for every 43 people, in comparison with
one doctor for every 1,030 people. Perhaps the most devastating statistic
Sivard provides is that despite the extraordinary economic and technological advances since the end of World War II, there has in the past
forty years been no reduction in the number of people who live in absolute poverty. In fact, says Sivard, "the population lacking in basic hu-

man needs of food, water, shelter, health care, and education, is steadily growing larger."[18]

The Persian Gulf offers tragic confirmation that the arms trade has implications for the war on want, as well as for war in its literal sense. In 1985 Iran imported $5 billion worth of arms, $3 billion worth of essential foodstuffs, and $750 million worth of medicine. With oil revenues drastically down, imports will have to be severely restricted, with the result, as journalist Gwynne Dyer described it, that "there will be malnutrition in the cities, more unneccessary deaths in the hospitals and grave ammunition shortages at the front."[19]

As already argued, weapons transfers frequently have the specific objective of cementing the economic relationship between the supplier and the recipient. Weapons imports exacerbate foreign exchange shortages in developing countries, as they create a need for funds, not only for the weapons themselves, but also for additional imports generated by the acquisition of sophisticated weapons systems — infrastructure such as airports, repair facilities and spare parts, and domestic facilities for expatriate trainers and technicians. These requirements add to the pressures to pursue economic policies that will maximize the production of foreign exchange — inviting direct foreign equity and loan investment, accelerating resource exploitation, using agricultural land to produce cash crops for export. In cementing its relationship with a recipient country, a supplier may also seek such things as access to raw materials, access to cheap tropical foodstuffs, and places to invest surplus capital. The impact on the development process in the recipient country can be substantial. Resources are drained away from the countryside and concentrated in the urban centres where the military infrastructure is housed.

Attempting to replace imports with indigenously produced weapons can reinforce the pattern. Industrialization based on military production means that revenue from resource exports must now be spent on imported capital goods and components. While a larger share of the national product may be retained by urban elites, the increased demand for luxury goods and infrastructure for the military industry still mean the transfer of rural resources to urban centres. In the process, real production capacity responsive to local development needs is not improved.[20] While the process of militarization represented by the arms trade has many direct implications for human rights, perhaps its most serious impact is on what Canadian churches have called "the inviolable rights" of access to the "basic needs" of "food, water, and shelter." In this area, the arms trade is an assault on the most fundamental rights of people.[21]

Militarization and Human Rights

The militarization of life in an increasing number of developing countries takes place in a seemingly endless cycle of poverty, political frustration, dissidence, repression, the import of weapons, the exacerbation of poverty, more political frustration and dissidence followed by more repression, and so on and so on. Developing countries, facing chronic shortages of the capital or wealth without which very little progress in meeting human needs can be made, find it close to impossible to step off this treadmill of despair. The political leadership is unable to maintain stability without appropriate redistribution of wealth and social welfare programs, but it is also unable to sustain longterm economic growth if such programs are implemented. Insufficient capital for both growth and redistribution leads to discontent throughout the political spectrum. This in turn leads to an unstable situation ripe for a takeover by those forces and institutions willing and able to introduce and impose discipline on the social and political order.[22]

It is in the exercise of this discipline that the transfer of "repression technology" is most relevant. The major powers, anxious to maintain stable and controlled regimes in their spheres of influence but unable to exercise control as directly as they once could, now must take a subtler approach to applying discipline. The preferred system is to supply and train indigenous military forces in the recipient countries so that these forces can look after the interests of the supplier nation under the guise of nationalism and the pursuit of national pride. Repression technology is designed, in other words, not to defend the state against an external aggressor but to attack and control internal military and political "enemies" of the regime. Moreover, even supplying a repressive regime with military equipment that does not appear directly relevant to repression can contribute to the overall strength of the military within the national political economy. Unlike sales of nonmilitary equipment or civilian sales to nongovernmental customers in the state, such transactions can be taken to represent political support for, or even endorsement of, the recipient regime, fortifying it politically and psychologically in its repressive policies.

The equipment used covers a wide range:

- crowd control systems (tear gas, rubber bullets, batons, etc.);
- small arms (pistols, rifles, submachine guns);
- police and prison hardware (handcuffs, leg irons, etc.);
- torture devices (truncheons, thumbscrews, electric shock devices);
- surveillance equipment (eavesdropping and phone tapping equipment, night vision, etc.);

- data processing equipment (computers and command, control and communications for police and military forces);
- vehicles (police patrol cars, armoured cars, helicopters);
- counterinsurgency gear (aerial reconnaissance systems, helicopters and transport planes, light planes and armoured cars);
- training and services (riot control, surveillance computer operation).

The most dramatic manifestation of this process of repression is the military coup — the assumption of political control by the same institution that exercises the disciplining role. As already noted, the assumption by military forces of social and political authority is almost always associated with the elimination or restriction of the right to vote, as well as with forms of institutionalized violence against citizens.

The coup, however, is merely an advanced stage in a process that begins under civilian rule.[23] Two conditions are generally needed to produce a situation in which authoritarian government structures are maintained through increased coercion, assisted by "repression technology": first, rising expectations that move wide segments of the population to seek greater and more equitable participation in the political and economic life of the country; and second, a military establishment of sufficient strength to prevent the development of more democratic institutions.

The military, by virtue of characteristics intrinsic to it, is inclined to obstruct increased popular participation in decision-making for a variety of reasons. Military authority is likely to be less disposed towards a self-reliant economy to the extent that this would weaken the possibility of obtaining foreign exchange to cover arms imports and other technologies related to the military buildup. Furthermore, participatory democracy tends towards decentralization and more appropriate (and labour-intensive) technology, which in turn gives priority to basic needs. The military, on the other hand, represents an entirely different organizational structure, with a high degree of centralization and hierarchy. The emphasis is on command and subordination, on discipline rather than creativity, with alternative thinking and approaches frequently defined as "subversive."

These are generally characteristics well suited to carrying out traditional military functions, but when they come to dominate civilian political structures they involve heavy social and human costs. As the military's role in denying popular participation in government increases, respect for fundamental human rights diminishes and individuals are required to forgo normal rights in favour of "order" and "stability" in the nation. Technology from the industrial nations — or, as is now also the case, from semi-industrial developing countries — is used to control local populations and suppress dissent. The economic disparities that result, of course, inevitably produce forces seeking to overthrow economic injustice and in turn increase the authorities' perceived need for, and use of, this repression technology.

The most serious violations of human rights occur when the military intervenes either to reverse a process that has already gone a long way towards participatory decision-making or to maintain an authoritarian system when consensus among the people is nonexistent or very low. Early in the process the usurping military regime frequently declares a state of emergency, which allows it to suspend the constitution and guarantees of individual rights. The regime then justifies extensions of the "state of emergency" with claims that there exists a state of "internal war." From there the constitution is regressively modified. A new distribution of power takes place. The traditional independence of the executive, the legislature and the judiciary disappears. The military junta concentrates political power in its own hands and assumes control — directly or indirectly — over the legislative body. Military tribunals and courts martial, using summary procedures, are given wider jurisdiction. Arbitrary detention without charges and without trial become common. Prisoners are mistreated or even killed during detention, as the legal remedies against arbitrary detentions no longer apply and the right of defence for the accused is abolished or made ineffective.

The arms trade, therefore, undermines the rights of individuals in developing countries in several direct and indirect ways. Its most direct impact is on what Canadian churches have described as the right "to be free from disappearance, from arbitrary arrest, detention, torture, and extra-judicial execution and from systematic state-sponsored racial discrimination."[24] The arms trade has a direct impact on human rights violations inasmuch as the acquisition of the means of control and repression assists the state in denying political and human rights and in imposing repressive policies and practices. It also has an indirect impact on the right to be free from the violations listed by the churches inasmuch as weapons transfers contribute to the state's capacity to circumvent or undermine the political process. A further indirect implication, as already noted, is the effect of weapons imports on people's ability to meet their basic needs.

A Competitive but Bullish Market

The international arms market, though more competitive than it used
to be, remains bullish. Despite its political and human consequences,
the arms trade functions increasingly according to commercial considerations — and it is inevitable that an industry dominated by commercial interests will not yield easily to political control. Commercial
enterprises prefer to be left to the open market without interference
from governments. Hence the primary pressure, in Canada and internationally, is to reduce controls on the export of military commodities.
Military manufacturers, already operating in a highly competitive environment, are anxious to keep the obstacles to sales at a minimum. And
government review and control of military exports is seen as an additional, domestically generated impediment to success. So the present
trend is the opposite of what it should be. Rather than moving towards
more responsibility in military sales and more concern for their ultimate social and human consequences, the trend is now towards depoli-
ticizing military sales and denying the social and political responsibility attached to them.

Thus, there is now no international discussion of possible ways of
controlling the international arms trade. No disarmament forum currently has the arms trade on its agenda. Both suppliers and recipients of
military commodities are reluctant to enter into international agreements that could interfere with their particular national or economic
interests.

The prospects are therefore for the arms market to remain bullish for
the rest of this decade. Military conflicts persist and weapons are still
obviously being consumed; there has been no retreat from military research and development as weapons systems innovation continues
apace; there is a large world weapons production capacity that is encouraging increased sales; and with gradual recovery from recession it
can be expected that the demand will increase. While the current surplus capacity will tend to discourage new entries, it is likely that governments will increase credits available to buyers in order to support indigenous industry. The International Monetary Fund has demonstrated a
reluctance to require reductions in military spending in its usual demand for economic restraints — no doubt a tribute to the critical role
of military forces in maintaining discipline in environments of economic austerity.

The proliferation of suppliers clearly makes it much more difficult to
control arms exports. With a much broader range of choices for many
weapons systems, buyer countries are now less dependent on a small

number of suppliers. The possibility that supplier countries will reach agreements to restrain the introduction of new weapons systems into unstable regions is correspondingly reduced.

Canada's Substantial Share

The Reagan arms boom has been a bonanza for Canadian military producers (see table 2). Since 1980 there have been rapid increases in Canadian military exports, with sales to the U.S. tripling in the first half of the 1980s. Canada's $2 billion annual export of military commodities exceeds Canada's total exports to Central America and the continent of Africa combined. Canadian military exports are the equivalent of almost 5 per cent of the world annual trade of about $50 billion. Non-Canadian sources do not accord Canada that level of prominence because the high level of trade in components between Canada and the United

TABLE 2
Canadian Military Exports
1959-1985
($ million)

Year	United States	Europe	Other*	Total
1959–1969	2,418.8	439.8	207.0	3,065.6
1970	226.5	41.2	68.5	336.2
1971	216.3	67.2	53.0	336.5
1972	175.0	73.7	51.7	300.4
1973	198.8	72.8	37.6	309.2
1974	150.0	45.6	84.9	280.5
1975	188.5	58.6	33.7	280.8
1976	191.1	113.1	31.9	336.1
1977	314.1	76.0	163.9	554.0
1978	267.0	129.6	87.9	484.5
1979	367.7	145.6	55.0	568.3
1980	481.7	142.1	97.9	721.7
1981	826.6	149.4	174.8	1,150.8
1982	1,027.9	157.8	248.4	1,434.1
1983	1,207.4	128.6	145.2	1,481.2
1984	1,360.5	243.1	149.8	1,753.4
1985	1,644.2	154.0	104.5	1,902.7
Total	11,262.1	2,238.2	1,795.7	15,296.0

*This category primarily represents sales to the Third World, although some sales to Australia and New Zealand may be included.
Source: Department of External Affairs

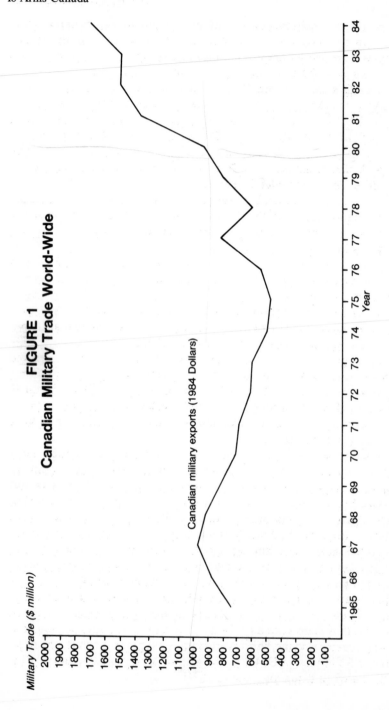

FIGURE 1
Canadian Military Trade World-Wide

Canadian military exports (1984 Dollars)

Military Trade ($ million)

Year

States is essentially treated as domestic U.S. production. From the point of view of Canada, however, the sales of components to the United States represent the international transfer of military commodities and become part of the military capability of a foreign power.

Canada's share of the arms trade with the Third World is more difficult to calculate. By the mid-1980s this trade totalled about $35 billion — having slipped somewhat from the peak year of 1982, largely as a result of worldwide recession. During the 1980s to date, Canada's direct sales to the Third World have averaged $150 million per year, with a peak of $250 million in 1982. This means that Canada's share of the world trade is just under 0.5 per cent.

Once again, however, because of Canada's special military production relationship with the United States, not all Canadian military commodities that regularly go to the Third World are accounted for in direct sales. Canadian military commodities sold to the United States become part of total U.S. military production, at least 10 per cent of which goes to the Third World each year. In 1983, for example, the U.S. military procurement budget was US$80 billion, and military exports were about US$18 billion, of which US$11 billion went to the Third World. Thus of the US$98 billion in total production, more than 10 per cent was exported to the Third World.[25] If one-tenth or more of U.S. military production goes to the Third World, it is reasonable to assume that at least one-tenth of Canada's part in U.S. military production also goes to the Third World. In 1985, for example, this would mean that 10 per cent of the $1.664 billion worth of Canadian military exports to the United States — about $160 million — could be expected to find their way to the Third World.

Exports of military components to other industrial countries must also be considered. A special case is the export of Canadian aircraft engines to aircraft industries in countries such as Brazil, Indonesia and Israel. Many of these engines leave Canada classified as "civilian" but are then used in the production of military aircraft such as Israeli Aravas, Brazilian Embraer patrol and trainer aircraft, or Indonesian-built Bell helicopters. Similar sales to industrialized countries such as Switzerland and Italy also result in Canadian "civilian" engines being used in military aircraft sold to the Third World (including, as Canadians learned in late 1986, Iran). While these sales are not tabulated as military exports, they are in fact exactly that, and a conservative estimate is that these sales add another $30 million per year to Canadian military exports to the Third World (annual engine sales to Brazil alone were $30.3 million in 1984, with the majority of Canadian-powered Brazilian aircraft being for military use[26]).

All told, this means that in 1985, when direct Canadian military sales to the Third World were reported at $104,500,000, about $300 million in Canadian military commodities reached the Third World, while in the peak year of 1982 the combination of direct and indirect military sales to the Third World was probably well in excess of $400 million. This means that Canada's share of annual arms sales to the Third World is about 1 per cent. Since 1945 arms transfers have provided the fuel for more than 100 wars in the Third World, producing more than 20 million military and civilian combat deaths. One per cent of those deaths amounts to 200,000 — about twice the number of Canadians who have lost their lives as the result of war during this century.

Canadian Arms and Prosperity

Canadian military production for export is pursued in support of a combination of defence and economic objectives. Canada pursues its defence objectives largely in the context of a military alliance and a continental military partnership, through which it has incurred certain military obligations and equipment requirements. Most of this equipment, by virtue of a series of events and decisions discussed in chapters 2 and 3, Canadian industry is not currently able to produce. This means that in order to equip its own armed forces, Canada must go outside its borders for virtually all major equipment (even in the case of ships, which are built domestically, the major subsystems are imported or built in Canada with imported technology through international consortia). In the interest of mitigating the cost of these imports, Canada has sought to develop a capacity to participate in coproduction and to supply components — and in some cases complete systems — to foreign buyers. This arrangement is obviously most advanced with the United States (with implications for the Canadian economy and the independence of Canadian defence and foreign policies that will be discussed further on), but an active arms export promotion team within the federal civil service is trying hard to expand these sales to Europe and the Third World.

In support of increased military production, military spending in general is increasingly cited as an economic benefit. Since we have to spend money on defence anyway, isn't it lucky that it is good for the economy too! In fact, the Mulroney government has sought to mobilize Canada's growing "nuclear allergy" in support of increased Canadian expenditures on conventional forces in both Europe and North America, with the argument that increased conventional military forces will not only reduce our reliance on nuclear weapons but also strengthen our economy in the process.

When Robert Coates, then minister of national defence, officiated at a ceremony to celebrate the arrival of the new CF-18 fighter aircraft at Canadian Forces Base Bagotville in December 1984, he allowed that the sounds of the CF-18 aircraft in flight were "the sounds of security, in more ways than one."[27] Not only would the aircraft enhance national security, he said, but the attendant repair and test facilities for the F-18 would also bring *economic* security to the region. The argument that new military procurement programs will help lift this country out of the economic doldrums is probably inevitable in a period of accelerated military spending. Charged with generating political support for increased military programs, governments are clearly out to accentuate the positive. Prime Minister Mulroney suggested that Canadian participation in the U.S. Strategic Defense Initiative could be justified if it could be shown to create jobs, and the Ontario Ministry of Industry and Trade has prepared a confidential report extolling the growing potential of high tech defence-related work in the next ten years.[28]

Canadian defence expenditures currently consume about 2 per cent of all goods and services consumed (GNP) in Canada, about 10 per cent of federal government spending, and almost 40 per cent of federal discretionary spending (discretionary spending consists of funds over which Parliament exercises direct, annual control and hence excludes such items as debt charges, transfer payments, social expenditures such as the Canada Pension Plan, and payments to certain crown corporations).[29] This figure makes the Department of National Defence one of the top competitors in the annual scramble for public funds, and recent trends indicate that it has been holding its own. Defence spending has risen by an annual average of 13.5 per cent compounded over the past six years, compared with an overall average increase in federal spending of 10.8 per cent (the cost of servicing the public debt has risen an average of 20.1 per cent).[30]

This means that other public programs have not been doing as well. And with the present government having made a dual commitment to continuing to increase military spending and to reducing the federal deficit, nonmilitary public commitments are destined to be sacrificed. Indeed, we have already seen some of those sacrifices and attempted sacrifices: budget cuts to the Canadian Broadcasting Corporation, cuts to the Science Council of Canada and the National Research Council, the questioning of universality in social programs, and the attempted deindexing of old age pensions.

This competition for limited public funds is taking place in an environment of continued high unemployment, high real interest rates, high foreign ownership and high trade deficits in manufactured goods. Canada is facing an economic crisis, and the question of who bears the main burden of this crisis will remain the central domestic political question of our time.

Increased military spending is regarded as having direct implications for Canada's ability to export military commodities. The larger Canadian requirements get, according to this reasoning, the more opportunities there will be to develop indigenous military production capabilities, which in turn will then be better placed to compete in the international military market. Thus, exports are seen as an important spinoff of domestic military spending (armoured vehicles built for the Canadian Armed Forces, for example, can then be produced for export), as well as a means of recovering the costs of military imports. The result is a growing assumption that military spending and military exports are an essential part of prudent economic and industrial planning.

The Coy Arms Merchant

The Canadian government — unlike its U.S. counterpart — has never revealed the details of military exports. Under Ottawa's so-called "Access to Information" legislation, the details of Canada's military trade remain hidden from the Canadian people, and the only difference is that the government now charges for the service. The access laws exempt disclosure of military sales information on several grounds. None of these grounds is related to security; they are rather more mundane and are concerned primarily with the competitiveness of Canadian firms. On grounds of "commercial confidentiality," firms are protected from public disclosure of their business dealings which might give important information to either domestic or foreign competitors. Disclosure is also exempted on grounds that trade information is voluntarily submitted (this is so in particular in the case of military exports to the U.S., for which permits are not required) on condition that it will be kept confidential. A third prominent rationale for nondisclosure is that secrecy is sometimes a condition placed on a transaction by the importing country.

In one request under Access to Information regulations, the Department of External Affairs provided a sample copy of export permits requested with the explanation that "you will note that considerable information will probably be exempted." It was a remarkable example of understatement, in that the sample permit was essentially a blank piece of paper, with the company name, the country of destination, the description of the commodity, the price and the file number all blocked out. The notice from the department went on to say that if copies of all the permits requested were still desired (as mutilated), there would be a fee of $3,000. In other words, the costs which the department would incur in its censorship operation were now to be charged to the person requesting the information, in exchange for a substantial stack of blank paper.[31]

While respect for commercial confidentiality is a sensible condition for normal business operations, military trade is not "normal." It is an extraordinary trade in lethal goods that must be subject to extraordinary controls. Military trade, having moral and political implications not present in other trade, requires public intervention in a way that other trade does not. The requirement that military exports be reviewed by government authorities through the export permit process is an acknowledgement that military sales are not sales like all others. If greater regulation and disclosure of arms sales impede the free flow of military goods, that is to be taken as a desirable consequence of such regulation and disclosure. To that extent, disclosure must be taken as part of the process of restraint — and secrecy a sign of lack of restraint.

In Canada, however, it is in disclosure itself that there has been the most consistent restraint. In 1975, in answer to a written question in the House of Commons, the Department of Industry, Trade and Commerce provided a table showing all recipients of Canadian military commodities for the years 1963 through 1974. Dollar values for each country were not given, for the same reasons cited by External Affairs officials today in defence of nondisclosure: "Military equipment export sales figures as compiled by the Department of Industry, Trade and Commerce contain information provided by Canadian companies on a voluntary and confidential basis and, therefore, details cannot be made available since such disclosure could be considered a breach of confidentiality and could compromise a company's competitive position."[32]

This was the last time a comprehensive list of recipients, even without dollar values, was provided. During the 1970s the Defence Programs Bureau (the agency responsible for administering Canada's military export program, then a part of the Department of Industry, Trade and Commerce and now within the Department of External Affairs) did provide an annual list of the top twenty "overseas" (meaning non-U.S.)

recipients of Canadian military commodities. Dollar values were excluded, and the list included European as well as Third World customers. Since then the government has refused even to list the recipients. Besides maintaining that certain countries make nondisclosure a condition of sale, officials argue that the identification of recipient countries would, in instances of single or infrequent sales, effectively identify sales and give commercially confidential information to competitors.

Apart from the limits on disclosure of direct military sales, identifying the ultimate destination of Canadian military commodities is further complicated by the fact that much of the military equipment that Canada exports is destined to be used by someone other than the immediate customer (see appendix 1). This is so particularly in the case of Canadian exports to the United States.

These indirect sales do not represent direct Canadian decision-making beyond their original destination. They are a reflection of the international nature of military industry and the global reach of the arms trade. They are nevertheless instances of Canadian military products going to, and affecting the ultimate capabilities of, armed forces outside Canada's own borders. And while (as already noted) a precise accounting of the volume of this indirect trade is not possible, whatever responsibility accrues to the supplier of military commodities for their end use must apply to these exports as well as to direct sales.

As appendix 1 shows, Canadian military commodities end up in such politically disparate countries as Chile, El Salvador, Iran, Iraq, Libya, Syria and Taiwan. Canada has chosen not to exercise control over the ultimate destination of these components (see chapter 7), but it is not at all clear that such a decision can absolve a country of the moral and political responsibilities that attend the production and marketing of weapons of war. Certainly, the level of responsibility grows with the degree of foreknowledge of the likely destination and use of the commodities. When Canada exports engines for military aircraft to Brazil, which in turn is known as a supplier of military aircraft to countries such as Honduras and El Salvador — to which direct exports of military commodities should be prohibited under current Canadian guidelines — it is not credible to insist that no responsibility attaches to Canada as a supplier of components (especially when the component in question, the engine, constitutes a substantial portion of the total cost of an aircraft).

All the World's a Market

Direct sales to the Third World have fluctuated considerably over the past decade (see table 2). In the early 1970s these sales averaged $50 million per year. After that there were sustained increases, but since the peak year of 1982, when sales hit $248 million, the pattern has been more erratic.

During the 1950s Canadian military sales consisted primarily of major systems such as aircraft built in Canada under licence and sold to NATO partners (e.g. F-86 Sabres, F-5s, T-33s and Tudors). In the late 1950s and early 1960s, Canada's main emphasis was on maintaining access to the U.S. market and upgrading access to the European market, while sales to the Third World were primarily to newly independent Commonwealth partners.

In the early 1970s U.S. withdrawal from Vietnam, detente and U.S. balance-of-payments problems cut Canadian access to the U.S. market. The difficulty in maintaining access to the American market was heightened by Canada's own restraint in capital spending, which resulted in a low level of Canadian purchases in the United States. Canada-U.S. military trade was supposed to be kept in rough balance, which meant that reduced Canadian purchases in the U.S. would ultimately be reflected in lower American purchases in Canada. During that time, Canada sought to increase military sales to Europe, but these efforts were not aided by the Trudeau government's reassessment of Canada's role in NATO and the subsequent reduction in Canadian troop strength in Europe.

The main alternative market that remained was the Third World. But here too, there were obstacles other than a "restrictive" arms export policy. Canada, as a producer of component parts for U.S. weapons systems, did not have a broad range of equipment for sale to Third World military forces. Apart from military transport aircraft, Canada was producing few major systems. In addition, sales of military components for American weapons systems were effectively limited to Third World countries that were already recipients of U.S. major weapons systems. During the 1970s, for example, Iran was the object of major attention. Tehran was the one place in which the Defence Programs Bureau had a direct representative, and during the 1970s Iran purchased more than $50 million worth of military commodities from Canada, making it apparently the single largest customer for Canadian military commodities over the decade.[33] It is not surprising, therefore, that in 1986 helicopter engine parts were reported as going fron Canada to Iran. While the revelations made headlines, those and more explicitly military items had been going to Iran for years.

Table 2 shows that while Canadian military sales to the Third World increased during the 1970s, the increase was not dramatic. The Third World proportion of total Canadian military sales went from 7 per cent in the 1960s to 18 per cent in the 1970s, but this near-tripling of the Third World's share was partly due to the relative decline of the U.S. market. During the years 1975 – 79, the "other" category accounted for 15.6 per cent of exports, and unofficial sources indicate the following breakdown of this category; Africa 6.6 per cent (of total exports), the Middle East 4.02 percent, Asia 3.8 percent, Latin America 0.75 percent, and Oceania 0.48 percent.

In the 1980s there has been modest growth in sales to the Third World, although the very dramatic increases in sales to the United States mean that the Third World's share has dropped to 11 per cent. During this decade, however, Canada's ability to export directly to the Third World has increased substantially (even though the competition has been getting tougher and it is a struggle just to maintain the level of sales). Besides being able to produce a considerable variety of components and spare parts for major weapons systems, Canadian industry now builds military patrol and transport aircraft, armoured vehicles, military trucks and motorcycles, and a wide range of military communications equipment. Government assistance to military industry (see chapter 5) includes an assortment of promotional activities.

Canada's current approach to military sales reflects the worldwide trend towards the commercialization of the arms trade. Promoters of military exports now routinely describe them as "high technology and defence-related" sales in a conscious attempt to subsume military equipment under a broad commercial category of high tech. The guidelines for the government's primary grant program in support of military exports, the Defence Industry Productivity program, state that "the primary objective of the DIP program will be to enhance economic growth through the promotion of viable defence or defence-related exports."[34] By defining the objective of military exports as economic growth, and by obscuring the distinction between military and nonmilitary commodities with references to the industrial sacred cow known as "high tech," the government is trying to provide military sales with a commercial gloss and hence undermine the idea that the supplier of weapons of war bears some responsibility for where and on whom they are ultimately used.

The pressure to maximize high tech sales is leading Canadian decision-makers to minimize the administrative and political impediments to such sales. This is reflected in efforts to streamline the export permit process and make it less stringent in its attention to human rights and other political implications. As the restrictions on sales are reduced, secrecy is increased in the hope that what is out of sight will be out of mind.

A commercially motivated arms industry in any country, including Canada, runs counter to one of the most urgent requirements of our time — to stop the manufacture and proliferation of weapons of war that have made the second half of the twentieth century a period of unusual bloodiness. The continuing human slaughter made possible by the worldwide distribution of the instruments of destruction will continue as long as arms exports are considered good business. But they are not good business; they are a deadly business — a business that should be under the clear control of international law and subject to additional national constraints that place the security of persons ahead of commercial interests.

2

Canadian Military Production from the Great War to the Permanent War

With Canada's unemployment rate running in the neighbourhood of 10 per cent, and with rumours of layoffs and shutdowns a regular part of plant gossip, long-term military contracts look pretty good. "On the whole," says a worker at the General Motors of Canada Diesel Division works in London, "the military vehicles are the best thing to happen to this plant in years." And "with wars going on all over, somebody has to make these things and it might as well be us."[1]

"These things" are a line of light armoured vehicles (LAVs), available in up to a dozen models. The LAVs, built for the Canadian Armed Forces, were a welcome opportunity for General Motors when, at the end of the 1970s, the company could no longer sustain a viable operation building buses and heavy earth-moving equipment. It was soon obvious, however, that the Canadian order was only a temporary reprieve and that long-term employment would require export orders. Then came a $625 million sale to the U.S. Marine Corps and another lease on life for the plant. But by the beginning of 1986 the rumours of layoffs were once again circulating and the plant was again in jeopardy. So, with the U.S. contract due for completion in mid-1987, the LAVs are now available for worldwide export.

The livelihood of several hundred London families depends on an interest in Canadian-built LAVs on the part of some government somewhere in the world. "Without a new contract, we are looking at layoffs in eighteen months," a company representative said in February 1986.[2] These families once relied on a market for buses and graders for their economic welfare. Now they rely on a market for weapons. What began as a reasonable and widely supported contract to provide equipment to the Canadian Armed Forces ended up as a stake in the global arms race.

Armoured vehicles in various configurations support a wide range of battlefield functions, including reconnaissance, machine gun and small artillery combat, antitank operations, and battlefield taxi (ferrying armed troops back and forth to the war theatre). The U.S. Army has become keen on lighter armoured vehicles because they are more easily transported than full-sized tanks — a significant consideration for an infantry that is described as being "designed to be deployed for combat anywhere in the world."[3] Light armoured vehicles are also attractive to armed forces whose responsibilities may include internal combat with insurgents and functions such as crowd control. Military regimes that have placed limitations on popular political participation and are low on popular political support are frequently pitted against popular movements and guerrilla insurgencies, and they find light armoured vehicles useful in these circumstances. In fact, it is with regimes with a requirement for "repression technology" that much of the potential market for Canada's armoured vehicles lies. Efforts have already been made to sell them to Indonesia, Saudi Arabia, Egypt and Malaysia.

With the London GM plant now dependent on becoming a regular supplier of armoured vehicles to the global arms bazaar in order to continue to provide jobs to London-area families, and with the best potential for new customers being countries where political and human rights are severely restricted and violent conflict is either already occurring or threatened, the pressure will grow on the Department of External Affairs to open up its military export guidelines.

The GM London plant illustrates a prominent dilemma of Canada's heavily export-dependent military industry. The pressures are increasing to relax the export guidelines and to deny any political or moral responsibility for the ultimate uses to which the industry's products are put. The Canadian military industry, as currently structured, has relatively little to do with the Canadian Armed Forces and less to do with Canada's defence needs. Instead, it has become a commercial industry whose exports are promoted as a solution to Canadian economic problems.

The LAVs follow an eminent Canadian tradition of building weapons for other countries' wars. Canadian weapons, like Canadian soldiers, fight abroad rather than at home. Not since Confederation have the Canadian armed forces fought on Canadian soil — nor, for that matter, has there been any direct military threat to Canada. These are blessings for which Canadians are insufficiently grateful, but they are not the best possible conditions under which to raise public funds for a major state-of-the-art fighting force. Nevertheless, for Canada's weapons industry the lack of a serious threat of war at home has not been an unmanageable deficiency, but rather just one more challenge to be met. Its success in meeting the challenge can be gauged by the fact that military production in Canada now exceeds $3 billion per year, about two-thirds of it for export.

Indeed, the Canadian military industry has turned the absence of Canadian wars, and the presence of a relatively restrained military establishment, into a kind of advantage. Not only do Canadian-built military commodities have the merit of not being used on Canadian soil, but when they are used overseas it is the armed forces of other countries that are called on to use them.

The Canadian defence industry no longer even offers the pretence that it is there to support Canadian defence requirements directly. It is avowedly part of a North American defence industrial base, and is primarily, and openly, designed to supply U.S. defence requirements. Brigadier General William J. Yost, writing in support of a more extensive military production capability in Canada, notes with approval that the "defence industry in Canada . . . is part of a continental defence industry which is largely responsive to United States military procurement orders."[4] Accordingly, it is changes in American, not Canadian, military deployments or perceptions of threat that have the most immediate impact on Canadian military production. And sustained American bellicosity is generally better for business than are detente and American restraint in military spending.

American withdrawal from Vietnam and the Nixon/Kissinger detente of the mid-1970s put the Canadian aerospace industry into severe decline. In fact it was during this period that the federal government purchased two large aircraft and aircraft-components manufacturing firms, Canadair Limited and de Havilland Aircraft of Canada Limited, both heavily dependent on U.S. military orders, rather than risk having them closed by their foreign parent companies. But an American military on the move, whether in Vietnam or in response to the Reagan/ Weinberger mission to make America great again, sends the Canadian industry into overtime. These swings in U.S. interest in Canadian military goods (down during detente and up the rest of the time), accentuate the vulnerability of Canadian firms for which the Pentagon is an important market.

As a means of mitigating this dependence and diversifying and increasing the potential market, the government and industry have looked to Europe and the Third World for additional sales. Foreign wars and military adventures, in other words, have not been at all bad for Canadian business. For the president of a Canadian electronics firm the point is not lost: "What would hurt us is if the world suddenly declared peace tomorrow and there was zero defence spending. But that's my nine-millionth worry right now."[5] This is not to say that this country has produced a coterie of Canadian Krupps willing to sell anything that shoots to the highest bidder. But as we have seen, Canadian military commodities do find their way onto a variety of the planet's battlefields, and in the two European world wars of this century, military production was a key element of the Canadian war effort.

Given the experience of those two wars, Sir Wilfrid Laurier's famous 1914 declaration that "when Britain is at war, Canada is at war" might appropriately be restated as "when Europe is at war, Canada is at full employment." This again is not to suggest that Canadian industrialists are William Randolph Hearsts promoting war for the economic fun of it.[6] But a long-term economic stake in military procurement is not likely to be the best base for a vigorous rejection of military solutions to political disputes. Nor do the direct economic returns from military production promote a forthright assessment of some of the less tangible, though no less real, costs — for example, the implications for Canadian political and economic independence. Canada's participation in the great wars of this century, from World War I to World War II to the Cold War, included, and ultimately focused on, the production of military commodities for export, accompanied by a persistent push towards industrial integration with, and dependence on, the United States. The process began in World War I.

World War I

Canada entered World War I with a serious unemployment problem, and when the military recruiters sent out the call, there was a substantial pool of surplus labour on which to draw. After the war, fully a fifth of the Canadian Expeditionary Force was estimated to have come from the ranks of the long-term unemployed.[7] The war eventually brought full employment, but not without a struggle and, more significantly, not without a little help from our American neighbours.

The war was openly greeted as an economic opportunity. The prospect of capturing markets that had been held by Germany was eagerly anticipated, and the Montreal *Star* editorialized that commerce and industry lost by Germany "will be parcelled out among the other nations and it is believed a large proportion of it will come to Canada."[8] Besides the opportunity to capture new civilian markets, the economic potential in the supply of war materials to both the British and Canadian forces did not go unnoticed. While the development of the needed production facilities proved to be rather more difficult than expected, the Imperial Munitions Board put together an industry of unprecedented size in Canada, which by 1917 included "600 factories, a quarter of a million workers (including 40,000 women) and a turnover of $2 million a day."[9] Canada had found what economist Tom Naylor has called a new staple — artillery shells.[10] Prolonged trench warfare, with its high rate of consumption of explosives, created a sustained market, and Canadian industry produced between one-quarter and one-third of the ammunition used by the British artillery. Canadian artillery shell shipments went from 5,000 in 1914 to 23,782,000 in 1917.[11]

In spite of this industrial surge, in 1917 Canada faced a crisis. While Britain had promised to pay for the Canadian war effort, by 1917 it was broke. The British threatened to reduce their orders to Canada unless Canada could itself help to pay for them.[12] In addition, Canada had built up a serious trade deficit with the United States, largely because in order to meet its commitments to the British, Canada had to import large quantities of steel, coal, machine tools and, in some instances, even ready-made munitions from the U.S.[13]

The solution Canada sought was twofold. First, it would increase borrowing and thus fight the war on credit. "We are justified," the minister of finance of the day declared, "in placing upon posterity the greater portion of the financial burden of this war, waged as it is in the interests of human freedom and their benefit."[14] Second, it would appeal to the United States to increase its military purchases in Canada. It was not the last time that Canada would respond to a military production crisis with an appeal for freer access to the frequently buoyant U.S. military market. And the American response to Canada's request would also not be the last of its kind. According to historians R.D. Cuff and J.L. Granatstein, when Prime Minister Sir Robert Borden went to Washington in February 1918 to promote U.S. munitions purchases in Canada, the Americans "expressed the view that the resources of the two countries should be pooled in the most effective co-operation and that the boundary line had little or no significance in considering or dealing with these vital questions."[15]

The insignificance of the 49th parallel when it comes to military issues has been a consistent theme of Canada-U.S. relations throughout the twentieth century. Just prior to World War I Canadians had been exercised over the issue of reciprocity, which had been the major focus of the 1911 election campaign. The reciprocity debate was characterized by prominent fears of the political consequences of extensive economic integration with the United States, but then came World War I. Trade between the two countries grew rapidly, and "from the time of World War I, the Canadian economy has remained closely tied to that of the United States."[16]

In the immediate postwar years Canada-U.S. economic integration continued to advance rapidly. While a significant industrial capacity had been built up by the end of the war, the wartime industrial infrastructure proved not to be easily adaptable to peacetime requirements. Shells, the wartime Canadian staple, were not in great demand in the 1920s. The main peacetime markets that were available were for such things as pulp and paper, chemicals and automobiles, all of which were underdeveloped in Canada and for which major injections of capital were needed. Canada had emerged from the war with a major debt burden and a scarcity of domestic capital. The United States, on the other hand, emerged as the world's primary source of capital, and since the pattern for economic and industrial cooperation between Canada and the United States was all in place as a result of wartime integration, it was inevitable that U.S. capital would fill the Canadian gap. Britain was in no position to reinforce its economic links with Canada, so the economic control of Canada effectively shifted from Britain to the United States.[17]

Demobilized at the end of World War I, the military industry in Canada remained out of action through most of the interwar period. There being no foreign wars to fight, the Canadian armed forces once again lacked serious purpose, and the Canadian military industry lacked an external market. The absence of a serious purpose for Canadian military forces was not the fault of one Colonel J. Sutherland Brown, who was the author of Defence Plan No. 1, a scheme to mobilize Canadian forces for war with the United States. Historian Desmond Morton has pointed out that the plan seems less absurd in the light of the fact that the Americans had a "Red Plan" for the invasion of Canada, and that both plans really served to provide scenarios for war games and military exercises.[18] But war games do not a military industry make, and it was not until the late 1930s that Canada began to follow the example of other Western countries and rearm.

In the early 1920s the Canadian Air Force was formed with aircraft provided by the British and the Americans, and several aircraft plants were established in Canada. Canadian Vickers Limited and de Havilland Aircraft, both then subsidiaries of British firms, and several American branch plants (Fairchild Aircraft, Fleet Aircraft, and Boeing Aircraft), were established in the late 1920s and 1930s. In the late 1930s

Canada built substantial numbers of air frames that were shipped to Europe for assembly and completion. At the outbreak of World War II the aircraft industry in Canada employed 4,000 people, with a peak production of forty planes per year.[19]

While the Canadian military leadership initially turned to Britain for equipment, Britain's own production rate at the time was having difficulty meeting its internal military demands. In fact, Britain was already turning to Canada for military industrial support, helping to set the pattern for what would again be a crucial element of Canada's later war effort — the supply of equipment and munitions to the allied European forces.

World War II

World War II produced some remarkable parallels to Canada's World War I military production effort. C.D. Howe's legendary war effort as minister of munitions and supply depended upon the same three-way trade relationship that had functioned so unsteadily in the earlier conflict. To meet Britain's demand for equipment, Canada depended upon British and American designs and on the supply of machine tools and components from the United States. Immediately, World War I – style balance of payments problems emerged. To buy from the United States, Canada needed dollars. But Britain, with its foreign reserves depleted, had no dollars with which to pay for its military imports from Canada. In the meantime Canada built up a useless surplus of British sterling.

For Canada the situation was intolerable. Even in peacetime Canada had run a perennial trade deficit with the United States and frequent surpluses with Britain. Canada was forced into the same twofold solution it had sought in World War I — to finance increasing portions of Britain's purchases out of its own borrowings, and to appeal to the United States to increase its purchases of war materials in Canada. Once again, it was Washington that provided the long-term solution. Besides agreeing to permit Britain to spend some of its U.S. dollar borrowings in Canada, the United States by 1941 was also engaged in a major armament program and was in a position to increase the level of its purchases in Canada sharply. In the summer of 1940, President Roosevelt and Prime Minister Mackenzie King had articulated principles of military "cooperation" between their two countries at a meeting in Ogdensburg, N.Y. At that meeting the Americans, well aware that the defence of the continent gave them a particular interest in the defence of Canada, proposed a "Permanent Joint Board on Defence," and King accepted it. The PJBD, which remains a central instrument of Canadian-American defence planning, opened Canadian territory to U.S. defence installations.[20]

In addition, as the precursor to the next year's Hyde Park Declaration, Ogdensburg paved the way for industrial integration. The declaration, signed when King and Roosevelt again met on April 29, 1941, said in part that "it was agreed as a general principle that in mobilizing the resources of this continent each country should provide the other with the defense articles which it is best able to produce, and, above all, produce quickly, and that production programs should be coordinated to this end."[21] Taken together, Ogdensburg and Hyde Park constituted a restatement of the World War I accord that Borden had reached with Washington, to the effect that the border was to be considered of "little significance" for purposes of the war effort.

For Canadian noncombatants, World War II turned out to be another successful foreign war. The war began in economic depression and high unemployment (500,000 unemployed in 1939), but by 1942 the country enjoyed full employment, and in just two years the GNP grew by 47 per cent.[22] By the end of the war Canadian industry had produced an extraordinary array of military materiel, including 487 escort vessels, 17,000 aircraft, and 38,000 tanks and personnel carriers.[23] After 1941 Canadian military sales were so successful that Canada ended the war with a surplus U.S. dollar account and was able to buy the American military installations that had been built in Canada during the war.[24] In the immediate postwar years, after some early adjustments, the economy grew rapidly. By 1948 the GNP had exceeded its wartime record, prompting Desmond Morton to comment that "Canadians had done well out of the war."[25]

The Cold War

Between the first two world wars of this century there was two decades of recovery time, but the third war was to follow much more quickly. There was a rapid reconversion of World War II military industries to civilian production after the war, but within two years it was clear that the Cold War would not permit the extensive demobilization that had followed World War I. The Cold War was another foreign war which Canada could not ignore. And with the United States taking over from Britain the role of Canada's imperial centre, Laurier's declaration could now be more accurately restated: "When America is at war, Canada is at war."

And America was at war. Unlike the European wars, the Cold War was and is capital-rather than labour-intensive. Expeditionary forces are not central to this war, and Canada's contributions are appropriate to its requirements. First, Canadian territory is placed at the disposal of "our side," and second, Canadian industry contributes to its capital base or infrastructure.

America's leadership in this war is clearly based on its economic, as well as military, strength. In 1946 the GNP of the United States accounted for nearly half of world production.[26] America's economic dominance meant that the dollar would set the standard for the international economy, and its military strength meant that America would be key to the development and maintenance of a stable international political order. With real American power joined by a sense of American manifest destiny, Canada now shared a continent with a superpower that would more than ever before take to heart the Borden/King rhetoric about the insignificance of national boundaries in the context of a common war effort. Where was Col. Brown when we really needed him?

In fact, there were some diplomatic Col. Browns for whom a political defence against U.S. influence became a major preoccupation. Canadian prominence in the formation of the United Nations was premised on a concept of "collective security" in which the relevant collectivity was not the North American continent but a global international community that, it was hoped, would be rationally ordered by a global institution. By acting collectively through the United Nations, nations would be able to discipline a member state that violated the consensus of the community and committed aggression against another member state.

At its beginning, Canada looked upon the United Nations not only as a means of resolving conflict and preventing war, but also as an antidote to the influence of its superpower neighbour. Canada turned to the United Nations, just as it turned to Europe and the North Atlantic Treaty Organization a few years later, as a means of managing its continental relationship. Like Col. Brown, Canadian diplomats in the immediate postwar period had a prevailing interest in holding off an American political invasion, and thus sought an international context within which Canada could act with confidence and the overwhelming impact of the United States would be mitigated.

When it became clear that the United Nations, with a veto system that effectively immobilized it as a mediator of international disputes, would not live up to its expectations as the guarantor of international security, Canada modified its interpretation of collective security to include regional collaboration for collective defence — outside the jurisdiction of the UN Charter but not, it was thought, in violation of it. Here too, the pursuit of "collective" defence stemmed from a concern that unless Canada joined others in common defence arrangements, the influence of the United States would be so strong as to imperil and finally erode Canadian sovereignty. The historian and diplomat John Holmes participated in the formation of Canadian security perceptions and policies in the immediate postwar years and concluded that "world events moved Canadian thinking in a pattern that might roughly be described as passing from collective security to collective defence and peaceful settlement and then, in 1950, by reason of the Korean invasion, to another look at collective security."[27]

By 1947 the idealism of global collective security arrangements was giving way to what was considered the more practical consideration of regional collective defence agreements. This new orientation was reflected in a joint Canada-U.S. statement on defence cooperation, which served as a confirmation of the principles elaborated at Ogdensburg and an acknowledgement of the fact of a shared continent. The statement encouraged common designs in military equipment between the two countries, as well as the reciprocal availability of their military, naval and air facilities.[28] Some cautions were raised about the need for specific approval from each country for the use of such facilities, but the implication was unmistakable — North America, at least North America north of Mexico, was for defence purposes to be viewed as a single unit.

The economic context once again included a foreign exchange crisis. Canadian imports from the United States were still largely being financed by exports to Britain, but British economic fragility proved not to be a good foundation on which to build Canadian economic renewal, and Canada did what has become habitual — explore ways of increasing access to the cornucopia that Canadian eyes always manage to discern in the United States. For at least some Canadians, then as now, economic solvency seemed only a free trade agreement away. In 1947 and 1948 secret free trade negotiations at the civil service level produced a detailed draft agreement to reduce trade restrictions and move towards common trade policies. The agreement did not make it beyond the bureaucracy, largely because of Canadian fears over sovereignty.[29]

Following the 1947 political-military declaration, complementary military industrial cooperation was again confirmed, as surely as Ogdensburg was followed by Hyde Park. Having concluded that the only way to mitigate the costs of Canadian military equipment upgrading would be to gain enhanced access to the U.S. military market, Prime Minister Louis St. Laurent carried on a public campaign for a renewed Hyde Park arrangement.[30] The U.S. Congress was decidedly reluctant to open its pork barrel to Canada, but this reluctance (which has endured for forty years) was mitigated by acknowledgement of the wider strategic interests of the United States — and strategic concerns at the time were focused prominently on the Korean conflict.

The U.S. Department of Defense, which has always had a keener sense than Congress of the strategic payoffs from military-industrial cooperation, moved on its own to improve Canadian industry's access to the U.S. military market (the Air Force, for example, exempted Canada from the "Buy America" provisions related to its purchases). The Pentagon knew that Canada would have to buy U.S. equipment in order to rearm rapidly in support of the Cold War, and any hot wars the cold one might contain. It also knew that Canada would be in no position to do this if Canadian industry did not have reciprocal access to the U.S. market. In October 1950, four months after the outbreak of the Korean War, the two governments exchanged notes endorsing a "statement of principles for economic cooperation." The principles called for the two countries to coordinate production, procurement, and controls over the distribution of scarce raw materials and supplies, towards the end of facilitating cooperation between the two governments "in all respects practicable, and to the extent of their respective executive powers, to the end that the economic efforts of the two countries be coordinated for the common defence and that the production and resources of both countries be used for the best combined results."[31]

Korea: Heating Up the Cold War

It was in the Korean War that Canada, and indeed the world, most directly confronted the new strategic environment that the Cold War had begun to shape. While the ideal world order was represented by a multi-lateral, UN-based system of mutual and collective security, the inescapable reality that the Korean War confirmed was a Pax Americana sustained and disciplined by a new and pre-eminent imperial power. The confrontation of these two principles — the pursuit of mutual and common security through a managed system of global cooperation on the one hand, and the acceptance of protective custody under the wing of an imperial eagle on the other — would help shape Canada's postwar approach to international security and to its military procurement and production arrangements in support of its national security policies.

Canada attached high importance to developing and nurturing security arrangements that would encourage and preserve a stable "world order" in which individual nation-states could expect their territorial integrity and sovereignty to be honoured. This goal was to be attained initially through the United Nations — established, as already noted, with Canada's active involvement and enthusiasm — and then, once it became clear that this "grand coalition" would not on its own preserve the peace, through regional "collective defence" efforts as well.[32] The Soviet Union and international communism gradually came to be viewed as the chief threat to a stable world order. The prevailing testimony of Canadian historians is that this conclusion was reached after extensive debate within Canada and was not simply borrowed from the United States, although it would have been influenced by U.S. interpretations. In the end Canada became convinced that, as Lester Pearson said, it must join "the struggle of free, expanding progressive democracy against tyrannical and reactionary communism."[33]

Even this, however, was not a simple acquiescence in the idea of a Pax Americana. A world order policed by a superpower was too much at odds with the idea of collective security for Canada to embrace it. And indeed, it never was easily embraced, although it was gradually accepted and even enjoyed. While Canada viewed the United States as the pre-eminent world power on which the primary burden for maintaining a stable world order would rest, a major objective of Canadian diplomacy between 1945 and 1950, through the creation of the UN and NATO, was to develop international structures that would engage the United States in this global task while at the same time restraining it and making it subject to collective discipline. As John Holmes wrote, "The ambivalent Canadian policy was to avoid weakening the United States while assisting in the weaving of a web to control the behaviour of states including the United States."[34]

For some the equation seemed obvious: on one side was an expansionist empire bent on domination, while on the other side were those committed to preserving the integrity of states within a peaceful international order — and the latter were just lucky enough to have the support of the extraordinary economic and military power of the United States. There was also a less self-serving equation, though not one with great currency in Ottawa. According to this view, one side was still credited with expansionist ambitions and a bent for domination, but the other side was recognized as another superpower with its own expansionist ambitions, combined with a near-religious sense of its destiny to lead or prominently influence — if not dominate — events in the international community in support of its widening interests.

Canadian attitudes towards the sale of military commodities to the United States are directly and extensively bound up with these two differing perceptions. If the arms for which Canada produces components are assumed to be dedicated to collective defence against an external aggressor within the framework of UN collective security ideals, military sales are likely to be widely supported. If, however, these arms are assumed to be part of the commitment of a superpower to maintain its imperial ascendance by conducting a prolonged rivalry with another superpower and by intervening politically and militarily in the affairs of sovereign states, such support is obviously more likely to be guarded, or even withheld.

The Korean War, to the extent that it was legally defined and publicly portrayed as a collective UN peacekeeping operation, may have been a propaganda victory for the former view, but it also gave clear indications of the latter. Canada entered the war as part of its commitment to a UN-based collective security arrangement, and its rearmament program was premised on this principle. Could Canada credibly support a prominent security role for the United Nations if, in the first instance in which the world body required the military commitments of its members in order to carry out its security functions, Canada declined to contribute for lack of means? Canada did contribute, but its contribution turned out to be more in support of American hegemony than of international order. Preoccupied with taking action against China and enhancing its influence in Indochina, the U.S. was predisposed towards pursuing its own objectives in Korea rather than simply acting on behalf of the UN's responsibility to discipline an aggressor and neutralize the results of aggression, as was formally required.

"Defence," in the process, was a acquiring a new meaning. With Canadian "defence" forces now operating in Asia, it was hard to sustain the view that "defence" was the application of a state's force in support of its sovereignty and the integrity of its national territory. Under collective security, it was of course participating in a collective action in support of the defence of a fellow member of the collectivity, but America's own policies and rhetoric pointed to another view. There was growing evidence that U.S. military forces, and whatever allies could be persuaded to join them, were being used, not so much in the defence of national territory and those national institutions that facilitate political participation and the mediation of justice, as in the protection and enhancement of America's influence within the international community. The United States was acting out of the desire to maintain a place of economic prominence, if not dominance, in an international order that can bestow substantial benefits on countries near the top of the hierarchy — in other words, in Korea the U.S. was practising what in today's parlance is referred to as "competitiveness."[35] National defence was still undertaken in the service of national security, but national security was quickly becoming synonymous with the national economic interest.

Prominent objects of the American national interest were (and remain) raw materials and markets. At the time of the Korean War access to raw materials was very much on the minds of the U.S. administration. In November 1950 a presidential commission declared that "it is vital not to lose the sources of these needed raw materials to the forces of Communist aggression."[36] During the same period diplomat Averell Harriman told a Senate committee: "I do not believe this country can survive if the sources of the raw materials are in the hands of unfriendly people who are determined to destroy us."[37] With the competition for resources cast in these East-West terms, it was part of the assumed prerogative — if not duty — of a superpower to use its economic and military resources to assure the presence of friendly regimes in those places where coveted raw materials were located. In December 1951, Harriman extended this mandate even further to include the right to shape the overall international environment in line with the interests of the United States. The U.S., he said, must be "more mindful than ever before of creating either climate or mechanisms of one kind or another which would make it easier for us to get these materials from foreign sources at lowest prices possible under circumstances which are most advantageous to us."[38]

A second concern, that of maintaining access to world markets, was also well established at the time. As early as the turn of the century a U.S. State Department circular had recognized that the country's strategic commercial interests would have to become the concern of government: "It seems to be conceded that every year we shall be confronted with an increasing surplus of manufactured goods for sale in foreign markets if American operatives and artisans are to be kept employed the year round. The enlargement of foreign consumption of the products of our mills and the workshops has, therefore, become a serious problem of statesmanship as well as of commerce."[39]

In Korea, Canada described itself as supporting U.S. actions on behalf of the UN's collective security responsibilities. In North America, Canada described itself as contributing Canadian territory and resources to the collective defence of the continent. Canada did not, of course, publicly describe itself as supporting the use of military force to forge an international "climate" that served the economic interests of the United States.

There was no direct economic rationale for the U.S. intervention in Korea. Nevertheless, the U.S. preoccupation with developing a worldwide network of sources of raw materials and markets suggests that even in Korea the United States was taking care to illustrate its willingness and its capability to protect its interests whenever they were threatened, whether directly or indirectly. Just as the atomic bombing of Hiroshima and Nagasaki was a signal to the Soviet Union of America's military power and its willingness to use it, so U.S. military and paramilitary interventions in the late 1940s and beyond were another signal to the Soviet Union and the international community that America willingly assumed the burden of empire. The Soviet Union's own interventions at the close of World War II, along with the active programs of military aid both powers began in the 1950s, signalled the arrival of an international environment in which national defence, in the strict sense of the protection of national boundaries and public institutions, had become a minor element in superpower national security preoccupations.

The Korean War, along with the prominent attention to military cooperation among Western allies that accompanied the establishment of NATO, launched Canada on a major military buildup. The 1950 statement ensured that this would be done in cooperation with the United States, and in 1951 the Department of Defence Production was established to coordinate the rearmament program. Inevitably, balance of payments problems emerged once again, and once again the government turned to the proven practice of currying special favour with the rising military presence of the United States. As the historians R.D. Cuff and J.L. Granatstein wrote: "Astronomical defence budgets, the arms race, arms sales, and a permanent military-industrial complex all became characteristic of the post-Korea institutional setting. These were among the most obvious ramifications of America's imperial power, and they underscored the utility for Canada of securing a continuing and cooperative economic relationship with the United States."[40]

The pursuit of a renewed arrangement for defence production cooperation with the United States had become urgent by the mid-1950s.

From a high of $127 million in 1953, U.S. military procurement in Canada had dropped to $49 million by 1956. While the Korean War had temporarily sustained military production in Canada, there would be little business from the new war, the Cold War, until Canada had sorted out the nature and extent of its own commitment to it. Several questions were involved. Despite the obvious failings of the United Nations, it was still not clear what the UN's long-term role would be in giving leadership in collective security. What kind of defence posture — given a combination of UN, European and North American commitments — would be appropriate for a smaller power sharing a continent with a superpower? And finally, what should be the military production arrangements of a small industrial nation with clear limits on internally generated demand for military commodities?

Throughout the postwar period, protectionism has been integral to American military production, and any joint production arrangement would inevitably confront this reality. The Joint United States – Canada Industrial Mobilization Committee accomplished very little in the initial period after its creation in 1949. One obstacle to its success was a prohibition on American military exports in force at the time, except in cases where the commodities in question had been declared surplus to the needs of the American armed forces.

A more serious restriction on shared defence production, however, was imposed by "Buy America" laws which specified that American military supplies were to be purchased only within the United States — except when it was "in the national interest" to buy them elsewhere because stocks were not domestically available, because costs were out of line with foreign prices, or because an emergency existed.[41] At the same time there was an effective mining and manufacturing lobby insisting that American industry was perfectly capable of producing all the military equipment the country required. The escalation of the Korean conflict in mid-1950 eased American protectionist sentiment long enough for the Joint Committee to develop a set of guidelines for the coordination of the two countries' resources and production facilities for the common defence, but the zeal to maintain this spirit of cooperation beyond the war was lacking. Vested American interests once more sought preferential treatment for American producers, and by 1954 Canada was once again running a defence trade deficit.[42]

The Permanent War

In the post-Korea 1950s it was becoming clear that the new strategic environment and changing technology would require sustained military production for a permanent war footing. The Cold War was the continuing struggle for global influence cast in East-West terms, and while there was little pressure on Canada to participate directly in the American mission to maintain a favourable international "climate" for the control of resources and markets, there was no doubt that Canada was expected to show political solidarity and provide support. In this century's earlier wars, that support had included a prominent role in military production. As Canada prepared again to lend industrial support to the war effort, it was inevitable that this process would once again lead towards further coordination and integration of Canada's military production with that of the United States.

In North America the military/strategic concern was to close America's back door. There could be no convincing global role for the United States if this back door was not secure, and it was soon clear that the Americans would take whatever measures were necessary to ensure that it was. In other words, if Canadians did not secure their own territory, the U.S. would do it for them. It is a position that has become known as Canada's need for "defence against help."[43]

The focus of the pressure was on the air defence of North America. The United States, from the end of World War II until the advent of the intercontinental ballistic missile at the end of the 1950s, continually sought Canadian cooperation for plans to mount an extensive air defence operation from Canadian soil.[44] The U.S. was interested in stationing fighter-interceptor aircraft in the Canadian Far North, and while Canada resisted this proposal, the two countries did eventually agree to three radar lines across Canada, the most important (and most expensive) being the Distant Early Warning (DEW) line. The DEW line, in the farthest reaches of the Canadian North, was a string of radar stations designed to provide early warning of a Soviet bomber attack to the nuclear bombers of the U.S. Strategic Air Command, enabling them to avoid pre-emptive attack and to be available for retaliation. In other words, the DEW line was designed to enable the SAC to appear to be a credible deterrent to Soviet attack.

In Europe, Canada was under considerable pressure to expand its contribution to NATO, while Ottawa tried to persuade European governments that defence spending in North America was part of its commitment to the North Atlantic community. In the rest of the world, Canadian support for Pax Americana was confined to general expression of political solidarity (at least until Vietnam).

Throughout this period Canada faced the difficult question of how to arrange for the production of the military equipment needed for this sustained Cold War. The nature of developing military technology itself turned out to be an impediment to self-sufficiency, or even a modest measure of independence, in military production.

Modern military technology is, of course, expensive, highly complex, and rapidly consumed in war. Even in the 1950s, the Soviet nuclear threat demanded a constant state of readiness in North America, and while costs had not yet reached today's absurd dimensions, they were rising.[45] In 1954 – 55 Canada's defence spending was 37 per cent of the federal budget.[46] The complexity of modern weapons meant that the lead time from conception to production was growing, and with the advent of nuclear weapons designated for battlefield use it was clear that the rate of consumption of these weapons in battle was likely to be formidable.[47]

In consequence of this combination of characteristics, it was no longer possible to follow the traditional practice of maintaining low levels of armed forces in peacetime with the expectation that in wartime there would be rapid mobilization of both personnel and industry to supply the weapons for a sustained war. Canadian analyst D.W. Middlemiss noted that there is a "technologically induced" need for "extensive forces-in-being," with the result that "for most countries, the new era of war-in-peace has dictated that matters of military weapons procurement now constitute an important and continuing function of Government."[48] Since modern weapons take a long time to build, are costly, and are consumed in war much faster than they can be built, there is little option but to have assembled, at the beginning of the war, all the weapons you think you're going to need for its duration. In other words, the age of permanent wartime preparedness had arrived. And since the West was now essentially integrated into a militarized Pax Americana, potential wars were no longer confined to North America and Europe.

The problem of the Permanent War is particularly acute for a smaller power. Even in the 1950s the trend was suggesting that few countries would be in a position to undertake decade-long research and development programs for the production of sophisticated weapons systems. But Canada, with its record of World War II production schedules still ringing in C.D. Howe's ears, did not give up without a try. In the mid-1950s Canada was an important manufacturer of military aircraft — Canadian designed CF-100 fighters and U.S.-designed F-86 fighters, Harvard and T-34 trainers, and Beaver and Otter transport aircraft.[49] Canada's attempt, and its ultimate failure, to use that expertise to reach for a place of prominence in the high-stakes game of modern weapons manufacture produced industrial and political ramifications which three decades have not been able to erase.

3

From the Arrow to Offsets:
The Perils of Production Sharing

In the mid-1950s, Canada was a successful producer of military aircraft, but to attain this position it had been required to make a costly sacrifice. At the close of World War II Canada had embarked on a bold manufacturing initative. In 1946 A.V. Roe of Canada, in consultation with Trans-Canada Airlines (TCA), undertook to design a transcontinental jet passenger aircraft. The British were already working on such a plane, but no American company had begun any work on commercial jet transports. The first flight of the Avro Jetliner took place in 1949. An industrial and technological triumph, the Jetliner was equally spectacular as a commercial failure.

E.K. Shaw, a technician who worked on the Jetliner, blamed changing TCA and Department of Transport specifications for the cancellation of TCA's option on thirty Jetliners.[1] Meanwhile, European airlines continued to show interest. Howard Hughes had the Jetliner flown to California where he tested it for a month, concluding with a series of strong endorsements of the aircraft, and in April 1950 the Jetliner flew from Toronto to New York, carrying the world's first jet airmail. It continued to fly as a company plane for eight years, apparently without the development of any design defects.

In 1950 a second Jetliner was under construction when the word came down from C.D. Howe to clear the company's floor of the plane in order to accelerate the pace of CF-100 fighter aircraft production. After TCA cancelled its orders, Howe insisted, as minister of trade and commerce, that "you can't build a plane without orders." Instead, he demanded that the company concentrate its efforts in an area where there were not only orders, but pressures to speed up production — military aircraft.

At the time of cancellation, the company had been in a position to be a world leader in the design and production of civilian aircraft, and the one completed Jetliner continued to fly until it was inexplicably cut up for scrap metal in 1957. But in the early 1950s the military market appeared to be the more buoyant. The fact that, for Canada to take advantage of the buoyancy of the military market, the Canadian military production industry had to be fully adapted to U.S. military requirements and policies was, for Howe, apparently not a crucial consideration. However, the experience of the Jetliner flies in the face of current conventional wisdom, which insists that the development of a viable commercial aerospace industry depends on the availability of military work. It was indeed wartime aircraft production that made the Jetliner such an early possibility, but it was also military aircraft production that prevented that early potential for commercial jet aircraft from being effectively exploited.

Aiming an Arrow at the Big Time

While more than 600 CF-100s were built, the sheen went off military aircraft production with the CF-100's successor. The Avro Arrow was aimed to provide Canada with an entry into big-time military production — but it turned out to be a monumental misfiring.

It was originally estimated that the next generation of fighter aircraft would cost from $1.5 to $2 million per copy (as compared with an ultimate cost of $650,290 per copy for the CF-100). But then things started to get more complicated. While initial plans were for only the airframe of the Avro Arrow to be developed in Canada, with the expectation that the engine, fire-control system and weapon (air-to-air missile) would be imported, by 1957 the engine and weapon were being developed in Canada, with the fire-control system being developed at full Canadian expense by RCA in the United States.[2]

At the same time costs were escalating, while the government's assessment of its total requirements was reduced from 400 to 100 planes. In 1955 the estimated cost per plane was given as $2.6 million. In early 1957 it was down to $2 million again. In late 1957 there were rumours that the price would be $8 million each, but in early 1958 an estimate of $6.1 million was given. By July of 1958 the estimate was back down to $4.5 million, but in September of that year Prime Minister John Diefenbaker suggested a price of $12.5 million per plane. It was estimated that if the government was to acquire both the Arrow and the Bomarc missile as planned, there would have to be a 30 per cent increase in Canadian military spending.

By 1957 the dying government of Louis St. Laurent had developed severe doubts about the future of the project. The succeeding Diefenbaker government made efforts to sell the aircraft to both Britain and the United States. The main prospect was the United States, and the Canadians argued the importance of Canada-U.S. integration. They noted that military integration, as represented by joint air defence operations involving the joint radar systems and ultimately the North American Air Defence Agreement (NORAD), was already a reality. This made equipment standardization and industrial integration essential, and if industrial integration was to work, then the United States would have to buy in Canada when Canada produced a superior product.

And the Arrow was widely acknowledged to be a superior fighter aircraft (although when the first test model was rolled out on October 4, 1957 the occasion was robbed of some of its glow by the day's news that the Soviet Union had launched the first Sputnik satellite). In subsequent flight tests the Arrow reached a speed of 2,250 km/h while climbing, and it was praised as far superior to any other aircraft, either flying or under development, in the "free world" at the time. But the equally spectacular climb of the aircraft's costs, the lack of success in marketing it outside the country, and the growing suspicion that with the imminent introduction of the ballistic missile the days of the bomber threat were numbered all combined to make the cancellation of the project almost certain. On February 20, 1959 the announcement came. Fourteen thousand A.V. Roe employees were left without work, as were perhaps an equal number of Canadian workers whose jobs were indirectly sustained by the Arrow project.

Both the Avro Jetliner and the Arrow demonstrated Canadian industry's capacity to develop technologically advanced products of unusual quality. In the case of the Jetliner the company was denied the opportunity to demonstrate its capacity to carry the product through to production. The Arrow, on the other hand, raised doubts about the industry's efficiency and its ability to meet deadlines. In consequence, Canada faced another difficult defence production decision. On the one hand it had an obvious interest in preserving its industrial capability and jobs, and in particular in improving its balance of payments with the United States. On the other hand, it had already committed itself, through NORAD, to a long-term collective defence arrangement on the continent — an arrangement premised on the integration of Canada's military forces and roles into a U.S.-led Western alliance.

Given the imbalance of the Canada-U.S. military relationship, NORAD was less a vehicle for the joint defence of North America than one for placing Canada under the wing of the United States. NORAD was never given the objective, nor has it ever had the capability, of providing comprehensive defence against a major invading bomber force. Instead, its primary function was to maintain a peacetime surveillance system capable of detecting and identifying unknown aircraft and providing a limited defence against bomber attack. It was designed to provide early warning to the U.S. Strategic Air Command, so that U.S. bombers would have time to respond and attacking Soviet bombers would be denied a pre-emptive strike against the U.S. airborne deterrent. Since then the role of NORAD has been substantially changed and augmented. Renamed the North American Aerospace Defence Agreement, NORAD now has responsibility for warning and assessment of ballistic missile attack, space surveillance to keep track of satellites in earth orbit and provide warning when there is a threat of attack, and assisting in the command and control of U.S. nuclear weapons.

Canadian governments have always treated joint defence and joint production as the two sides of a single coin. In 1967 Prime Minister Lester Pearson responded to suggestions that the Defence Production Sharing Arrangements be ended with the claim that such action "would be interpreted as a notice of withdrawal on our part from continental defence and even from the collective defence arrangements of the Atlantic Alliance."[3] Whether in defence production, continental defence, or the acquisition of nuclear weapons, the governments of the 1950s and 1960s were proceeding down a military-industrial path from which they saw no exit.

Old Problems, Old Solutions

The Arrow debacle placed in sharp focus Canada's need to find a longer-term solution to its military production problems. One possibility, at least in theory, was that Canada would pursue a more autonomous defence policy using military equipment within its own industrial capability. However, this possibility had been effectively eliminated by Canada's entry into the NORAD agreement and its commitment to military integration. Following the second option, a full-fledged pursuit of a broad state-of-the-art military industry capable of producing equipment to meet the military needs defined by the alliance leadership, had turned out to be at best extremely difficult, as the experience of the Arrow had shown, and that option had died with the Arrow's cancellation.

Given Ottawa's full commitment to integration, there was only one option left. Circumstances had simply confirmed that what Canada had done in World War I, World War II, and the Korean War, it would do again in the Permanent War — in exchange for U.S. technology and capital it would seek preferred access to the U.S. military market. Once again, unless the United States would buy the industry's end product (as it had so conspicuously failed to do in the case of the Arrow), Canadian military production could not continue.

Well before the death of the Arrow, the separate interests of the two countries were converging to lead towards a more formal set of defence production sharing arrangements. For the United States, the primary consideration was a need to make sure that the back door was closed. America's role as a global power required a reliable security arrangement for its home territory. Even though there neither were in fact nor were assumed to be any immediate threats to the homeland, the United States still had to create confidence that no such threats would develop and that it had in Canada a reliable neighbour.

The Americans, in effect, wanted a tangible renewal of Mackenzie King's pledge that Canada would take appropriate care to ensure that no third party could use Canadian territory to attack or threaten attack on the United States. Canada had gone a long way towards updating that pledge by building the DEW line and by entering into the NORAD agreement, but American military planners always felt that military integration of the two countries should be reinforced by industrial integration. As John Holmes has written, "the friends of Canadian defence production were in the Pentagon and the State Department."[4] While the United States obviously sought access to Canadian territory for early warning and bomber defence, it also had a security interest in what University of Toronto political scientist John Kirton has described as a "wider dispersal of production facilities, establishment of supplemental sources of supply, and determination of Canadian production facilities available for the supply of the United States."[5]

For Canada, a primary interest was in making defence procurement affordable. The more the costs of the Arrow soared, the more Canadians recognized that Canada would in the long term be substantially dependent upon external sources for major defence equipment. To mitigate the costs of these imports, Canada sought a sustained export capability in defence products. Economically, of course, there was no reason why exports to compensate for military imports would also have to be of military commodities. The effect on the balance of trade with the United States would be no different if Canada sold such things as wheat or automobiles or tractors to the United States in return for importing fighter aircraft. But even though Canada's primary concern was economic, and there was no strictly economic imperative for defence production sharing as such, Ottawa was not ready to forgo all military production. Politically, it would be much easier to develop support for the import of military commodities if it could be shown that the export of military commodities would flow from and, in effect, be made possible and enhanced by such imports.

Gideon Rosenbluth, who provided the first substantial study of the impact that disarmament would have on the Canadian economy, also pointed to the differing rationales for defence production sharing on the two sides. For the Americans the rationale was cooperation and integration in military planning, while for the Canadians it was nurturing a viable Canadian defence industry.[6] From Hyde Park to the present, the interest of the United States in production sharing has focused on military and defence policy issues.[7] The Americans viewed military-industrial cooperation as a means of encouraging Canadian political support for U.S. defence policy and North American defence planning. A 1958 U.S. National Security Council document supported Canadian industrial participation in the production of major weapons systems and emphasized the importance of Canadian defence cooperation and the need for the U.S. to be mindful of Canada's economic requirements. "Unless Canadian defence industries do remain healthy," it warned, "the United States probably will not receive the same excellent cooperation in the joint defence effort that has prevailed in the past."[8]

Indeed, when the Defence Production Sharing Arrangements (DPSA) were established in 1959 by an exchange of letters between the U.S. secretary of defense and the Canadian minister of defence production, virtually all the economic concessions were made by the United States. Canada was able to maintain tariffs to protect Canadian subcontractors until 1966, and continued a policy of giving a 10 per cent domestic price preference in Canadian military procurement in order to provide Canadian firms with a competitive advantage.[9] In 1966 Canada waived customs duties on the import of defence goods over $250,000, but retained duties for contracts under that figure so as to increase the competitive advantage of small Canadian firms.[10]

This economic imbalance in the DPSA lends additional credence to the view that the United States was pursuing primarily strategic objectives through the DPSA — to maintain broad Canadian compliance with American defence policy and to ensure a sufficient level of Canadian military spending and preparedness — while Canada was pursuing economic objectives (the political costs to Canada of this situation are evaluated in chapter 8). A U.S. Defense Department directive issued in 1960 described the purpose of defence production sharing as being "to continue the principle of economic cooperation with Canada in the interests of continental defense, and [to] stipulate the policy of maximum production and development program integration in support of closely integrated military planning between Canada and the United States."[11] John Kirton concluded:

> To put the case most dramatically one must enquire why, in the face of considerable opposition from its own defence industries, the American government not only allowed foreigners to compete for the supply of goods required for the national security, but also gave them access to American military "secrets", and later, American government funds in the form of research grants to enable them to do so effectively. American participation stemmed from an assessment, reinforced by Canadian negotiators, that in the absence of such measures, the political realities of the Canadian situation in the light of the Arrow cancellation would make it extremely difficult for the Canadian government to continue its defence expenditures at any significant level. From the American perspective, the economic concessions were a small price to pay in order to ensure a meaningful Canadian contribution to continental defence.[12]

In 1985 government officials told the Commons External Affairs and National Defence Committee that the objectives of defence production sharing are "greater integration of military production, greater standardization of military equipment, wider dispersal of production facilities, establishment of supplemental sources of supply."[13] The DPSA permit Canadian firms to compete for U.S. defence prime contracts and subcontracts. To facilitate this, the U.S. agreed:

- to waive regulations of the "Buy America Act" for U.S. purchases of military goods in Canada;
- to waive import duties on most defence goods[14];
- to relax security restrictions to permit freer Canadian discussion with the U.S. Armed Forces and U.S. defence contractors.

In turn, the Canadian government undertook to assist the Canadian industry in becoming more competitive by underwriting partial costs of preproduction and tooling for firms bidding against U.S. companies whose preproduction and tooling costs had already been written off under previous contracts (currently, this activity is the purpose of the Defence Industry Productivity program). In addition, Canada promised to pursue a variety of promotional efforts, such as increasing Department of Defence Production staff in Washington and providing Canadian industry with up-to-date information about U.S. procurement programs (this activity currently is the responsibility of the Defence Programs Branch of the Department of External Affairs).

For the Canadian workers who had built the Avro Jetliner and the Arrow, the directives to Canadian industry must have been particularly galling. Canadian industry was urged, in the exchange of letters, to "be efficiency conscious," to "use imagination and engineering skill of a high order," and to "concentrate Canadian development and production on the things Canadian manufacturing industry can do best."[15]

By agreement between the two governments, Canada's military industry has been structured to specialize in and focus on supplying equipment to meet U.S. military needs. In return, the United States "recognized" that Canada would buy the majority of its major weapons systems from the U.S. This is not a formal requirement of the agreement, but it does not have to be. Without a fully developed industrial base of its own, Canada had no choice but to import its military equipment, and so confident was the U.S. of its position that it saw simply taking note of that fact as being sufficient.

The result of the agreements has been a Canadian industry that relies primarily on a single customer, the Pentagon. The question of the costs (taken up in chapter 8) remains. What happens to Canadian defence policy when it is to be carried out by equipment designed to fulfill U.S. policies and strategic objectives? What price must Canada pay to continue to enjoy access to the lucrative U.S. defence market?

Historian John Holmes acknowledged that the DPSA have undermined Canada's independence: "There was no doubt that Canada, in pursuit of its legitimate economic interest, had got itself into a position that placed a constraint on its freedom of movement in foreign policy."[16] Holmes, however, went on to say that this constraint was never tested — which only begs the further question of whether Canada has become so attuned to working within the constraint that it is no longer understood as being a constraint.

Economic Interests and Political Acquiescence

Canada's interests in defence production sharing have, from the beginning, been self-serving and impractical. When the Cold War was heating up in the 1950s, history and geography were kind enough to provide Canada with a convenient bargaining chip, an expansive northern territory situated between the world's most celebrated adversaries. Canada lost little time in putting this chip on the table. The deal Canada sought was, in effect, to give the Americans the run of its territory in return for a go at the American defence market — a market that has always seemed, at least to Canadians interested in military production, a bottomless pit to be filled with wing tips, microcircuits, shock absorbers and all the other bits and pieces that Canadian industry hustles to the Pentagon. Canadian military sales representatives like to tell of the $100 billion-plus U.S. military market and of how Canada supplies a mere 1 per cent of that market. Visions dance in their heads of high technology and full employment as Canada scrambles to feed a monster they fondly see as both benign and insatiable.

For the three decades since the cancellation of the Arrow, military production in Canada has been premised on the hope that we can build a military industry of note, a military industry that will contribute to our national security and economic prosperity, on the strength not of Canadian but of American military spending. If we could just land that one crucial foreign customer, security and plenty would be ours. Of course, Canada has always acknowledged that this strategy might involve a cost, but at the same time it has assumed that, with a little luck, we might avoid paying that cost in hard currency. Perhaps it could be paid instead in two commodities that Canada has in rather more generous supply — territory and political acquiescence. Both of these were in fact promised to the Americans, in a cooperative Canadian spirit.

But cooperation was one characteristic with which the ample personality of John Diefenbaker was not notably endowed, and as a result his government had some momentary problems in delivering it. In the early years of defence production sharing, when patterns of behaviour were being established and it was especially important for goodwill to be manifested, the Diefenbaker government, if not overtly uncooperative, was at least confused. What confused John Diefenbaker was that he had not understood that, having put Canadian territory and cooperation in defence policy onto the bargaining table in exchange for access to the rich U.S. military market, he would have to forgo many of the prerogatives of sovereignty and independent decision-making. Diefenbaker claimed that he had not known that Bomarc missiles and Voodoo aircraft were useless without nuclear warheads, but his confusion was not so much technical as political. He was still under the impression that, having integrated Canada into a single North American air defence command and a single North American defence industry, he would have something to say about the continent's policies.

His impotence found its most eloquent expression during the Cuban missile crisis in 1962. With unconscious temerity, the Chief wanted independent verification that the blurred photos of Cuba sent him by the

U.S. State Department were in fact evidence of Soviet missile installations there. He said he would need this before complying with an American request to put Canadian forces on a wartime alert. While he was playing the role of an in-charge sovereign leader not about to be stampeded, his minister of defence, acting on his own initiative, quietly moved to put his forces on the requested alert. The last laugh, however, was on the minister of defence who, thinking he was acting out of courageous loyalty to a trusted ally, was unaware that his military commander's courageous loyalty was more fervent than his own and that, on orders from Washington, Canadian forces had already been placed on alert.[17]

Even with the real centre of Canadian military authority thus established, the "sharing" of defence production with the United States still proved problematic. While Canadian officials were pleased with the cooperation displayed by U.S. procurement officials and with the way in which the production sharing procedures were being implemented (they were even extended to include NASA[18]), they were not yet fully prepared to accept that the limits of American cooperation would ultimately be defined by American interests rather than by Canadian desires. A preliminary indication of what these limits might be was provided by the Eisenhower Administration in 1960, when it announced measures related to military procurement in an effort to reduce the growing U.S. balance of payments deficit. Included as a directive to the Department of Defense was the requirement that it "take promptly all possible steps to reduce by a very substantial amount the expenditures from funds appropriated to the military services . . . that are planned for procurement abroad during the calendar year 1961 . . . "[19]

Defense Secretary Thomas Gates did issue a memorandum exempting Canada from the provisions, and U.S. purchases in Canada grew from $96.3 million in 1959 to $112.7 million in 1960 and $142.6 million in 1961. But the Kennedy Administration that followed had an unabashed disdain for Diefenbaker and his disarmament-prone external affairs secretary, Howard Green, and it showed little interest in promoting defence production sharing. The Pentagon, mindful of U.S. economic difficulties, understandably sought to steer procurement to those domestic areas which had been hard hit by the unemployment that accompanied the slight recession of the early 1960s.[20] However, despite the adverse economic and political climate, U.S. procurement in Canada — aided by Canadian acquisitions in the United States, including the CF-101 and CF-104 aircraft and the Bomarc missiles — was growing.

These developments lend themselves to two contradictory interpretations. On the one hand it could be credibly argued that, despite a
climate that was adverse to defence production sharing, the program
was working, and that once the bugs were out of the system, things
could only get better. Another credible view was that the early difficulties encountered by the arrangements were confirmation that they
would inevitably and perhaps incessantly run up against conflicting
national interests and that Canadians would have to be constantly vigi-
lant to protect their newly found U.S. market from the ever-present
threat of erosion.

Whichever interpretation one preferred, they both clearly implied
that each country would have to pay a price to keep the arrangements
working. For the Americans, the DPSA impinged upon at least two sets
of conflicting interests: the interest in promoting full Canadian cooperation in the defence of North America on the one hand, and the commitment not to become dependent on external suppliers for major military equipment — coupled with the obvious interest in using defence
expenditures to maximize employment at home — on the other. So the
extent to which the Americans honored and supported shared defence
production was evidence of the value they placed on the political/secu-
rity payoffs inherent in the arrangements.

For the Canadians, the extent to which the Americans cooperated in
shared defence production and made their market available to Canadians, despite adverse economic conditions, was a measure of the extent to which Canada would have to continue to make political concessions. This equation was a consequence of the fact that, unlike Canada,
the United States was pursuing political and not economic objectives
through the DPSA. The immediate American objective was to gain Canadian cooperation in a North American air defence system under
NORAD, while the long-term objective was overall Canadian cooperation in U.S. defence policy, particularly in North America and Europe.

Canadian industry officials at the time recognized this connection
between defence production sharing and political solidarity. During
the early days of the DPSA the issue of consuming controversy was the
question of whether or not the Canadian armed forces should be
equipped with nuclear weapons. Aircraft industry representatives assumed a direct relationship between Canadian nuclear policies and
Canadian access to the U.S. military market, and they showed no hesi-
tation in calling on Canada to pay the political costs of their economic
interests. At the first annual meeting of the Canadian Air Industries Association at Niagara Falls, Ontario, in 1962, its president, David Gold-

en, described what he considered to be the economic implications of the political decision on whether or not Canada ought to accept nuclear warheads:

> It will be a disaster if defence production sharing is ended. We cannot go on expecting Washington to take politically difficult decisions like allowing us an equal break in their defence market and yet refuse to take the politically difficult decisions that face us. If we won't take nuclear arms we must be prepared to take the consequences. This year we will have sold $200 million worth of items and equipment to the U.S. under the deal. It is this business which forms the solid base on which our most advanced technology has grown. With this under our belt we have been able to go on to win substantial export orders in other parts of the world. But if we lose the U.S. market we are finished. The Canadian demand cannot support an advanced industry by itself.[21]

Journalist Maurice Cutler commented that in general the Canadian defence industry feared that the United States "might reduce defence expenditures in Canada until this country moves its policies more into line with Pentagon thinking."[22] In sum, much of the story of Canadian military sales to the United States is the story of the efforts to manage the conflicting interests that both countries bring to defence production sharing. The Americans have been looking for the stable ground between the economic concessions that would ensure Canada's political cooperation and the protectionism that would satisfy the well-developed sense of economic self-interest in Congress. The Canadians, meanwhile, have been searching for the proper compromise between unrestricted access to the U.S. military market and the maintenance of some semblance of defence and foreign policy independence.

Finding the Fair Share in Production Sharing

From the beginning, Canadian industry and government officials have been convinced that Canada is not getting its "fair share" of the U.S. defence procurement pie. Apart from security restrictions, in the early years there was a feeling that Americans were simply having a hard time getting over their habit of buying military goods from American suppliers. They simply weren't accustomed to looking to the tundra for microcircuits. For the Canadians the temptation was to find a structural solution to this problem.

In 1960, Diefenbaker's minister of defence production, Raymond O'Hurley, thought that perhaps there should be additional measures taken to assure the equalization of Canada-U.S. military trade.[23] Some industry officials, with a somewhat surprising, if charming, political ingenuousness, thought that Canadian firms should be guaranteed a certain percentage of U.S. defence purchases.[24] No doubt Washington State and California, which at least had the merit of being paid-up members of the American union, would have been happy with as much (it's little wonder that the Americans regularly accuse Canadians of wanting a free ride). Unable to build a defence industry on the erratic levels of military spending in Canada, industry officials in Canada obviously thought it would be nice to be guaranteed that benefits would immediately accrue to them from any increases in U.S. spending.

Canadian naivete turned to audacity when industrialists and editorial writers alike began promoting the idea of Canada's being given sole responsibility for certain areas of continental military production. Through specialization, it was argued, a prescribed field within the overall market could be reserved for Canadian industry.[25] In their apparently boundless innocence, the Canadian industrialists deemed it entirely sensible that the U.S. Congress should decide to take measures to guarantee that a portion of its annual spending authorization for weapons be reserved for Canadian industry — all this in a climate of American restraint and military cost reduction.

Rather than giving Canada additional guarantees, it is hardly surprising, at least in retrospect, that the Americans were moving in the opposite direction. While U.S. military procurement in Canada reached an initial peak in 1962, the trend in 1963 was sharply down. That, combined with Defense Secretary Robert McNamara's public resolve to cut down costs and to make procurement more competitive, once again left Canadian officials nervous and in need of a trip to Washington. Bud Drury, minister of defence production in the newly-elected Liberal government of Lester Pearson, headed the delegation. The Canadians heard McNamara reassure them that U.S. balance-of-payments problems would not interfere with American military purchases in Canada. When Drury reported on the meeting to the House of Commons, however, he added that "the maintenance of a general balance in our cross-border procurement of equipment seems the best answer to concern at the drain on foreign exchange reserves through such procurement."[26]

During the discussions with the Americans it was clear that the issue of the trade balance, or imbalance, between the two countries was a central point of contention, and in addition each side was dealing with a different set of figures. As a compromise it was agreed that Canada would keep the tally of what each side had purchased from the other, and that, as seems in retrospect to have been inevitable, the two countries would try over the long run to maintain a balance in military trade. To the Canadians, this seemed, as O'Hurley had suggested earlier, to be to their advantage. American protectionism, a seemingly permanent element of the American political economy, was best dealt with through structural adjustments in the trade relations between the two countries — it's a familiar tune that the free traders of the 1980s have also learned to play.

On the assumption that it would be a constant struggle for Canada to gain systematic and growing access to the U.S. military market, and that Canadian equipment purchases would naturally be made in the United States, it seemed like a good idea at the time. Canada had just purchased two American planes, the CF-101 and CF-104, and wanted the U.S. to buy more from Canada. This way, the U.S. would have to buy as much from Canada as Canada bought from the U.S. Of course, it also meant the opposite. Canada would have to buy as much from the United States as the U.S. bought in Canada. In the mid-1970s (as discussed later in this chapter) the United States was able to use this provision to exercise direct influence on Canadian defence policy and spending by suggesting that the U.S. would have difficulty sustaining high levels of military procurement in Canada if Canada did not undertake some substantial — even specific — purchases in the U.S.

In 1963, few anticipated these repercussions. However, the *Financial Times of Canada* expressed intimations of what was to come with this explanation of the operation of the "rough balance" principle: the U.S. Defense Department would reopen the door for Canadian manufacturers only on the condition that the Canadian government kept an exact tally of U.S. spending in Canada and then matched it, dollar for dollar, with its own purchases in the U.S.[27]

Canadian government and industry officials were still convinced that Canada was not being given the full access to the U.S. military market that had been promised in the Defence Production Sharing Arrangements. These arrangements had been entered into with visions of an invisible border and full acceptance of Canadian companies as equal partners with American military contractors. Thus, it was a harsh irony that the Canadians encouraged a specific limitation on Canadian access to the U.S. military market, by virtue of the "rough balance" provision, hoping thereby to expand their access to that market.

Meanwhile, the Canadians were also undertaking efforts in other areas to improve their competitiveness in the North American military trade. Another point of contention early on was Canada's fear that it would be permanently disadvantaged as long as research and development activity was concentrated in the United States. This fear grew out of a general American inclination not to purchase complete, fully developed military commodities offshore. Canada had faced this American predilection for made-at-home weapons in the Avro Arrow episode, when the United States showed no interest in purchasing a fully developed aircraft from Canada, whatever that aircraft's merits might have been. If the United States was not about to buy complete systems from Canada, the Canadians argued that it should at least make parts of its overall research and development activity available to Canadian firms, on the same basis that it made its production contracts available to Canadian firms through the Defence Production Sharing Arrangements.

In a campaign to increase the overall research and development work done in Canada, Canadian industry representatives called both for greater access to U.S. research and development contracts and for increased spending on research and development within Canada's military budget. In the latter case, however, they were eager for the border to become visible again and for Canadian military research and development to give preference to Canadian firms. When it came to defence research and development sharing, it seemed, Canadians were determined to have their cake and eat it too. While they claimed their right of access to their "fair share" of U.S. military research and development, protectionism was to be the order of the day for Canadian military research and development.

Canada did not manage to get the United States to fund the Canadian industry's research and development activity in quite that neat a fashion, however. In November 1963, representatives of the United States Department of Defense and the Canadian Department of Defence Production signed a memorandum of understanding in the field of cooperative development, providing for Canadian firms to undertake development projects with the costs shared by the American and Canadian governments and the Canadian firm. Referred to as the Defence Development Sharing Program, the memorandum of understanding identified three principal objectives: to permit Canadian firms to undertake research and development work on behalf of the U.S. armed forces, to "utilize better the industrial, scientific and technical resources of the two countries in the interests of mutual defence," and to promote the standardization and interchangeability of defence equipment between the two countries.[28] The agreement committed the United

States to fund 25 per cent of mutually agreed upon research and development projects.

From Boom to Bust through Vietnam

Appealing as the "rough balance" provision may have seemed at the time, what it did not count on was Vietnam. Little more than a year after agreement on the provision was reached, the United States was heavily enmeshed in the conflict in Indochina and embarking on a major military buildup. In the Pentagon's rush to equip and send forces to Vietnam, the availability of duty-free military goods from Canada became rather more attractive, so that the rest of the sixties was a boom time for Canadian military industry. Canadian manufacturers readily took advantage of the windfall, and neither they nor the government gave much thought to the day when the "rough balance" provision would call for similarly extravagant purchases by Canada in the United States.

Immediately upon the American government's decision to commit combat troops overtly to Vietnam, there was a dramatic increase in Canadian military sales to the United States. Between 1964 and 1966 sales doubled to reach $317.1 million (about $800 million in 1986 dollars). While Canadian officials sought valiantly to place this bonanza within the context of normal defence production sharing, there was no hiding the fact that Canadian military production had hit upon good times and that these were coincident with the war in Vietnam which the Canadian public generally opposed, and for which even the Canadian government occasionally professed distaste.

What was not widely recognized during the military export boom years of the late 1960s was that the boom would inevitably turn to bust. Even during the boom years, the ongoing management of the DPSA was a delicate matter. As one analyst commented, "the industrialists of one country can hardly be expected to welcome the entry into the home market of competitors from another country. Legislators, sensitive to domestic interests and pressures, are likely to raise embarrassing questions as to why the manufacturers and workers of a foreign country should be accorded equality of treatment with those of the home country."[29] Over the first decade of the DPSA, Canadian access to the American market was gradually restricted through amendments to the annual Defense Appropriations Act.

In a report to the Commons External Affairs and National Defence Committee, the director of the Office of International Special Projects of the Department of Industry, Trade and Commerce, Frank Jackman, listed the restrictions which at the time limited American defence purchases to U.S. sources: the Berry Amendment on food, clothing and certain textile materials; restrictions on specialty metals that were not melted in steel manufacturing facilities within the United States or its possessions; the Byrnes and Tollefson Amendments regarding naval vessels or "major components" of naval ship hulls or superstructures; small business set-asides; labour surplus area set-asides; minority group – owned business set-asides; programs for depressed industries; restrictions in the Military Assistance Program requiring that prime contractors be American; restrictions on U.S. military construction contracts and materials for those contracts; restrictions on areas of technology and weapons considered to be in the national interest; and balance of payments (gold flow) restrictions on goods specified for overseas destinations.[30]

These problems were overshadowed, however, by the riches deriving from the war in Vietnam. At the time, the war seemed to be a genuinely insoluble problem, and American foreign affairs doctrine did not suggest that America's military requirements were likely to take a sharp downturn. Nevertheless, that is exactly what happened. America's withdrawal from Vietnam came at a time of dramatic balance of payments problems in the United States, and while it may be rash to describe the withdrawal as a "solution," it did result in a precipitate decline in American demand for imported military commodities. Between 1969 and 1974 U.S. military purchases in Canada were cut in half. This resulted in a major dislocation within Canadian industry — especially the aerospace industry — and once again set Canadian policy-makers on the road to Washington.

In 1971, when the trend in military exports was already sharply downward, President Richard Nixon put Canada into a general state of shock with the imposition of a 10 per cent surcharge on all manufactured goods entering the United States. Nixon's objective was to counter the growing U.S. deficit in its balance of payments and to increase domestic sales of American manufactured goods.[31] The real surprise was not that Nixon had taken drastic measures to protect U.S. economic interests, but that Canada's appeal to the "special relationship" between the two countries as a basis for a Canadian exemption from the American measures was unsuccessful. A Canadian delegation led by Finance Minister Edgar Benson went immediately to Washington to seek an exemption, and it was during these and later discussions that it became clear that among the "trade irritants" identified by the U.S. administration were the Defence Production Sharing Arrangements.

In particular, the Americans wanted greater Canadian defence procurement in the United States to redress the defence trade imbalance.[32] In calling for such a redress, the Americans were invoking the 1963 rough balance provision, but that provision had not been committed to writing at the time and even government officials appeared unaware of it in 1971. In the House of Commons, the opposition Tories hinted at a "secret pact" that could mean the loss of Canada's military trade surplus with the United States. Neither the defence minister nor the trade minister in the Liberal government seemed to be aware of the 1963 agreement, but Treasury Board President Bud Drury, who had been minister of defence production in 1963, soon acknowledged that there had been an "oral understanding" between himself and Robert McNamara, then U.S. defense secretary, on the matter of a rough balance. Drury said that Ottawa felt bound to honour that agreement and that this would "likely have some effect on the Argus replacement."[33] This reference was an acknowledgement that Canada's intended purchase of a long-range patrol aircraft to replace the Argus then in service would be directly influenced by this apparent requirement that Canada increase its military purchases from the United States.

The timing of the revelation that Canada was committed to buy as many military commodities from the U.S. as we sold to them thus had a dual significance. First, it came on the eve of a meeting between Prime Minister Trudeau and President Nixon at which the matter of the Argus replacement would be high on the agenda. And second, it came towards the end of direct American involvement in the Vietnam War, concluding a decade in which unusually high U.S. military purchases in Canada had resulted in a substantial military trade surplus in Canada's favour. The Americans had, in effect, decided that Canada would not have very effective access to the U.S. military market as long as this "unfair" surplus existed.

In the meantime, however, Canada had become accustomed to the buoyant U.S. demand for Canadian military commodities — and Canadian industry would have a hard time learning to live with less once more. The Vietnam demand years generated an artificially high Canadian capacity in military goods — a capacity that could not be sustained by current levels of Canadian defence spending or by post-Vietnam American spending. The result was that Canada would have to do two things: first, it would have to increase Canadian military spending, and second, much of the increased spending would have to take place in the United States if Canadian industry was to recapture access to the American market.

The Offset "Solution"

In the context of a major Canadian aircraft purchase, that left Canada with very little choice but eventually to buy a U.S. aircraft. Impressed with the magnitude of the purchase, the Canadians were anxious to ensure that buying a long-range patrol aircraft in the United States would in fact mean expanded access to the American market. The Americans, on the other hand, were not impressed with Canada's search for guarantees. As Clive Baxter wrote in the *Financial Post*, "it is that $509 million surplus in our favour that appears to have attracted the attention of the men in the U.S. Treasury. A $250-million order for Orions, they argue, would go a long way toward setting things in balance — and Canada should just put up the money and buy the aircraft without trying to wheel and deal on the side to get extra business in return."[34] That "wheeling and dealing on the side" produced an innovation in Canada-U.S. military trade which both government and industry officials have since learned to regret.

In contemplating a major equipment order from the United States (that $250 million order eventually turned out to be in excess of $1 billion), Ottawa sought guarantees that this would contribute to military production in Canada and thus sought to negotiate as part of the purchase deal a commitment by the prime contractor to undertake "offset" purchasing in Canada. As a result, Lockheed, the American manufacturer with which Canada placed an order for eighteen long-range aircraft in 1976, was asked to give formal assurances that it would place major reciprocal orders in Canada.

These offsets included some traditional U.S. purchases in Canada — such as tail assemblies for all of Lockheed's long-range patrol aircraft (not just the ones sold to Canada) — and an overall contractual commitment to purchase $400 million worth of Canadian products in the first ten years of the contract. Two-thirds of these purchases were to be in the aerospace industry, while the remaining third were to be purchases of any manufactured goods (raw materials, food and automobile products were excluded). As the Canadian Senate Committee on Foreign Affairs explained it, "the aim is to take advantage of the enormous buying power of Lockheed ($35 million of supplies annually, all ordered through a central procurement agency within the company) and of the buying power of the thirty-odd subcontractors, some of which are larger than Lockheed itself."[35]

During a 1976 appearance before this same committee, Frank Jackman of the Department of Industry, Trade and Commerce was asked whether it was "really in accordance with the spirit of the DPSA agreement to seek to maximize Canadian content — is that contemplated by the agreement?" Jackman replied that American officials had asked the same question. The question had arisen, he said, because of an uncertainty as to whether or not a $1 billion peacetime purchase was within the normal course of trade that was contemplated by the Defence Production Sharing Arrangements. "We have agreed amongst ourselves," he said, "that a $1 billion purchase is not a routine purchase, and, therefore, would distort the roughness of the balance to the extent where it might not be tolerable. It was therefore accepted by both sides that some extraordinary measures had to be taken to improve the Canadian content of a major purchase of that sort, be it from Lockheed, or some other manufacturer."[36] Since then offsets have become a prominent practice in military trade, and Canada has itself been the "victim" in similar reciprocal arrangements with other countries.

But Canadians always seem to be willing to believe that they are on the verge of a major breakthrough, and that a new American attitude of cooperation is in the offing if only Canada is sufficiently forthcoming and willing to spend enough. In 1977 the custodian of official Canadian optimism was Defence Minister Barney Danson. Canada had just ordered a billion dollars worth of long-range patrol aircraft from the U.S. and was about to place an order for several billion dollars worth of fighter aircraft. An update of the DEW line was under discussion and Canada was putting money into European AWACS aircraft. In other words Canada was in the early stages of a major increase in military capital spending and felt that it was in a good position to negotiate a better defence production sharing arrangement with the Americans.

Danson's plan was to change the division of labour involved in the DPSA. Rather than have Canada buy all its equipment off the shelf from the U.S. and supply the U.S. only with component parts in return, he arranged to meet the U.S. defense secretary, Harold Brown, to try to persuade him that Canadian industry should be allowed to produce some complete systems which the U.S. would buy off the shelf from Canada. "Perhaps," he said, "it makes sense if we supply the DHC-7R [a maritime patrol version of the Dash-7 passenger aircraft] coastal patrol vessels for all North America or antisubmarine equipment or even destroyers for their navy as well as ours. In return we would then buy all NORAD equipment off their shelves."[37]

As it turned out, however, 1977 was not a good year in which to persuade Americans that they should use public funds to import more goods. In the second half of the 1970s the United States was busy becoming a debtor nation, as the American trade deficit grew towards the point where foreign investment earnings ultimately were unable to compensate for it.[38] And in early 1978 continuing U.S. protectionist sentiment manifested itself in a variety of measures to ban the purchase of foreign goods or materials for use in publicly financed projects in the United States.[39] While the DPSA were negotiated specifically as an exemption from that kind of protectionism, that was not a sufficient reason for an Alabama congressman to refrain from making an effort to prohibit the U.S. Department of Defense from purchasing equipment that contained foreign specialty metals. The measure, had it been successful, would have been a direct restriction on Canada's access to the U.S. market and a threat to the DPSA, and as such was opposed by both Canadian and U.S. defence officials.[40] Meanwhile, Canadian Ambassador Peter Towe complained about the proliferation of Buy America laws across the U.S., noting that in 1978, 30 per cent of purchases by the Canadian government were of U.S. origin.[41]

The 1970s turned out not to be happy years for defence production sharing. Canadian military producers had hitched themselves to an uncertain star, but at the end of the decade a new star appeared, this time from Hollywood. From out of the West, riding not into, but out of, a setting sun, Ronald Reagan had a mission to make America great again. And many Canadians, notably those charged with trade promotion and military production, would also be able to shine again in this new star's reflected light. We will return to this development in chapter 6, but first we will look at the structure of the Canadian military industry, along with Ottawa's efforts to support and promote military exports.

4

Canadian Military Production for Export

A respectable country these days doesn't keep an arms industry —instead it maintains a defence industrial base. And while national economic planners show no overt interest in weapons plants, high technology defence production capabilities are another matter. You won't hear industry or governnment officials extolling the economic advantages of the arms trade, but they do routinely claim that military research and development are "essential to our ability to continue to be world competitive," or that "there is no doubt that high-technology defence requirements are a major driving force" behind successful industrial development.[1]

The "defence industrial base" has become the matter of some worry in Canada. That is, government and industry officials now publicly worry that Canada doesn't have one. It is true that Canada currently produces about $3 billion worth of military commodities annually (about two-thirds for export), with the Toronto *Globe and Mail* describing "aerospace and defence [as] the second most important group of high-technology companies (after telecommunications)" in the country. But volume alone does not make a defence industrial base.

The journal of the aerospace industry in Canada, *Aerospace Canada International*, defined a defence industrial base in the following terms: "The defence industrial base provides the resources to supply and support a country's armed forces, and to sustain this fighting capability in times of national emergencies."[2] By this definition Canada does not have a national defence industrial base. Canadian industry is not capable of supplying even the most basic requirements of the Canadian Armed Forces as defined by current policy. All major equipment, such as supersonic aircraft or tanks, must be imported, and even Canadian-built systems, such as the patrol frigates currently under construction, depend heavily on foreign technology and systems management. In fact, since the late 1950s, as noted in chapter 3, it has been Canadian policy to reject the development of a Canadian defence industrial base in favour of linking up with the Americans as part of a North American defence industrial base.

Like any other economy with a reasonable measure of industrial and technological capability, Canadian industry could in wartime be quickly mobilized to support a broad range of military objectives (assuming that the war is not a nuclear spasm but a civilized war that drags on and on and thus permits orderly mobilization over a period of several months). But in peacetime, Canada's military industry is not properly defined as a national defence industrial base. And that is because it has relatively little to do with Canada's defence policy and posture. The arms industry in Canada is, in other words, not so much a "defence" industry concerned with Canadian military needs as it is a military industry with economic objectives.

It is the conventional wisdom in Ottawa that Canada does not have the means to maintain a mature defence industrial base: commercially viable military production in Canada cannot be sustained by Canadian defence requirements. It is this "reality" that is offered to account for the integration of Canadian military production with that of the United States to form a North American defence industrial base. The conventional wisdom is based on the assumption that a defence industry is essentially a commerical enterprise that develops a product and looks for a market, and sustains itself either by developing new products as the market changes or by using promotion to develop the loyal repeat business or new markets needed to make long-term production possible.

But "realism" could also be based on an alternative assumption — that military production must take place outside normal market conditions. According to this assumption, military production is not a commercial activity like other commercial endeavours (just as prescription and other restricted drugs do not operate under usual market conditions). Thus, commercial viability is not a central question. This view of military production prevails in wartime, when military needs are defined without reference to economic opportunity or viability. They are externally defined needs and the industrial resources of the country are simply mobilized to meet those needs. Clearly, there is no prominent sense in wartime that long-term economic viability has to be built into military production. The diversion of resources from meeting ordinary human needs to meeting military needs is considered to be a short-term, emergency requirement. The assumption is that when the emergency is over, the country will revert to a more proper and sensible use of resources.

The same assumption could obtain for "war in peace." But in most contemporary industrial countries, and in a growing number of semi-industrialized Third World countries, it is assumed that the extraordinary social requirement for weapons of destruction can be used to build an ordinary industrial base. The current effort in Canada is based on this assumption. The effort is based on the belief that military-induced economic demand, like any consumer economic demand, can be sustained and made part of the basis of long-term economic planning.

But to convert military objectives into a long-term economic demand takes an unusual level of government intervention and manipulation. Even in the United States, where military demand is not currently characterized by restraint, extraordinary efforts — ranging from arm-twisting on Capitol Hill to Hollywood blockbusters in which brave Americans face the communist menace — are needed to maintain that demand at economically viable levels. The extensive literature on the military-industrial complex describes the symbiotic relationship that has developed among industry, the Defense Department and the White House to manage and sustain military economic demand. Industry engages armies of engineers, for example, not so much to respond to military needs as to work on developing products for which military needs and therefore markets can later be created.[3]

In Canada the whole enterprise operates on a somewhat different scale, but the principles are similar. To sustain commercially viable military production in Canada, several conditions must be met. First, Canada must maintain access to the U.S. military market. Without access to that market, as officials repeat over and over again, only a very few Canadian firms could remain in the military production business. Second, in order to mitigate its vulnerability to shifts in that market, Canada must reduce its dependence on the U.S. and expand alternative markets. This means more concentrated efforts to increase sales to Europe and the hotly contested Third World military market (the Third World is probably crucial in that it accounts for roughly two-thirds of the global demand for imported military products). Third, Canada's own military expenditures must be increased. Growth in equipment purchases by the Canadian Armed Forces serves to expand the size of the market available to Canadian firms, to provide a base for generating new technologies, to improve competitiveness in the international military market, and to increase imports from the United States so that Canada maintains access to the U.S. market through defence trade reciprocity.

Fulfilment of all of these three conditions — access to the U.S. mar-

ket, increased overseas sales, and increased Canadian procurement —
is heavily dependent on government intervention. Furthermore, fulfilling these conditions requires the government to make military policy
decisions in pursuit not of national security objectives but of economic
objectives. While national security objectives are frequently invoked as
a rationale for military production, the promotion of military production in Canada is in fact an economic activity — albeit an economic
activity that has direct and particular foreign policy implications in
ways that other commercial activities do not.

Does Canada Need New Military Production Capability?

Industry and government officials charged with managing the public
relations of Canada's nonexistent defence industrial base are indignant
at the use of the term "arms industry." The former Liberal defence
minister and arms industry booster, Barney Danson, used to tell
whoever asked that "Canada doesn't make anything that goes bang."
Aside from the fact that some of the things that Canada makes do
indeed go bang, the term "arms" is a generic one and includes both
weapons and the support facilities and equipment that make weapons
usable. Radios don't go bang, but they are essential to establishing field
locations and coordinating an armed force. Computers don't usually go
bang, but they are essential for locating targets and aiming the things
that do go bang at those targets. Military transport aircraft also don't go
bang, but they are essential for delivering those things that do to the
field of battle.

Canada's traditional approach to the production of arms is currently
undergoing a major reassessment. This new interest in expanding Canada's military production capacity does not, as already noted, exactly
come in the context of a global arms shortage. In fact, there now exists a
surfeit both of arms and of the production facilities to make them (this
surplus goes some way towards explaining the absolute inability of governments to control the worldwide arms trade). Any country that now
proposes to add to this surplus of supply and production capacity therefore has to have available a convincing set of supporting arguments —
it is a tribute to human ingenuity, if nothing else, that every new arms
factory seems to be built for the best of reasons. Canadians are not particularly wanting in ingenuity, and so, even in the context of a level of
global military production that defies rationality and is excessive to the
point of obscenity, Canadian officials make a credible case for increasing Canadian military production.

Canadian officials have for years been talking about the need to develop a more extensive indigenous defence industry. And, noted the *Financial Post* in 1984, "starting with military jeeps (Quebec-based Bombardier, Inc.), ammunition (Diemaco Ltd. of Kitchener, Canadian Arsenals Ltd. of Montreal), and small arms (IVI Ltd. of Valcartier), that's exactly what Canada is trying to do."[4] This signals a shift in official attitudes to military production — away from continental integration and towards the development of more national capacity in complete systems production.

The argument is basically twofold, strategic and economic. Not surprisingly, in the Department of National Defence, greater importance is given to the strategic concern. Enthusiastic as it tends to be about its close relationship with the Pentagon, National Defence has grown increasingly uncomfortable with its dependence on foreign suppliers. Especially during times of crisis, when the traditional foreign suppliers are likely to experience a surge in local demand that would take precedence over export sales, Canada could be vulnerable to shortages and resupply delays. For strategic reasons alone, DND therefore argues, Canada's military equipment requirements cannot be left entirely to foreign sources. Added to this is the reasoning that given Canada's commitment to the defence of Europe and its shared responsibility for the defence of North America, this country has growing military obligations and must improve its internal capacity to support those obligations.

Not only are Canada's obligations growing, but their nature is also changing by virtue of changing conditions and strategies.[5] In the 1950s and early 1960s, it was assumed that any war would be basically "fight-as-you-are," with no time for mobilization. In the 1960s, however, NATO moved to a "flexible response" doctrine. Because of the terror of the nuclear threat and the consequences of the use of nuclear weapons, a prolonged World War II–style conventional war was once more deemed a possibility. It seems to have taken Canada a while to adjust its own strategy accordingly. When Liberal Defence Minister Gilles Lamontagne said in 1983 that "the Government has agreed that, in principle, the Canadian Forces should be able to meet and fully maintain their commitments in an emergency and, if so directed, further expand their capabilities," this was taken as the significant shift in Canadian policy.[6] Canada's previous heavy reliance on forces-in-being was no longer adequate. It now became necessary to develop mobilization plans and a sustained source of supply of military equipment for extended war.

And no source can be assured in an emergency, say defence analysts, except your own. Regardless of peacetime arrangements for joint projects and production sharing, "it is understandable that, when a surge in production is required, foreign manufacturers will give first priority to the military requirements of their own governments. Clearly Canada requires a domestic defence industrial base to fulfill her wartime military tasks."[7]

But to have a "defence industrial base" available for those emergencies, it has to be maintained throughout peacetime. The maintenance of an extensive military production facility during peacetime is politically not so simple. It requires the promotion either of a sense of danger or imminent threat or else of the idea that the maintenance of an extensive military industrial base will return many economic benefits to society. Through this latter idea, the strategic rationale for military industry is intimately related to the second major argument for an expanded defence industrial base — the argument that military production promises special economic opportunities. Enthusiasts soon go on to claim that defence production not only will produce economic benefits but is almost a prerequisite to prosperity. The Canadian aerospace industry, for example, argues vociferously that its long-term viability is dependent on participation in military production. Failure to revitalize aerospace defence, says the industry's journal, "will likely result in serious problems for all sectors of the aerospace industry. It has been estimated that more than 50 per cent of current civil production utilizes technologies originally developed in the defence area."[8]

Besides the appeal to job creation and technological innovation, proponents of military industry also commonly argue that domestic military production helps lessen the tax burden by reducing the costs of military procurement. This can occur in two ways. First, the economic benefits of military production are kept in Canada if procurement is done in Canada (this reasoning even includes the possibility that we may have to be prepared to pay a premium on military equipment in order that it can be built in Canada). Second, the costs to Canada can be reduced if the industrial capacity used to supply Canada is also used to increase exports of military commodities.

Underlying these assumptions is the prevailing wisdom in Ottawa that Canadian diplomatic influence is directly related to the extent to which this country demonstrates that it is prepared to "carry its weight" in Western collective defence arrangements. Canada can be expected to have a voice within the councils of the powerful, runs the argument, only if it is prepared to carry a fair share of the burden of power. Our willingness to bear this burden is expressed notably through military spending, and the idea of a more substantial defence industrial base in Canada is based on an assumption of continuing expansion of capital spending by the Canadian Armed Forces. By developing a broader range of capacity in military production, Canada seeks to demonstrate its firm commitment to making a sustained contribution to Western collective defence and its willingness to be counted on to participate directly and immediately in a common war effort should the need arise. Finally, there is a less tangible but still strong sense that a measure of indigenous weapons production capacity contributes to national pride — something that helps you hold your head up during those long hours at the tables of the powerful.

Anatomy of Canada's Military Industry

Current Canadian military production for export is concentrated in two provinces, Ontario and Quebec, and two industries, aerospace and communications. Since 1959 these two industries have provided 75 per cent of Canadian military exports (see table 3). In recent years vehicles have become more prominent — primarily Bombardier trucks and jeeps and General Motors armoured vehicles. Shipbuilding has traditionally not been a major export industry, mostly because access to the U.S. military marine market is restricted by U.S. protectionist legislation regarding naval vessels and their major components. The relatively low level of exports of actual armaments (about 7 per cent of the total) reflects the fact that such armaments, things that go bang, make up a relatively small element of the equipment required by modern armed forces.

That leaves the electrical and electronics industry (roughly coinciding with the Statistics Canada designation of communications equipment) and aerospace as the mainstays of Canadian military exports. Both characterized as high technology fields, these two industries are closely related to each other and overlap extensively. Much of the production in aerospace is electronics, and much of electronics production is for the aerospace industry. To some extent, therefore, the division between the two categories is arbitrary.

A number of electronics or communications systems that *Aerospace Canada* describes as specialized products of the aerospace industry are in fact not supplied to the aircraft or space sectors but to naval systems. Examples include Canadian Marconi's AN/SPS-503 surveillance and target-indicating radar specified for the CAF Destroyer Life Extension Program (DELEX); Litton Systems Canada's ADLIPS (Automatic Data Link Plotting System), a modular command, control and tactical

TABLE 3
Military Exports by Industry Sector

Industry Sector	1985				Total 1959–1985			
	U.S. $ million	Other $ million	All Countries $ million	% of total	U.S. $ million	Other $ million	All Countries $ million	% of total
Aerospace	447.9	114.2	562.1	30	4,203.5	2,221.0	6,424.5	42
Armaments	79.8	23.6	103.4	5	799.9	239.9	1,039.8	7
Electrical/electronics	558.8	87.4	646.2	34	3,668.8	1,310.3	4,979.1	33
General purchasing	58.1	4.0	62.1	3	268.6	45.4	314.0	2
Shipbuilding	161.0	22.7	183.7	10	971.6	112.6	1,084.6	7
Vehicles	338.6	6.6	345.2	18	1,349.7	104.7	1,454.4	9
Total	1,644.2	258.5	1,902.7	100	11,262.1	4,033.9	15,296.0	100

Note: Data for "other" (non-U.S.) countries not available for 1959–1961.
Source: Department of External Affairs

data communication system that has been purchased for the Canadian navy; and Computing Devices' SBP 1-1 (AN/UYS-503) sonobuoy processor, designed for a variety of antisubmarine warfare platforms and on order to Canada and Sweden. A clear delineation between aerospace and electronics production is obviously not possible. For purposes of general description, the generic term "high technology" may be more useful, precisely because it is imprecise.

The "armaments" sector of the military industry is by its nature exclusively dependent on military customers, but the remaining four major military-related industries (aerospace, electrical and electronics, shipbuilding and vehicles) are primarily civilian industries with varying proportions of military production capacity. The extent to which each of these industries has been dependent upon military production and exports has been far from constant over the past two decades, and there is no fully reliable means of measuring the share of each industry that is devoted to military production. Figures 2, 3 and 4

FIGURE 2
Aerospace Defence Exports as a Per Cent of Total Aerospace Exports 1965–1984

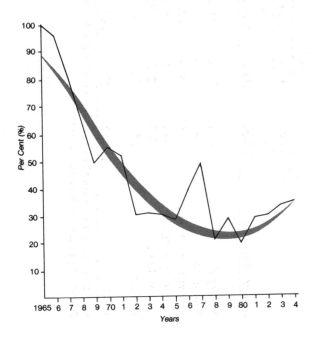

FIGURE 3
Electrical & Electronic Defence Exports as a Per Cent of Total Electrical/Electronics Exports, 1965–1984

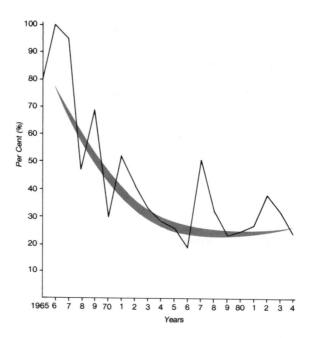

show the proportion of military exports in the aerospace, electrical and electronics and shipbuilding industries. These figures are necessarily approximations, and military exports cannot be meaningfully compared with total exports in any one year. Nevertheless, by comparing the two sets of figures over time, significant long-term trends are revealed.[9]

In each of these industries military production represents a significant proportion, but still a minority, of total output. During the late 1960s and early 1970s, all categories except vehicles showed much greater dependence on military exports. In the middle and late 1970s the military proportion fell (a reflection of reduced U.S. military spending in Canada), and then in the 1980s military sales increased sharply, so that the trend line once again begins to show military sales as a more significant share of exports. In some instances the level of military exports is likely to be understated. As noted in chapter 1, commodities such as aircraft engines sometimes leave Canada designated as civilian

FIGURE 4
Shipbuilding Defence Exports as a Per Cent of Total
Shipbuilding Exports, 1965-1984

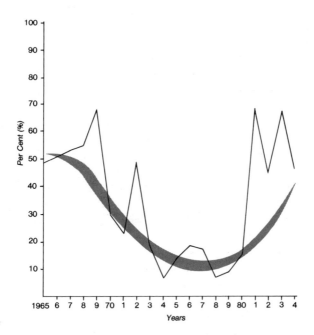

goods but are subsequently used in military systems. While Canada considers the famous Canadarm — the remote manipulator arm developed by Canada for the U.S. space shuttle — a civilian device, it has been used extensively to deploy military payloads. (When the space shuttle resumes flights, the proportion of military payloads, initially at least, will be significantly expanded. By the mid-1990s there may be a backlog of as many as seventy-five military satellites waiting to be hauled into space. By the time it flies again, says an analyst quoted by *U.S. News and World Report*, NASA might as well "paint the shuttle Air Force blue."[10])

Aerospace

The Canadian aerospace industry — which until recently was the aircraft industry — produces both complete aircraft and components. It has always been highly dependent upon government policy and could almost be regarded as a state industry.[11] Until 1986 the government directly owned two of the key firms in the industry, Canadair Limited and de Havilland Aircraft of Canada Limited. Along with substantial subsidies for both military and civilian products and preferential procurement practices, this has created a unique relationship between the industry and the federal government.[12] This relationship has been reinforced by a 1985 "Memorandum of Understanding for Industry Development Planning" between the minister of regional industrial expansion and the Aerospace Industries Association of Canada (AIAC). The memorandum is intended to outline areas of industry-government cooperation in the pursuit of a "secure" and "more certain environment" in which aerospace firms can operate.

The main role of government in the aerospace industry, however, is to provide a market for the industry's products. In this, says the AIAC, Ottawa lags behind other governments.[13] According to the AIAC, government is typically the aerospace industry's primary customer, so that the industry serves a domestic market with exports as a side benefit. In Canada the situation is reversed — 80 per cent of production is for export.

The Canadian industry supplies about 6 per cent of the world aerospace trade and ranks fifth in the world in gross sales, behind the U.S., France, Britain and West Germany and slightly ahead of Japan and Italy.[14] In 1985 the industry's sales reached about $4 billion, of which $3.2 billion consisted of exports. The aerospace industry comprises some 150 companies, a number of which could also be classified as electronics high-technology firms. Fewer than a third of these companies account for about 90 per cent of the industry's business. In the past decade, the number of firms has grown substantially, reflecting an increased focus on components and subassemblies and reduced potential for the full production of complete aircraft.[15] The industry is concentrated in Quebec, with 50 per cent of industry sales in 1984, and Ontario, with 42 per cent. The West had 7 per cent of the business, with the Atlantic provinces receiving the remaining 1 per cent. The industry directly employs about 45,000 people.

In rough terms, three levels of firms operate in the Canadian aerospace industry. At the first level are companies with an integrated capacity to design, develop, manufacture and market complete aircraft and aeroengines. Companies capable of manufacturing aircraft, space and aeroengine subsystems and possessing some design and development capability constitute the second level. The third level consists of companies, most of them small businesses, that supply components and provide machining, sheet metal, casting, heat treatment, plating and other services. The defence segment of the industry can be divided into the same three levels. The first level supplies complete systems, such as transport aircraft, surveillance drones and flight simulators; the second supplies subsystems, which include inertial navigation systems, marine surveillance radars and ballistic computers; and the third level engages in the manufacture of components such as landing gear parts and hybrid microcircuits as well as providing machining services. The industry also undertakes substantial repair and overhaul work.[16]

While these three levels of industry could be mutually supporting, they do not in fact represent a self-sustaining Canadian industry, as the lower-level companies are not primarily engaged in supplying the higher-level companies in Canada. The industrial hierarchy to which these companies belong is the North American aerospace industry. Canadian second- and third-level companies may supply first-level companies in Canada, but their survival depends on their ability to penetrate the first-level market in the United States. Even the first-level companies in Canada must also be able to supply components to U.S. companies in order to survive.

Canadair

The two most advanced aerospace manufacturers in the country are Canadair Limited of Montreal and Toronto-based de Havilland Aircraft of Canada. Both companies have just come through a stormy decade, passing from private foreign ownership to Canadian government ownership and back again to the private sector.

Canadair, a manufacturer of jet and utility aircraft and remotely-piloted vehicles, was sold to the Canadian-owned Bombardier Inc., also based in Montreal, in 1986. The federal government bought Canadair in the mid-1970s in a rescue operation designed to prevent the company from being shut down by its American parent, General Dynamics Corp., during a period of sharply reduced U.S. procurement in Canada. As rescue operations go, this was not a cheap one. During the decade of public ownership, the company received $2.1 billion in federal financing.[17] Having been relieved of major long-term debts, the company has operated profitably since 1983.

Government financing has left a legacy of development and production capability in major civilian systems. The company's urgent need to expand its market for these products has led it to pursue military applications. Canadair's CL-215 amphibious water-bomber, for example, has been offered as a search-and-rescue and maritime surveillance aircraft, in addition to its primary role as a water bomber. In its military and search-and-rescue applications, the water tanks are removed and replaced with appropriate equipment. Spain operates eight CL-215s in search-and-rescue and coastal patrol, and Thailand operates two in maritime surveillance roles.

The company's business passenger jet, the Challenger, is operated as a VIP passenger aircraft by the Canadian and West German armed forces, but the company also offers it as a potential vehicle for maritime surveillance, antisubmarine warfare, and airborne early warning operations. The Canadian Armed Forces operate seven Challengers as electronic support and training aircraft and one as a test bed for DND's Aerospace Engineering and Test Establishment.

Canadair's new owners are eager to reduce the company's reliance on sales of its two aircraft, and are looking to pilotless airborne surveillance vehicles for future activity.[18] Pilotless and driven by an aircraft engine, a surveillance drone is a kind of cruise missile, except that it carries electronic and photographic information-gathering equipment rather than a warhead. Drones are operated from ground stations and are flown over enemy positions to gather battlefield intelligence. The CL-89, a recoverable vehicle, is operated by the British, French, West German and Italian armies. In 1985 Canada, France and West Germany signed a memorandum of understanding for the development of a successor, the CL-289. In 1986 the vehicle was being tested in West Germany, with production expected to begin in 1987.

While Ottawa has financed 25 per cent of the development and preproduction costs, Canada will not be buying it. Canadian forces in Europe, as currently assigned, have no need for surveillance drones. Thus, the CL-289 is true to the general pattern of Canadian military production in that it responds to foreign rather than Canadian defence needs. Similar circumstances apply to Canadair's CL-227, a "real-time surveillance and target acquisition system." A peanut-shaped pilotless aircraft, the CL-227 lands and takes off vertically in the manner of a helicopter, and can hover or fly horizontally. It is now under further development, with the Canadian government funding half the $62 million cost of this phase (as a loan repayable out of future earnings from sales). The CL-227 has the potential to be used in a much wider range of activities, including coast guard and search-and-rescue operations. The market currently being explored is the U.S. Army, although the Canadian Armed Forces may have an interest in acquiring the CL-227 in the 1990s.

Canadair also serves as a components manufacturer, particularly for the U.S. aerosapce industry. In 1985 subcontracting for major aircraft manufacturing companies accounted for 18 per cent of Canadair's sales.[19] The company produces components for the U.S. F/A-18, F-15 and F-5 fighter aircraft, cargo doors and other elements of the U.S. C-5B Galaxy military transport aircraft, and structural components for the U.S. P-3C antisubmarine warfare aircraft.

De Havilland

The federal government's sale of de Havilland Aircraft of Canada Limited to Boeing Corp. of Seattle, Washington (for a price less than one-fifth of the total provided to the company in grants during the past decade), places the Toronto-based firm within one of the world's pre-eminent commercial and military aerospace empires. One of the top five U.S. military contractors, Boeing is also a world leader in civilian passenger aircraft, and de Havilland will add to both capacities.

De Havilland has become a world leader in short takeoff and landing aircraft capable of operating from unprepared landing strips. Promotional material in the government-published *Defence Products Guide* describes the company's DHC-5D Buffalo as "the world's only medium tactical transport which is capable of providing logistic support to front line areas." The aircraft was developed in cooperation with the U.S. Army and now flies with nearly twenty military forces, including those of Abu Dhabi, Brazil, Chile, Ecuador, Ethiopia, Peru and Zaïre. In 1986 de Havilland was competing with Spain and Italy to supply fifty-two Buffalo aircraft to Turkey — possibly in a joint production arrangement.[20] The Buffalo can carry forty-one combat-equipped troops, thirty-five paratroops, or twenty-four stretchers and six seated troops. A smaller military transport plane, the Twin Otter (DHC-6) flies with military forces in about a dozen countries, including Argentina, Chile, Panama and Paraguay. The military transport version can carry fifteen combat troops, while counterinsurgency and maritime reconnaissance versions have provisions for mounting bombs, rockets and machine guns. Both the Buffalo and the Twin Otter also have civilian versions sold throughout the world.

De Havilland's fifty-passenger Dash-7 commuter aircraft has been sold to the Venezuelan navy, and a longer-range surveillance and patrol version of the aircraft, the Dash-7R, has also been developed. The more recent thirty-six–passenger Dash-8 is being considered for an antisubmarine warfare role. According to Boeing's Canadian chairman, a proposal has been submitted to "an unspecified foreign government" for use of the Dash-8 in this role. Two Dash-8s have been sold to Sierra Research of the U.S. for use as airborne monitoring platforms in the context of the firm's contract to supply the U.S. Air Force Systems Command with a "flying data link that will relay telemetry, voice communications and drone tracking data while simultaneously performing radar surveillance functions."[21] Dash-8M (M for military) ads declare: "Many missions — the Dash-8M does them all." The listed missions include flight calibration, range control, medical evacuation, surveillance, early warning, search-and-rescue and antisubmarine warfare.

On the whole, de Havilland's sales in the mid-1980s have consisted primarily of civilian aircraft and components, with the U.S. accounting for about 40 to 45 per cent of sales. In 1983 only 10 per cent of total sales were military, although company officials hope to raise that to 20 per cent. The Dash-7 and Dash-8 are regarded as key to increasing military sales.[22] Attention to the military market is also reflected in research on technology for a new generation of short takeoff fighter aircraft. The Canadian-funded system has been under development for nine years and is aimed at participation in a U.S.-British project to produce a short takeoff and vertical landing fighter aircraft for the twenty-first century.[23]

Simulators, Engines and Components

By most accounts a Canadian company is the world leader in the design and production of aircraft flight simulators. CAE Electronics Ltd. of Montreal, a subsidiary of CAE Industries Ltd. of Toronto, produces both civilian and military aircraft simulators to reproduce actual conditions and aircraft performance characteristics for pilot and crew training. The armed forces of at least twenty countries operate CAE military flight simulators for such aircraft as the European Tornado fighter aircraft, the French Alpha Jet trainer, the E-3A AWACS aircraft, the C-130 Hercules transport, and the P-3C Orion and CP-140 antisubmarine warfare aircraft, as well as a variety of military helicopters. Currently the company is developing simulators for the U.S. Army's LHX helicopter program to evaluate crew workload and combat performance. The system is intended to simulate five types of missions: antiarmour, armed reconnaissance, antipersonnel/antimateriel, security operations, and command and control tasks. Other systems include a helmet-mounted display for presentation of computer-generated images, airborne "magnetic anomoly detection" systems used in antisubmarine warfare operations, and machinery control systems for hydro stations and for the Spar Aerospace Canadarm. About 30 per cent of the company's sales are military.[24]

While aircraft engines are obviously subsystems, their design and production represents a major systems capability. Another of the giants of the Canadian aerospace industry is the manufacturer of an extensive series of turboprop engines, designated the PT6. Pratt and Whitney Aircraft of Canada Ltd. is a subsidiary of the U.S.-based United Technologies Corporation, which has granted the Canadian subsidiary a mandate for design and manufacture of these engines for the world market. About 20 per cent of the company's sales of $800 million in 1986 are acknowledged to be for military purposes.[25] Pratt and Whitney turboprop and helicopter engines power military aircraft produced in a wide range of countries, including Brazil, Switzerland, Israel, France, West Germany, Italy, Britain and the United States.

Canada does not control the ultimate destinations of these engines, which now operate extensively throughout the West and the Third World. In 1986, Pratt and Whitney sold $10 million worth of "Twin Pac" helicopter engines to Indonesia, which is assembling a fleet of Bell 412 helicopters. This order was the second of its kind; the first received financing from the Canadian government's Export Development Corporation.[26] Aircraft with Pratt and Whitney engines fly with military forces in a very large number of countries, including Angola, Chile, El Salvador, Honduras, Iran, Iraq, South Korea, Libya, Paraguay, the Philippines and Syria.

Fleet Industries, founded in 1930, was an early manufacturer of complete aircraft, but now operates as a supplier to the North American aerospace industry. The company concentrates on components, as opposed to self-contained subsystems, and its product list indicates a diversity of both markets and production capabilities. Fleet provides wing components and spares for two versions of the U.S. AWACS aircraft and for the KC-135 refuelling aircraft (the kind that provided in-flight refuelling to the U.S. F-111 long-range bombers that attacked Libya from their bases in Britain). It also supplies flight stations for the P3C antisubmarine aircraft, as well as wing and structural components for the A6 fighter, a carrier-based aircraft designed for low-level bomb attacks and capable of delivering conventional or nuclear weapons. Blade subassemblies from Fleet go to the Sikorsky Black Hawk, a land- and sea-based troop transport helicopter, and the Seahawk, a multipurpose helicopter armed with missiles, machine guns, mine-dispensers and torpedos. The company also produces medical evacuation stretcher units for the Black Hawk. Graphite composite gunloader and avionics doors and precision radar racks go to the F-18A fighter, while speed brakes and flaps go to the A4E Skyhawk fighter. Fleet also supplies components to naval forces and radar systems. Pave Paws (Position and Velocity Extraction Phased Array Warning Systems) — land-based devices on the coasts of the United States designed to detect submarine-launched ballistic missiles — contain phased array antennas from Fleet Industries.[27]

In 1983 Fleet Aerospace Corporation, Fleet Industries' parent company which also has holdings in other high-technology firms, had total sales of $35 million, with 65 per cent of that in military commodities.[28] Since then sales have doubled and the company has expanded into the United States. Fleet Aerospace President George Dragone explained his company's acquisition of Aeronca Inc. of the U.S. by saying that "no matter how good a Canadian manufacturer is, it will be excluded from many U.S. defence programs unless it establishes a base in the United States."[29]

Garrett Manufacturing Limited is a prime example of succesful world product mandating. In 1961 Garrett's American parent, Garrett Corporation, itself in turn one of the U.S. Signal Companies, transferred responsibility for design, development and manufacture of its temperature control systems to the Canadian subsidiary. These systems fly on more that 70 per cent of the commercial and military aircraft in the Western world.[30] The temperature control systems are used in aircraft cabin, cockpit and compartment air-conditioning systems; wing anti-ice temperature control systems; window heat control systems; and equipment bay temperature control systems. Military aircraft using the system include the U.S. F-18, F-16, F-15, F-14, and F-4 fighter aircraft; the EF/F-111 and B-52 long-range bombers; and the C-141 and C-5A/B military transport aircraft.

Many of the same aircraft use microcircuits from the company's microelectronics products plant. The company's "thick and thin-film hybrid microcircuits" are used in missile guidance systems, inertial navigation systems, and radar and other systems. Missiles using these microcircuits include the Chaparral, AMRAAM (a "fire and forget" medium-range air-to-air missile), Shillelagh, Phoenix (an air-to-air missile with a high-explosive warhead) and Wasp. Garrett Manufacturing is currently developing a "peripheral vision display" (PVD) system for fighter aircraft, designed to help pilots maintain their orientation during complicated manoeuvres. The PVD uses a helium-neon laser to shine a line of red light across the surface of the cockpit. The line maintains its position relative to the horizon, so that it moves relative to the aircraft as the plane pitches and rolls. As a result, the pilot is always visually aware of the horizon even when involved in other tasks. The intention is to reduce disorientation, the cause of an estimated 15 per cent of aircraft accidents. About 50 per cent of Garrett Manufacturing's business is military.[31]

The Helicopter and Space Segments

In an attempt to broaden the base of the Canadian aerospace industry in the early 1980s, Canada invited two major helicopter firms to set up assembly operations in Canada to service what was expected to be a major domestic requirement for civilian helicopters. MBB Helicopter Canada Ltd., a subsidiary of Messerschmitt-Bolkow-Blohm GmbH of West Germany in which Fleet Aerospace holds a 5 per cent interest, set up its $7.1 million plant in Fort Erie with $1.1 million contributed by the federal and Ontario governments. The two governments are committed to contributing another $35 million towards a promised $70 million development plan. In the meantime the market for civilian helicopters has all but disappeared. As a result of the downturn in the oil industry, the number of helicopters registered in Canada has dropped from 1,500 to 1,200. In 1985, says MBB vice-president James Grant, there were only five helicopters sold in Canada.[32] His company sold four of them. For the foreseeable future the government is going to have to act as the market for helicopters if its investment is to survive. Twelve MBB helicopters have been ordered for the Canadian Coast Guard, at a cost of $24 million. Currently, the Canadian subsidiary imports 70 per cent of the content of its helicopters from West Germany.

The government's other helicopter venture, a Bell Helicopter plant in Montreal, could turn out to be — as the *Financial Post* noted — "the most expensive job-creation program in Canadian history."[33] Ottawa is committing $165 million to the plant, while the Quebec government's contribution is $110 million. However, revised estimates are that the venture will create only 500 jobs over the next few years — $550,000 in government money per job — and by mid-1986 the company had yet to produce its first helicopter. The plant had intended to produce a series of lightweight civilian helicopters. Instead, its operations will for the moment be confined to the production of tail beams for Bell's UH 1-H military helicopter and the assembly of single-engine jet ranger 206 BL helicopters.[34] The most substantial prospect for both companies is for orders to replace various helicopters operated by the Canadian Forces.[35]

The AIAC identifies forty-three companies in Canada that are in the space end of the aerospace business. Of these, eight to ten are considered major space producers — that is, companies that have the bulk of their business in space technology.[36] That group includes Canadian Astronautics Ltd. of Ottawa; ComDev Ltd. of Cambridge, Ontario; DSMA Acton Ltd. of Toronto; MDA Ltd. of Vancouver; SED Systems Inc. of Saskatoon; and Spar Aerospace Ltd. of Toronto. The space industry is primarily civilian-oriented and represents less than 10 per cent of the aerospace industry in sales and employment. Spar Aerospace Ltd. of Toronto is clearly the best known of the space companies, and is described by its president, Larry D. Clarke, as the only Canadian company to have handled a space contract in its entirety and one of the few companies in the world able to do so.[37] Best known for the Canadarm, the company has also served as prime contractor for Anik satellites and supplies communications systems for a large number of satellites. Since 1968 the company has been working on an infrared surveillance and tracking system (IRST) for military use. It is currently building three production models under joint contract to the U.S. and Canadian navies, and if production contracts follow, the company's overall orientation will shift noticeably towards military work.[38] Currently about half the company's sales are military – related.[39]

Political Niceties

Overall, the Canadian aerospace industry is export-oriented and will continue to depend on the support of government to market its products. Governments are a prominent customer for its products — in the case of military products, the only customer — and its commercial success depends heavily on government support in the political and marketing spheres. The federal government's marketing role for military commodities is a magnet for controversy, so that there are obvious incentives to hide the whole enterprise from public view. So far, the key to political management of the government's role as arms merchant has been the dubious claim that the production of components and nonlethal elements of weapons systems is really nonmilitary. When whole systems are developed and sold, however, new controversies will arise. As the aerospace industry's journal has commented, "government will have to grapple with the political niceties of promoting a product that is clearly identified in the public's mind as a complete weapons system. It may not be an activity that is politically palatable."[40]

Electronics

For most of us, military combat has to do with bombs, missiles and machine guns — the things that go bang. While that may be the proverbial bottom line, the primary military activity is the collection, transmission and interpretation of information. As the saying goes, what we have here is a problem in communication. Electronic communications devices operate the complicated machinery that aims and fires weapons, disclose information about enemy forces' strength and movements, and facilitate contact between the field and command centres. This means computers, radar, photographic equipment and all the other technical wizardry which most of us don't understand but without which neither civilian nor military life in the present style would be possible. While the term "electronic warfare" is usually used to refer to the specific attempt to interfere electronically with the military communications systems of the other side, it could just as well describe modern warfare in general.

The Canadian electronics industry is primarily a civilian industry, encompassing a wide range of common consumer goods as well as the more elaborate systems that are part of modern civilian and military communications systems and operations. By all accounts, this industry is regarded as weak in Canada. A government task force concluded in 1978 that "in present circumstances, the outlook for Canada's electronics industry is not encouraging."[41] Almost a decade later, Canada is still considered to have the worst overall high tech trade deficit (without distinction between military and nonmilitary) among the "economic summit" countries. In 1984 the deficit was $12.1 billion, and in 1985 it reached $12.5 billion.[42]

The Canadian electronics industry consists of about a thousand firms, most of them small. The strongest subsector is the telecommunications industry — dominated by a few large firms such as Northern Telecom — while the consumer products subsector is probably the weakest. The components branch of the industry has also generally not kept pace with international developments. Only 20 per cent of the firms are foreign-owned, but these firms account for about 55 per cent of the industry's sales.[43]

The Devtek Group

The Devtek group of companies illustrates the broad range of activities included under the military high tech umbrella. A half-dozen companies in the group produce marine equipment and armaments, and undertake the precision machining of components for the small arms, computer and aerospace industries.

Diemaco Inc. of Kitchener, Ontario, began as a shop to repair and overhaul small arms for the Canadian Armed Forces, and subsequently was chosen to build new rifles for the Canadian Forces. The rifle is based on the M16 rifle manufactured by Colt Industries in the United States, and Diemaco produces it under licence. The company is eager to translate its technology into export orders. In fact, Devtek president Helmut Hoffman said at a ceremony marking the delivery of the first C7 rifles to DND that the company had received a request from the Pentagon to become part of its "mobilization base." As part of the U.S. "Planned Producer Program," the company would be awarded regular contracts to maintain its production capacity and ensure a long-range supply and emergency mobilization capability. In the case of Diemaco, this would mean supplying components to Colt Industries. Hoffman therefore called on the government to recognize and support Diemaco's gun-making capacity as an opportunity for exports and economic growth: "We seek [the government's] support since sales of this nature are generally on a government to government basis."[44]

A second Devtek company, Hermes Electronics Ltd. of Dartmouth, Nova Scotia, is also part of the Pentagon's Planned Producer Program for the supply of sonobuoys to the U.S. Navy.[45] Exports to other countries have included a West German order for an air-launched, non-recoverable sonobuoy that detects underwater sounds and relays the information back. A 1986 contract to supply 58,425 such devices to the U.S. Navy was valued at $22 million.[46] The company's other products include communications transmitting and receiving equipment, such as "receiving antenna arrays" supplied to the U.S. Army. Hermes is regularly within the top twenty Canadian companies selling to the Pentagon.

West Heights Manufacturing, another Devtek company located in Kitchener, specializes in precision machining of components for aircraft landing gear, fire control systems, and inertial navigational system components. Such components have been manufactured for the F-18 fighter aircraft and the A-6A low-level attack bomber. Grantech Manufacturing of Kitchener joined the Devtek fold in 1986 to supply components to the aerospace industry and to Diemaco's rifles, while the group's original company, Magna Electronics of Scarborough, Ontario, provides precision machining in titanium, beryllium and other exotic metals for space and military programs, including the U.S. space shuttle and satellite projects. It also makes machined castings for the fire control system of the M60 battle tank.

Canadian Marconi

One of the most remarkable "success" stories in Canadian military production for export is Canadian Marconi Company. About 80 per cent of the company's production is for military purposes, and Marconi President Philip Wheatley says that his firm "would like to increase commercial business, but most products are sold to the military before finding commercial applications."[47] Marconi is in the business of military communications, and its AN/GRC-103 lightweight, mobile, tactical radio relay equipment is used by armies all over the world. Other products of the telecommunications division include what is essentially a battlefield radio station and transmitter that can be mounted on a truck and taken into forward areas to provide multichannel tactical communications facilities. The unit is designed to be secure against unauthorized personnel and is compatible with voice-coding equipment. Since 1969 when they were first developed for the U.S. armed forces, about 7,500 radios have been sold to the U.S. and another 7,000 to almost thirty other countries, for total sales of $600 million.[48]

A twelve-line semiautomatic field tactical switchboard, another of the division's products, was the company's first sale to China. In 1985 Marconi signed a contract to supply tactical switchboard systems to the Chinese army, which will use them in extensive evaluations under field conditions.[49] A variety of Marconi airborne navigational systems, engine monitoring and display instruments and other communications hardware operate in weapons systems such as the F-111 long-range nuclear bomber, the Hughes YAH-64 Apache helicopter, the Bell 214ST, the Aerospatial Puma, and the Sikorsky Seahawk, UH-60A Blackhawk, HH-53, Nighthawk HH-60D and CH-124A Seaking helicopters. In 1984, the *Armed Forces Journal International* reported that Marconi's "vertical instrument displays have been selected for use in every new U.S. helicopter program begun in the last eight years."[50] The company also supplies electronics to control the launching of Hellfire missiles from the U.S. Marine Corps's AH-1J and AH-1T helicopters.[51]

The U.S. Navy uses Marconi's LN66 surface-search radar in ships of all classes from river patrol boats to nuclear-powered aircraft carriers. The radar is designed to provide accurate data for the location of targets, as well as navigation and weather information.[52] The American Trident strategic nuclear missile submarine uses the same radar for surface navigation.

Marconi could also acquire a stake in the Trident's submerged operations through the receiver sets the company is developing for the NAVSTAR system. The NAVSTAR Global Position System is a series of satellites able to provide simultaneous and continuous surveillance and communication coverage for the entire globe, enabling any craft lucky enough to have a receiver set to determine its location within an accuracy of 15 metres. While land-based vehicles have other means of determining location and direction and speed of movement, sea-based vehicles, without stationary reference points, have had to rely on much less precise information. This has had significant implications for sea-based strategic weapons systems, which have been less accurate than their land-based counterparts, as a result not of any deficiency of the missile but of the inability of the submarine — the firing platform — to know its precise location. You can't plot an appropriate flight path for your missile to a target 8,000 kilometres away if you don't know where you're shooting from.

The NAVSTAR system is out to change all that. And while the system, and the Marconi receiver sets, have a host of constructive civilian applications, some of their military applications are dangerous. The Trident's enhanced accuracy, for example, will make it available to threaten a pre-emptive or first strike against Soviet land-based missiles. This capacity gives credence to first-strike and nuclear war–fighting scenarios and has serious destabilizing implications. The NAVSTAR system will also be available for land-based military forces with extensive ramifications for counterinsurgency and intervention operations.

Inertial Navigators and Ballistic Computers

Litton Systems Canada Limited owes much of its public image in Canada to the U.S. cruise missile, for which it manufactures the inertial navigator unit. The company has provided the same basic technology for thousands of commercial and military aircraft. Among its other products is an airborne search radar supplied to, among others, the Royal Thai Navy and Israeli Aircraft Industries. At the time of writing, the company was gearing up to supply radar for the Canadian ADATS (air defence and antitank) system, in cooperation with a consortium led by Oerlikon-Buhrle of Switzerland. The Canadian order will give Litton a world product mandate for the radar and it hopes to win long-term military export orders in the process.

The fire control system of the M60 battle tank — the same system that receives machined castings from Magna Electronics of Scarborough — is run by a "tank ballistic computer" that is currently being upgraded by another Canadian company, Computing Devices Company of Ottawa, a division of Control Data Canada Ltd. The company developed the fire-control computer for the U.S. Army's M1 Abrams tank, and has been producing the devices since April 1986 at the rate of sixty per month.[53] The company has also supplied the computer to South Korea for its XK1 tank, and is now using the same technology to retrofit the fire control computer in the M60. In collaboration with Texas Instruments in the U.S., Computing Devices is developing a "universal tank retrofit package" which it hopes to market internationally, with Turkey identified as a possible first customer.[54] The company's export business also includes artillery computers, antisubmarine warfare signal processing equipment, projected map displays for aircraft, and electronic components for a variety of military systems. About 95 per cent of the company's production is for military purposes, and about 90 per cent of total production is exported.[55]

Military Vehicles

Two companies have changed the face of Canadian production of military ground vehicles. General Motors of Canada and Bombardier Inc. have both made recent and substantial entries into military production, with the result that, as a proportion of defence exports, the "vehicles" product category has been growing rapidly, from less than 5 per cent in the 1970s to more than 20 per cent in 1985 (see table 3). Through these companies, the central industry in Canadian manufacturing, the automobile industry, may be on the verge of a major entry into the military market.

General Motors of Canada

The U.S. parent of General Motors of Canada has indicated that it may no longer be satisfied with being the world's largest autombile manufacturer, and that its ambitions now include becoming "the leader throughout the world in the defence industry."[56] And the Diesel Division of General Motors of Canada in London, Ontario, has been doing its part. In mid-1987 the Diesel Division will complete delivery of 758 light armoured vehicles (LAVs) to the American armed foces. First produced for the Canadian Armed Forces, the vehicles were developed by the Swiss firm MOWAG AG and built under licence in Canada. The LAV is Canada's main entry into "a new group at GM: the General Motors Defense Group," which, as the ads modestly put it, has "energy, talent and brains" all "dedicated to supporting those charged with keeping peace around the globe."[57] The most concrete expression of that dedication to date has been the $625 million sale to the U.S. Marine Corps for rapid deployment to whatever may be deemed a trouble spot by virtue of White House reasoning.

The LAVs come in six- and eight-wheeled variations and at least a dozen versions, for purposes ranging from troop transport to antitank operations. A command and control version provides communications, map boards and what are called "planning tools" for field commanders. The armament is confined to a single machine gun for the commander, but an extendable shelter provides a "briefing room" for the commander and his operations staff. The antitank version is outfitted with missiles that can engage multiple targets and can be reloaded without exposing crewmen to hostile fire. Armoured vehicles are increasingly favoured over main battle tanks for their versatility and adaptability to a variety of "missions," from traditional front-line battlefield operations to urban street crowd control. The U.S. Marine Corps is currently developing a new tactical electronic warfare system to be mounted on the GM LAV. It is considered desirable to mount communications jamming and other electronic warfare equipment on an armoured vehicle rather than on a conventional truck so that the devices can be carried directly into the battle area for "tactical operations during intense combat situations."[58]

GM also produces military marine engines, mine clearance kits, and update kits for U.S. M113 armoured personnel carriers. In 1986 GM signed an agreement with a West German company to produce "high mobility tactical military trucks" under licence. It hopes to win a contract to supply these trucks to the Canadian Armed Forces, and then, following the pattern of the LAVs, to market them internationally.[59] The company also plans to team up with Hughes Aircraft Co. to prepare proposals for submarines to the Canadian Armed Forces.[60] If evidence that the defence industry cannot be neatly divided into air, space, ground transport and marine production is needed, it is provided by the example of an auto manufacturer teaming up with an aircraft manufacturer to bid on a submarine contract.

Bombardier

The second major Canadian company offering military ground vehicles is Bombardier Inc. Even before it purchased Canadair, Bombardier was one of the country's largest exporters of manufactured goods.[61] Like General Motors, Bombardier has used the purchase of foreign technology as a means of entering the military market. It purchased rights to a 2.5-tonne military truck, including some export rights, from the American firm A.M. General, with 2,700 vehicles to be supplied initially to the Canadian Armed Forces. Similarly, it bought the worldwide production and marketing rights for the Iltis, a jeep-like vehicle, from Volkswagen of West Germany, and supplied 1,900 of the vehicles to the Canadian Armed Forces. Bombardier has also acquired rights to an 8.5-tonne truck from the Oshkosh Truck Corp. of Wisconsin for possible supply to the Canadian Armed Forces and subsequent exports.[62] Other Bombardier military products include off-road motorcycles (sold to Britain and Belgium as well as Canada), snowmobiles, troop carriers and two-wheeled gun carriages.

Road Graders and Other Vehicles

A perhaps unexpected participant in the sale of military vehicles to the United States is Champion Road Machinery Ltd. of Goderich, Ontario. The company manufactures road graders and is a frequent supplier of road graders to the U.S. armed forces. In February 1986 External Affairs announced a $1.8 million sale of graders to the U.S. Army in Columbus, Ohio. If Congress votes the necessary funding and if all options are exercised, sales to the Army could reach $12 million.[63] And a Calgary company, Canadian Foremost Ltd., also offers its off-highway vehicles, used in the oil, mining and other industries, as heavy-duty military vehicles.

Shipbuilding

If the electronics industry is considered weak, the shipbuilding industry is near collapse and, for all intents and purposes, has become a ward of the federal government. While in 1975 the Canadian shipbuilding industry employed some 17,000 people, in mid-1986 — just over a decade later — it employed about 4,000.[64] The government has accounted for most of the recent work in Canadian shipyards. In 1982, the private sector placed orders worth $839 million for new ships and repair work, while government-related procurement amounted to only $110 million. In 1985, this pattern reversed itself. Commercial shipyard business was $291 million, while Ottawa accounted for $386 million in orders.[65] But now government orders may also be drying up. By the end of 1986, all but one of the ships ordered under a special program begun by the former Liberal government was to have been delivered. That program produced $600 million in orders for the Canadian Coast Guard and other ships. The survival of the industry may now depend on a new set of government orders — including an icebreaker, the updating of the Canadian Forces' Tribal Class destroyers, a second set of DND patrol frigates, submarines and other auxiliary vessels for the navy.

The Canadian shipbuilding industry's sorry state is not likely to be alleviated through access to the U.S. military market. A clause in the U.S. Defense Assocation Act prohibits the Pentagon from purchasing any naval vessel from a foreign source, and another clause prohibits the subcontracting to a foreign supplier of the production of "major components" of naval ship hulls or superstuctures.[66] Since "major component" is not defined, Canadian suppliers can still pursue marine subcontracting, but it is an uncertain business, as St. John Shipbuilding discovered in 1986. In January 1986 a Virginia shipyard announced that St. John Shipbuilding would receive a multimillion dollar subcontract to build a bridge structure for a U.S. navy nuclear aircraft carrier.[67] By midsummer, however, it was announced that the company had lost the $3 million contract when the clause on "major components" for naval vessels was invoked.[68]

One Canadian manufacturer that has not been prevented from making major sales to the U.S. Navy is Indal Technologies of Mississauga, Ontario. Indal produces a device to pull helicopters down onto a ship's deck, a matter of some risk and delicacy in heavy seas. The system works together with a horizon reference set — manufactured by another Ontario company, Sperry Aerospace and Marine Group of Rockland — which acts as a homing device to guide the incoming helicopter to the hauldown apparatus. Once attached, the helicopter is pulled down and secured to the deck. Indal has sold large numbers of these "recovery assist and traverse" (RAST) systems to the U.S. Navy and complements the hauldown system with shipboard telescoping hangars and other lighting and firefighting equipment for decks. In 1984 the company became the first non-U.S. firm to earn "validation" by the U.S. Navy as being capable of handling $500 million defence contracts.[69] The company's 1985 annual report said that its "mainstream business" would come from the shipment of RAST systems to the U.S. and other navies.

The $15 billion a year which the U.S. spends on antisubmarine warfare equipment is critical to Fathom Oceanology Ltd., also of Mississauga. With 80 per cent of its 1982 sales in military commodities, and the majority of that exported, Fathom is a good example of a Canadian firm that depends for its survival on access to the U.S. market. The company specializes in the development, design, testing and manufacture of towed naval acoustic systems. These are listening devices towed submerged behind a ship or attached to a helicopter for the purpose of

detecting submarines or other acoustic systems, or for mine coun-
termeasures. The systems have been delivered to a variety of defence
forces around the world, as have Fathom's hull-mounted sonar domes.
The company's military products also include various types of custom
deck equipment, such as davits and traction winches, that are also used
in civilian ships.

Things that Go Bang

A pacifist Mennonite community in southern Manitoba seems an
unlikely home for a member of the U.S. Defense Preparedness Association. But in Winkler, Man., Brown Armaments designs, develops and
manufactures a variety of small arms and related commodities. A current specialty is what the company calls "a revolutionary new muzzle
brake" designed to eliminate more than 90 per cent of the recoil forces
produced by hand-operated weapons. Other products described as being in the concept stage in mid-1986 include an "ultra-reliable," compact and lightweight machine gun; small arms and machine guns; a
low-cost pistol, also "ultra-reliable"; and a system of lightweight armour – piercing weapons and ammunition with an extremely compact
and lightweight antitank weapon, "theoretically possessing frontal kill
capabilities."[70]

But the flagship of the Canadian munitions industry is Canadian Arsenals Limited, one of two companies that account for most of Canada's ammunition production. Canadian Arsenals has long been a
supplier of armaments and related products to the Canadian Armed
Forces. Established in Mississauga in 1940, the company originally
produced small arms such as pistols, rifles and machine guns for the
Canadian war effort. Although it closed its small arms division in 1976,
when it was shifted to Diemaco in Kitchener, the company continued to
supply the Department of National Defence with medium-and large-
calibre ammunition and ancillary military equipment. Today its adver-
tised products include live and training ammunition for artillery (including 155-mm howitzers), naval and tank guns, infantry mortars and
hand-held antitank weapons. It also produces other equipment such as
gas masks, camouflage nets, fuses and demolition charges. All of its
production is for military purposes.[71]

In 1985, the company's sales reached $220 million, primarily to the
Canadian Department of National Defence. In that year, the federal
government sold the company to a Montreal engineering firm, the SNC
Group, which also owns the other major Canadian ammunition pro-

ducer, IVI Inc. of Montreal, a supplier of small-calibre ammunition to the Canadian Forces. Privatization of Canadian Arsenals signals an intention to pursue exports — currently less than 10 per cent of the company's sales — more vigorously. One reason why the SNC Group was chosen was its international contacts, which were thought to be best suited to meet what the *Financial Post* described as "a tough-to-fulfill mandate to turn Canada into a major munitions exporter."[72] The SNC Group has been involved in projects in the U.S., Peru, Nepal, Thailand and elsewhere.[73]

In the 1970s the Quebec-based Space Research Corporation earned notoriety and eventual closure following revelations that 155-mm artillery shells and long-range artillery technology had found their way to South Africa, in violation of the UN arms embargo, by various circuitous — but deliberate — routes. In 1986 the same technology and some of the designers turned up in China. *Jane's Defence Weekly* reported in October 1986 that Chinese test firings had reached a range of 40,000 metres. And just to prove that there's something in it for everyone, even cutlery manufacturers have a role to play in the arms business. Nella Cutlery Service makes the bayonet for the C7 rifle, which is manufactured by Diemaco for the Canadian Armed Forces.[74]

Systems Integration

Although the Canadian industries that produce military commodities have extensive capabilities, systems integration is less advanced. Systems integration is a specialized activity that involves developing the complete functioning and integration of all systems on an aircraft or ship and requires a broad engineering and management capability. As the aerospace industry journal *Aerospace Canada International* noted:

> In order to develop a total systems integration capability a company must employ a large group of experienced engineers and develop an extensive data bank to provide information, such as performance specifications, on all available systems worldwide. At this time, few Canadian companies can muster the resources to undertake such a task, and this effort will not be made in the absence of an actual defence contract.[75]

The Department of National Defence used to be the custodian of this systems capability in Canada. During the 1970s, however, Canada in effect did not procure any complete systems — except for the long-range patrol aircraft and the new fighter aircraft, both of which were off-the-shelf purchases of U.S. systems — and as a result DND effectively lost that capability. Thus, when it came time to acquire new ships, the systems integration function had to be contracted to a foreign firm. Sperry Corporation of the United States was given responsibility for systems integration of the new patrol frigates, with Sperry setting up a new company in Montreal, Paramax Electronics Inc., for that purpose. The technology is to be transferred to Canada as part of the agreement through which the frigates are being purchased, but it is not clear what will be done to ensure that the capability is maintained. There would have to be either a steady stream of Canadian government purchases of complete systems, or else a stepped-up effort to market the technology overseas.

A Significant but Truncated Industry

Military production has, by definition, a single market: governments. For any military production capability to be sustained over the long term, extensive public support, political and financial, is required. An individual company that develops a particular commodity with high demand in the international defence marketplace — such as Marconi military radio sets — will be able to function essentially as a an independent commercial undertaking. Overall, however, military production is a public enterprise, even when actual production is done by private firms. Hence, the long-term viability of military production depends upon government planning. For Canada, through the Defence Production Sharing Arrangements, the long-term planning and design function has essentially been carried out by the United States. Canada has acted as a regional contributor to the overall North American enterprise and Canadian financial support has been largely confined to funding individual companies to help them compete more effectively in the North American defence market.

The main base for a successful defence industry is government procurement. As long as the government finds public support for a major defence equipment budget, there is little difficulty in maintaining a defence industry. The U.S. government has managed continued high levels of procurement, while the Canadian government has not. But because the industry is continentally integrated, this has not meant the total demise of the Canadian industry. It has instead meant the radical restructring of that industry — from the systems capability it possessed in the 1950s and 1960s, primarily through licensed production of aircraft, to a new focus on component production.

By the mid-1980s the government was shifting its strategy again —

this time, towards the development of complete systems capabilities and greater efforts to market military products beyond the North American continent. None of this is easy. To be sure, the planet has a gargantuan appetite for military paraphernalia, but on a worldwide scale supply is currently outpacing demand. That means you've got to hustle, and in the next chapter we look at how this northern hustler operates.

5

Promoting the Industry

The *Canadian Defence Products Guide* is the Eaton's Catalogue of the Canadian arms business. In a nine-by-twelve glossy full-colour format, the *Guide* advertises military paraphernalia ranging from jet aircraft to plastic watercans. Published by the Defence Programs Bureau of the Department of External Affairs, the *Guide* is not widely distributed in Canada, and in fact is only reluctantly provided to Canadians. Its intended audience is foreign governments and foreign military contractors.

The focus of the *Guide* is on dull competence, not excitement and noble causes. It sells reliability and durability and its rallying cry is loyalty rather than freedom. It is a uniquely Canadian style of military hype that eschews rhetorical flourishes about the defence of liberty (a prominent element of advertising in industry journals), appealing instead to the advantages of international coordination of military production and relying on matter-of-fact, technical descriptions of the commodities offered. The hundreds of colour photographs avoid scenes of military action and concentrate on close-ups of microcircuits, display terminals, instruments with protruding wires and the world's largest selection of sturdy black and olive-green metal boxes. The only human forms are those of technicians in lab coats hovering intently over wires and those metal boxes. The message is that defence is not about guns but about high tech and cautious innovation.

Thus, the *Guide* promises "protection, safety and comfort" to the purchaser of "nuclear biological chemical (NBC) overboots and chemical warfare (CW) gloves." In the case of the CW gloves, "the soft butyl rubber plus finger and palm of curved configuration allows excellent manipulative dexterity together with dependable durability." This display is complemented by another offering simple pocket-size devices to detect the presence of chemical warfare agents, or more elaborate kits "with carrying case" to test the environment and determine when it is safe for soldiers to unmask.

Canadian Arsenals Limited, Canada's premier producer of munitions, is a bit more daring and displays its shells and mortars on a background of advancing tanks silhouetted against the setting sun. But the text of the ad is all business. Offering "experienced and innovative engineering" and "rigid quality control," it says that "with an enlarged line of defence material, Canadian Arsenals is offering, at competitive prices, an ever-increasing variety of high-quality products."

An introduction to the *Guide* explains that "Canadian policy has encouraged the domestic defence industry to specialize in certain product areas on the basis of natural advantage." As examples of natural advantage, it mentions "vast distances and extreme climate," so it is no surprise to find that Magline of Canada Limited of Renfrew, Ontario, offers a line of snowshoes, parkas and other equipment for the Arctic traveller. More extensive clothing lines are offered in a separate publication in the same format, the *Canadian Cold Weather Clothing and Equipment Guide*. Here, the clothing is complemented by ads for portable heaters and Yukon stoves, sleeping bags, survival kits and "magic pantry" — vacuum-sealed field rations.

The *Canadian Security Products Guide* is the government's offering of Canadian goods for the export market in response to increasing demand for "systems, equipment and services to provide security protection for military, paramilitary, and commercial facilities." A variety of surveillance and detection devices are included, along with protective clothing, prison furniture, security information systems, and even a S.W.A.T. (special weapons and tactics) consulting service.

Three Levels of Support

The military industry is not an industry of the free market. Its wares are purchased almost exclusively by governments, and in Canada as in other countries, its commercial success depends heavily on government administrative and political support. While individual firms advertise their products, governments are the primary arms export promoters. In testimony before the House of Commons Standing Committee on External Affairs and National Defence, Defence Programs Bureau officials pointed to three main tasks the government must carry out to ensure a successful run at military exports.[1] First, "government support has to be political — the government must decide where and how and with whom you will do defence trade." Second, there must be financial support. Particularly within NATO, "financial support is to ensure that you develop the technology and develop the right product with your friendly nations to get the best economies of scale and the most efficient defence forces." Third, there must be direct government guidance and assistance in arranging contracts, inasmuch "as this is a highly regulated type of trade."

Accordingly, four government departments and one government agency are mobilized in the encouragement of Canadian military exports or, as it is officially referred to, the administration of the Defence Trade Program. The department with primary responsibility is the Department of External Affairs, whose Defence Programs Bureau is in charge of the overall management of the Defence Trade Program. Also involved is the office of the director general of international programs in the Department of National Defence, the industry sector branches (such as aerospace) of the Department of Regional Industrial Expansion, and the Department of Supply and Services. In addition, the Canadian Commercial Corporation serves as a liaison between Canadian suppliers and foreign buyers of military commodities.

Besides its military export promotion functions, External Affairs administers Canada's cooperative defence production programs with other countries — chiefly the Canada-U.S. Defence Production Sharing Arrangements, but also arrangements with other NATO countries (see chapter 6) — and the control of military exports through the export permit program of the Export and Import Permits Act (see chapter 7). The latter responsibility in particular must be seen as being in conflict with the department's promotional role. In a single department of government, ultimately accountable through a single senior cabinet minister, officials are charged with administering what is described as a "restrictive" export control policy, with developing political and administrative proposals for the international control of the arms trade, and with maximizing Canadian military exports in support of national economic objectives.

Before the Trudeau government's transfer of international trade responsibilities to the Department of External Affairs, the Defence Programs Bureau was housed in the Department of Industry, Trade and Commerce. While the government as a whole had to accommodate the conflicting needs of export promotion and export control, this was not required of a single minister. In the spring of 1986, External Affairs Minister Joe Clark had the unenviable job of guiding an internal departmental review of export guidelines, including the provision that Canadian military commodities not go to regions of active or imminent conflict, while at the same time publicly supporting and promoting a Canadian firm's interest in selling armoured vehicles to Saudi Arabia — a prominent actor in the Middle East, a region of the globe where conflict is not noticeably absent and where there is not a paucity of weapons. At the same time that the department was reviewing the policy of controlling arms exports to human rights violators, it was arranging for and financing the participation of Canadian military manufacturers in a defence communications sales fair in South Korea — a country that has not been known for its sensitivity to human rights concerns.

The Defence Programs Bureau

The department's military export promotion activities are carried out through the Defence Programs Bureau (DPB). The bureau was first established in 1963 "in recognition of the need for a highly specialized industrial and trade oriented Branch within the Canadian government to promote the export of Canadian defence products."[2] The DPB is concrete evidence of the proposition that, as the department's own documents describe it, military production and sales are not activities like other economic activities, and military exports contain unusual implications for which governments are uniquely responsible. The bureau was formed, says the department, because "the export of defence equipment, including research and development programs with foreign governments, was a unique, specialized and highly competitive market sector, [for which] there must be a single, qualified Canadian government organization to take the lead in these operations."[3]

The DPB has three main responsibilities. In the first instance, it undertakes contacts and negotiations with other countries to develop defence trade relations and increase Canadian access to those markets. Military exports do not fall within the General Agreement on Tariffs and Trade, which means that defence trade relations are conducted bilaterally or multilaterally through military alliances such as NATO. This activity includes arranging bilateral research, development and production agreements.

Second, the DPB is responsible for more general export promotion. This includes initiating and implementing new export promotion programs for defence and related products — for example by organizing seminars, conferences and trade fairs. Bureau officers also provide international marketing information, advice, and assistance on defence and high technology products. They provide assistance to Canada's trade commissioners stationed abroad, officials of the department's geographical bureaus, other federal departments, provincial governments and, of course, the industry itself. The DPB undertakes market research and analysis, and when, for example, Canadian firms apply for funds under the Department of Regional Industrial Expansion's Defence Industry Productivity program, the DPB provides analysis of the export potential of the commodity for which funding is sought. Another feature of market analysis is advising the government of "the international trade implications of any National Defence procurement."[4] In other words, the DPB indicates the extent to which export opportunities may derive from the domestic production of equipment required by the Canadian Armed Forces. This assessment takes place through a Procurement Review Committee involving the four departments with a direct interest in military exports, with particular attention paid to procurements of more than $100 million.

Finally, the DPB maintains official statistics for trade under the Canada-U.S. Defence Production Sharing Arrangements and for other bilateral defence transactions.

With 80 per cent of all Canadian exports — and 85 per cent of all military exports — going to the United States, it is not surprising that the government identifies the U.S. as the primary market area and focuses its main export promotion attention there. A *Production Sharing Handbook* published by the Defence Programs Bureau leads Canadian manufacturers through the intricacies of dealing with the U.S. Department of Defense. Export permits are waived for the sale of military goods to the United States, and the handbook identifies the appropriate agencies and procedures.

Identifying the Customers

Access to markets other than the United States and European NATO does not command the same level of attention within the DPB, but these have also been the subject of government publications. A now-dated survey of "World Market Opportunities: Defence," published in 1977 by the Department of Industry, Trade and Commerce, sought to provide Canadian military exporters with current information about military sales opportunities around the world. DPB officials themselves have criticized the publication as being politically naive and of little help to Canadian industry. By politically naive, presumably, they mean the somewhat ingenuous commentary on the defence needs of various countries and advice on how to approach them. Of Indonesia, the booklet said that "activities in the Indonesian defence field have been somwehat slow," but then noted that "recent trends" indicated "an increase in activities" and "significant potential." This was written in the late 1970s, when the Indonesian military was engaged in an extensive and bloody campaign to annex the former Portuguese colony of East Timor.

In Pakistan, the publication noted, the "predominant role of the military" meant that major purchases were expected, adding almost hopefully that "the government is expected to be under military law at least until the elections." The booklet also provided advice on how to deal with the Philippines: "The most effective way of achieving success in dealing with the Philippine military is to make a direct approach to the appropriate weapons board and once the requirement has been defined and articulated, to carefully select an agent or reprepresentative who enjoys good contacts with the purchasing entity concerned." For Thailand, the publication offered this hopeful prognosis for military sales: "The necessity of the Thai armed forces to have an adequate strategic capability, combined with the key role of the military in the government of Thailand, ensures that the defence budget is generous." And for Zaire, the Ottawa arms promoters turned uncharacteristically to frankness: "The armaments race has become a fact of life in Africa and the countries of Central Africa are in the running. Canadian exporters will find it advantageous to investigate the opportunities for aeronautical equipment, parachutes, and logistical and electronic backup materiel."

As part of its general trade promotion activity, External Affairs publishes a variety of materials on Canadian trade promotion and support, including pamphlets on the Canada-U.S. production sharing program and the role of the Canadian Commercial Corporation.

Summits and Subcommittees

The primary role of government, however, is political rather than informational, and it is at summit meetings between Canadian and American leaders that much of the political work gets done. Summit meetings are invariably occasions for "reaffirming" arrangements for defence development and production sharing between the two countries and mutual pledges to "stimulate the flow of defence products" between them.[5] These special political moments of high rhetoric and good intentions are then complemented by a quite startling array of additional programs and arrangements.

The Defence Development and Production Sharing Arrangements, as they are now known, are administered through a Canada-U.S. steering committee. In its role of overall manager of the Defence Trade Program, the Canadian Department of External Affairs is represented on this committee by an assistant deputy minister, and the U.S. Department of Defense is represented at an equivalent level. Other Canadian participants include the assistant deputy minister of materiel in the Department of National Defence, the assistant deputy minister of the industries branches in the Department of Regional Industrial Expansion, and representatives of the Department of Supply and Services and the Canadian Commercial Corporation. This steering committee is an umbrella for various subcommittees. The subcommittee on technology transfer is concerned with the control of technology transfer to Warsaw Pact countries. The subcommittee on the defence industrial base aims, as a Canadian official told the parliamentary committee, "to ensure that the North American industrial base concept is implemented" (in other words, to maintain and increase Canadian access to the U.S. market).[6] Another committee deals with administrative and security impediments to defence trade between the two countries.

Americans in Canada

Beyond the immediate political and administrative support it provides, the Department of External Affairs arranges for and funds incoming trade missions. One notable such event occurred in December 1984 when a team of procurement officials from the U.S. Defense Department undertook what was described as a "first-ever" tour of Canada. The aim of the exercise, financed by the Canadian government, was "to increase sales by Canadian manufacturers and suppliers to different branches of the American military."[7] The tour went to seven Canadian cities and consisted of briefings of Canadian industry representatives by about twenty Pentagon officials. While U.S. Defense Department officials regularly come to Canada to deal with defence contracts (in fact, the U.S. Defense Contract Administration Services Management office in Ottawa has about seventy U.S. civil servants servicing military contracts beteween Canada and the U.S.), this tour was given a high profile and touted in Canada as the result of new Tory attitudes towards the U.S.

Robert Wenman, parliamentary secretary to Defence Minister Robert Coates, had difficulty containing his enthusiasm for the tour. Citing job creation and economic renewal as its benefits, Wenman managed an unusual blending of metaphors in his insistence that "this visit is part of the bread and butter resulting from the chemistry that developed between Prime Minister Mulroney and President Reagan during Mr. Mulroney's trip to Washington."[8] The government designed the tour primarily to provide political support for military exports — it was to be what Wenman called "a strong statement about the new direction of the Conservative Government."[9] The Tories were publicly acknowledging that continuing access to the U.S. market would require the maintenance of a friendly political environment. It was clear that the demonstrators outside the briefing halls realized the same thing. They understood that the high-profile, Canadian-financed tour was a way of expressing overt Canadian political support for the military policies of the United States.

The U.S. Defense Contract Management office in Ottawa is the only out-of-country office of the Pentagon Defense Logistics Agency. In cooperation with the Canadian Commercial Corporation and the Department of National Defence, it administers contracts and manages a reciprocal system for audits, quality control, and inspection.[10] Under the U.S. Defense Acquisition Regulations administered by the U.S. office in Ottawa, all prime contracts in Canada over $25,000 are to be awarded through the Canadian Commercial Corporation, a Canadian crown corporation.

The Canadian Commercial Corporation

The Canadian Commercial Corporation is a contracting agency that aids Canadian firms in dealing with foreign governments. Only in the case of the United States are companies required to deal with the CCC. In all other cases, the CCC enters a trade deal at the invitation of either the foreign government or the Canadian firm. It arranges a prime contract over $25,000 by placing back-to-back contracts with the Candian firm to supply the commodity in question and with the foreign buyer to purchase it. The CCC then follows through to manage the contract, pay suppliers, and bill the overseas customer. Working through a government agency provides corporations and foreign buyers with quality control and financing assurances and generally simplifies the frequently complicated business of international trade.[11]

Most of the contracts the CCC administers are for military commodities, and the majority of those are with the United States. The

U.S. Defense Contract Administration sends Canadian firms bidding information on upcoming contracts, but before a Canadian firm can receive such information it must apply to the CCC to become listed for particular commodities. The CCC examines the firm's capabilities and decides whether to certify it as being eligible to be listed with the appropriate U.S. procurement agency.[12] When the CCC receives a U.S. bid request, it then determines whether there are Canadian firms capable of responding within the allotted time. After bids are entered and a contract is awarded to the CCC, it in turn makes the purchase from the Canadian bidder.

Historically, the federal government has covered all the costs of the CCC — $18 million in 1985 — but in 1986, at the recommendation of the Erik Neilsen task force reviewing government programs, the corporation began to phase in a user fee of 2.5 per cent.[13] However, the move appears to be backfiring, with major contractors suggesting that the CCC's role simply adds another level of bureaucracy and is not worth the fee. Smaller firms have most need of the CCC's services, but their contracts are largely exempt (contracts of $50,000 or less awarded to small firms with sales of less than $5 million and fewer than 100 employees are not to be charged).[14] By mid-1986 the U.S. Department of Defense was charging that the fee would in effect be added to its procurement costs and was threatening to stop dealing through the CCC — a move that would require adjustments to the American Defense Acquisition Regulations.[15]

Research, Development and DIP

Research and development funding is also available to Canadian firms looking for access to the U.S. defence market. While the U.S. Defense Department funds 100 per cent of military research and development, Canadian funding is normally limited to 50 per cent, with the company expected to pick up the rest. The Canada-U.S. Defence Development Sharing Program (DDSA), however, provides for jointly-funded projects, through which Canadian firms can get full R&D funding, with up to 50 per cent from the U.S. and the other half from Canada. The joint funding of R&D projects sparked particular interest within U.S. procurement agencies, according to a 1981 memo from the U.S. deputy secretary of defense to Pentagon procurement officials. The memo reminded the procurement officials that under the DPSA/DDSA Canadian military producers are "an integral part of the North American industrial mobilization base," and that "in DDSA projects, the Canadian Government also funds up to 75 per cent of the development costs. This cost sharing arrangement could save the U.S. Government millions of dollars annually." The memo was in turn circulated in Canada by the director general of the Defence Programs Bureau to remind Canadian industries and researchers that they should "refer to it as appropriate in your dealings with the U.S. military."[16]

The main vehicle through which the Canadian government subsidizes research and development within Canadian industry is the Defence Industry Productivity (DIP) program. It was begun in 1959, the same year that the Defence Production Sharing Arrangements were formalized, and focuses on assisting Canadian companies in competing within the American military market. The DIP program was first conceived as an element of defence policy rather than economic policy. The Administrative Directive for the program put out by the Department of Regional Industrial Expansion says that "the traditional objectives of the DIP program [have been] to provide a defence industrial base and to develop and maintain a defence technological capability." As part of a continental defence industry base, Canada helps to maintain an overall industrial capacity to meet the needs of the continental defence policy. But since Canada has little influence on the direction of either that defence policy or defence industrial development, the real focus of the DIP program has been to help Canadian companies get as much economic benefit as possible from the ever-buoyant American military budget. Even with the DPSA, Canadian firms do not have automatic access to that market. Rather, they have opportunities to compete in it — and it is the job of DIP to make Candian firms more competitive.

Hence, the primary focus of the program is now economic rather than defence policy. The DIP program's administrative directive describes its "primary objective" as now being "to enhance economic growth through the promotion of viable defence and defence-related exports." This commercial focus is reinforced by the declaration that "greater emphasis will be placed on the market analysis of candidate projects by industry and government, and on the improvement of marketing data bases within government against which the marketing risks associated with candidate projects may be more rigorously assessed." While this emphasis has also led to increased funding of civilian projects through the DIP program (e.g. the development of STOL aircraft and civilian aircraft engines), the current government has indicated that "future DIPP funding will be re-directed to its original purpose."

Only time will tell whether this means a reintegration with defence policy and planning or a narrower focus on developing the commercial viability of strictly military production for export.

There is an official expectation that export commodities funded through the DIP program will achieve sales equal to twenty times the amount of the contribution. For goods that are primarily for the Canadian market, export sales are expected to yield a ratio of about ten to one. The supporters of the program regularly claim that ratios of this order are achieved, but there is no public accounting of how these conclusions are reached. If annual total military exports are compared with annual total DIP contributions, the ratios are substantially less (see table 5), although the sales generated by the DIP program are understated here since civilian sales are not taken into account.

DIP funds support four categories of activities in defence and defence-related research, development and production:

• research and development;
• establishing a company as a qualified supplier of particular commodities;

TABLE 4
Top 15 Recipients of Defence Industry Productivity Program Payments, 1969–1985

Company	Amount received($)
Pratt and Whitney Canada Limited, Quebec	333,242,094
De Havilland Aircraft of Canada, Ontario	124,802,247
Canadair Limited, Quebec	123,101,286
Litton Systems Canada Limited, Ontario	70,736,442
McDonnell Douglas Canada Limited, Ontario	66,242,203
Bell Helicopter (Textron), Quebec	56,636,566
Canadian Marconi Co./CMC Elect, Quebec	46,158,013
General Motors of Canada, Ontario	29,170,169
CAE Electronics Ltd., Quebec	27,321,381
MICR Systems Lid., Ontario	25,826,442
Spar Aerospace Ltd., Ontario and Quebec	25,447,933
Garrett Manufacturing Limited, Ontario	14,625,094
Dowty Equipment of Canada Ltd., Ontario	12,431,904
DAF Indal Ltd., Ontario	11,459,312

Source: Public Accounts of Canada

TABLE 5
Annual Military Sales to the United States Compared with Annual Defence Industry Productivity Subsidies in Support of Those Sales, 1969–1985

Year	DIP Payments ($ million)	Military Sales to U.S. ($ million)	Ratio of DIP Payments to Sales (%)
1969	29.6	299.8	9.8
1970	48.5	222.6	21.4
1971	45.2	216.3	20.9
1972	48.8	175.0	27.9
1973	48.3	198.8	24.3
1974	57.5	150.0	38.3
1975	48.4	188.5	25.7
1976	39.0	191.1	20.4
1977	44.9	314.1	14.3
1978	43.2	267.0	16.2
1979	52.2	367.7	14.2
1980	57.9	481.7	12.0
1981	94.9	826.6	11.5
1982	154.9	1,027.9	15.1
1983	131.9	1,207.4	10.9
1984	144.2	1,360.5	10.6
1985	152.7	1,644.2	9.3

Sources: Public Accounts of Canada; Department of External Affairs.

- modernizing plants and acquiring advanced production equipment intended to upgrade manufacturing capabilities;
- marketing feasibility studies related to existing or new products or product ideas.

Bailouts, Trade Fairs and High Tech

Other programs, such as export financing and insurance through the Export Development Corporation and export promotion through the Program for Export Market Development (PEMD), are also open to military exporters, but are not specially directed towards military exports.

A significant element in government support for military production has been direct public investment in the two prominent aircraft manufacturers, de Havilland and Canadair. De Havilland was purchased in 1974 for $40.5 million and Canadair in 1976 for $46.4 million. In the 1980s, before the government sold the two firms back to the private sector — de Havilland for $155 million and Canadair for $120 million — it subsidized them to the tune of $2.5 billion.[17]

The Department of External Affairs also funds promotional activity through trade fairs and missions. For example, the 1984–85 External Affairs Annual Report notes that the Defence Programs Bureau supported security and defence trade missions to three Latin American countries and four Pacific Rim countries. And in 1984 the Canadian Consulate General in Philadelphia hosted an exposition of about seventy-five Canadian manufacturers of "high quality and advanced technology Canadian industrial/defence products." Designated CIDEX 84 (Canadian Industrial Defence Exposition), the event promised technical and marketing assistance for a wide range of commodities and activities: castings; forgings; precision-machined parts; electromechanical, electrical and electronic components; hardware; software; R&D; "and a great deal more."

The High Technology Export Conference organized by the Defence Programs Bureau annually since 1963 brings Canadian industry representatives together with government officials able to assist industry in the marketing of high tech and defence products. Government personnel include trade commissioners and commercial officers from Canadian embassies and consulates around the world, as well as representaitves of various government departments and agencies involved with military exports. While the conference originally focused exclusively on defence commodities, recent conferences have dealt with commercial high technology products as well.

Promotion of Canadian defence industry places major emphasis on high technology and what the Pentagon has identified as key "emerging technologies" in weapons development. At a 1984 symposium sponsored by the Canadian Advanced Technology Association and the U.S. National Security Industrial Association, U.S. officials said that much of the technology needed for things such as the detection and targeting of missiles would be purchased off-the-shelf — meaning that Canadian industry would have the opportunity to develop such technologies. The emerging technologies are intended for both nuclear and conventional weapons. Areas indentified as being ones in which Canadian industry could participate included microelectronics, optoelectronics, acousto-optic processing, high density monolithic focal plane arrays, sensor technology, super computer systems, and advanced algorithms for high speed signal processing. *Canada Commerce*, a magazine published by the Department of Regional Industrial Expansion, noted in its report on the symposium that "any Canadian company which has or is developing new processes in any of these emerging technologies would be wise to advise the Local Regional Office of DRIE which can steer it to the proper channels of the U.S. Defense Department."[18]

The emerging technologies emphasize the two commodity areas that have dominated Canadian military sales to the U.S. — aerospace and electronics. The American armed forces have placed a high priority on gaining information superiority, and U.S. military representatives told Canadian industry in the spring of 1984 that the push in the emerging technologies is to get the technology out of the lab and into the field. The United States, they said, cannot afford to do this alone and existing Canada-U.S. agreements put Canadian companies in "a very favoured position." A great deal of the Canadian government's promotional activity is directed at trying to maintain that position. This is not an altogether reassuring thought in the light of the attitude of the Department of External Affairs, as reflected in the statement before the Commons External Affairs and National Defence Committee referred to earlier, that first and foremost the government's support of Canadian industry must be political — that is, political support for the commodities that industry is trying to sell to the U.S. and elsewhere.

Support through Procurement

The Department of National Defence assists in the export of military commodities primarily through its own procurement. DND has been encouraged to make export potential a more conscious element of its own procurement decisions. The technology and production experience gained in supplying military commodities to a domestic defence department are considered to be one of the best means of developing export markets. For example, the light armoured vehicles purchased by the Canadian Forces from General Motors of Canada have been converted by the company, with more than a little help from the government (including almost $30 million in DIP grants), into a commodity with substantial export potential. The government is now all set to try the same thing with its new order for low-level air defence and antitank (ADATS) units. With the Canadian order assumed to represent only 5 per cent of the total sales potential of ADATS, the betting is that the Canadian purchase and arrangements for domestic production will mean that this too will find offshore customers.[19]

Almost a decade ago DND began to worry in earnest about the lack of domestic capability to manufacture such basics as rifles and feared that in a crisis this lack could lead to shortages of supply. Another worry was the growing deficit with the United States in defence trade. The solution was to promote the development of home-grown capabilities in basic combat systems. Hence, Bombardier was encouraged to develop jeeps and trucks, General Motors developed the light armoured vehicle, Diemaco of Kitchener was given the job of providing rifles and ammunition, and Canadian Arsenals and IVI Ltd. of Valcartier were awarded contracts in small arms and ammunition. Virtually all of these systems relied on foreign technology, but in each case the technology transfer included rights to pursue international sales. In 1984, speaking at a ceremony marking the delivery of the first Iltis jeep from the Bombardier plant to the Canadian Armed Forces, then–Defence Minister Robert Coates said that "by increasing the responsiveness of our defence industrial base, we not only reduce our reliance on foreign sources of material and enhance our ability to defend ourselves, but we also increase the possibility of sales to allied forces."[20]

In June 1986, Supply and Services Minister Stewart McInnes said that NATO, in considering a common design for multipurpose frigates, had expressed interest in the Canadian frigates now under construction. A Saint John Shipbuilding Ltd. spokesman echoed the same optimism about foreign ship sales: "Even if we don't sell the ships, we can sell the expertise, design and program management."[21]

The Aerospace Industries Association of Canada considers domestic procurement of defence products "crucial" in international marketing efforts, and welcomes any efforts by the Department of National Defence in that direction. According to the AIAC, the department is considering establishing a defence industry research program as part of its effort to develop a Canadian defence industrial base, and has pledged to use its R&D budget (about 5 per cent of its capital budget) to develop domestic industrial capabilities that can provide a greater portion of the Canadian Armed Forces requirements.[22]

Among the responsibilities of the director general for international programs in DND is the coordination of the department's support of sales of defence equipment and services. This includes the exploration and development of cooperative procurement and development projects within NATO, as well as direct sales support such as the loan of equipment not available in the private sector for demonstration purposes. For example, in reporting on the activities of the Defence Programs Bureau, the 1984 – 85 Annual Report of the Department of External Affairs refers to military equipment demonstrations in the Middle East — probably the demonstration of General Motors LAVs in Saudi Arabia. DND does not cover shipping and travel or other costs, but will provide personnel to demonstrate or accompany the equipment. The Canadian Armed Forces have also loaned LAVs to other prospective buyers. The current director general for international programs, Don Bell, argues that doing this is in the interests of DND. The department notes that it is concerned about maintaining a long-term repair and resupply capability for the LAV in Canada, but the company could not maintain an economically viable LAV operation if DND were the only user of its product. The more sales the company makes, the better it will be able to meet DND needs in the future.

The DND Defence Research Establishments also encourage military exports by developing commodities that may have an international sales potential. In these cases, the technology is transferred, through the facilities of the Canadian patent office, to an appropriate private firm to complete development and undertake production and marketing. In all of this, says Don Bell, DND supports exports, but does not promote them.

In the early 1980s Canadian officials became enthralled with the industrial possibilities related to the American use of space for military purposes and explored ways of developing greater Canada-U.S. cooperation in defence and space work. They were hoping for greater Canadian access to the U.S. defence market for "state-of-the-art" systems and components, and for the transfer of critical space technology to Canada. In particular, then–Defence Minister Gilles Lamontagne expressed the view that "the U.S. seems willing to get involved in the latest surveillance technology relating to the defence of North America."[23] Several Canadian firms were reported to have had preliminary meetings with U.S. defence suppliers, and Canadian government officials were negotiating with the U.S. Air Force Space Division in Los Angeles, which the *Financial Post* described as "the heart, brains and influence centre of the nation's space defence system."[24]

In an effort to get in on the high tech/space gravy train, Canada reaffirmed the DDPSA during a summit meeting between President Reagan and Prime Minister Trudeau and renewed the NORAD agreement as the North American "Aerospace" Agreement, the Trudeau cabinet almost tripled the annual funding base of the DIP program to about $150 million, and the Defence Programs Bureau placed a representative at the Los Angeles Space Division office of the United States Air Force.

Ottawa's promotion of military exports exposes a basic contradiction in Canada's pursuit of such exports. On the one hand, the industry is encouraged to function as an apolitical commercial enterprise that seeks out markets wherever they are available with a view towards maximizing sales in support of Canadian economic interests. Exports and associated promotional activities are thus portrayed as an element of economic and trade policy, unrelated to defence or foreign policy considerations. On the other hand, military exports, whether to the U.S., to Europe or to the Third World, require political support and promotion in a way that commercial exports do not.

Though military exports depend on the political support of the home government, neither government nor industry will admit to any political responsibility for the ultimate use of their products, or for the military doctrines and practices which those products may support. The next two chapters look at the destinations of Canadian military commodities and the military policies to which the traffic in those commodities contributes.

6

Rough Riding on the Reagan Arms Boom

As noted in chapter 3, the 1970s were a trying decade for Canada-U.S. defence production sharing. Thus, Ronald Reagan's pledge to unleash a ravenous military budget in the interest of making America great again was good news for Canadians in a position to help feed the Pentagon appetite. The Reagan years, it very soon became clear, would be boom years for Canadian military exports. Since Reagan's election, Canadian military exports to the United States have increased at an average of more than 35 per cent per year. In 1985, these exports were five times what they had been in 1978 — $1.64 billion as compared with $267 million.

But along with the boom this orgy of American military spending created for Canadian military manufacturers, Reagan-era military exports to the U.S. also produced two disquieting developments. First, they pulled Canada deeply and directly into controversial and disturbing changes in American military doctrine and posture. Second, they demonstrated that no matter how great the Pentagon's appetite for Canadian military production, the American Congress would remain staunchly protectionist and look for ways to get the Pentagon to eat at home more often. Even in boom times, Canada-U.S. military trade arrangements would require some deft management — not all of which would always be successful.

The 1970s had opened with Americans claiming that the Vietnam-induced American military trade deficit with Canada was a violation of the spirit of balanced defence production sharing. By the second half of the decade, following Canadian purchases of long-range patrol and fighter aircraft in the United States, the balance had gone the other way and Canada was looking for guarantees of reciprocal military trade through negotiated offsets. Neither offsets nor the Reagan arms boom has been able to reverse the balance.

For a newly-elected Ronald Reagan, Canada-U.S. military trade was, of course, not a central concern. In Reagan's eyes, the main event of the 1970s was what *Business Week*, in a special March 1979 issue, called "the decline of U.S. power." And for Canada, it was a classic case of bad tim-ing. Just as the American star was declining, Canada was yet again coming to the conclusion that its own place in the heavens depended on its being more securely hitched to this same star. The conclusion drawn from the "Third Option" attempt to draw away from the United States in the early 1970s was that it had "borne little edible fruit." For Canadian industry, military and civilian dependence on the American market was reconfirmed. As an External Affairs official would later put it, "it is on the basis of a North American economy that the private sec-tor [in Canada] makes its growth plans."[1]

Unfortunately, the fact of Canadian economic dependence on Amer-ica is no guarantee that America's economy will be worthy of such de-pendence. And in the late 1970s, American decline was very much on Ronald Reagan's mind.

Canada and the Drive to Make America Great

Ronald Reagan's concern about American economic decline was both overshadowed by and related to a more urgent concern: that the Soviet Union had reached military parity with America. And now the Soviets were busy pushing for superiority. If this were allowed to happen, he prophesied, the world would be headed for an unprecedented reign of terror and turmoil. He called for a reassertion of American will, and es-pecially American military power. Jerry W. Sanders, a Senior Fellow at the World Policy Institute in Washington, identifies three basic prem-ises from which Reagan's military buildup was launched. First, there was the assumption that international stability, American security, and American power — particularly military power — are inseparable: the first two cannot exist without the last. Second, there was the conviction that the world is filled with hostile forces whose primary aim is to chal-lenge American power and thus undermine American security and in-ternational stability. Finally, there was the belief that these hostile forces could be defeated if only the American people and their leaders had the courage and the will to restore and exercise that power.[2]

An impressive election victory provided President Reagan with some persuasive evidence that the American public had found the will to back up his view that international peace and stability would ultimately emerge from the barrel of an American gun. With a single-mindedness that has become rare among politicans (except perhaps in their determination to be re-elected), Reagan set out, as he put it, to rebuild American military might. He launched a simultaneous attack on all fronts. Strategic nuclear forces were to be "modernized" and were to provide the global umbrella under which America could exercise its military, political and economic influence with equanimity. In Europe, nuclear modernization and the development of new conventional military technologies were to remove the ambiguities, once and for all, in the military arena where the Soviet Union posed the most immediate and credible military challenge. Military forces available for intervention in trouble spots anywhere in the world received special attention. Restraint in military sales, which had been faltering even under the Carter Administration, was now abandoned in favour of a policy of arming any friendly states with military ambitions — and preferably a little hard currency — that could be found to promote American interests in key regions of the world.

Strategic nuclear forces were assumed to be the cornerstone on which all exercise of American military force must ultimately rest. Here Reagan made explicit what some American analysts and military leaders had been maintaining for some time — that the old deterrence doctrine of mutually assured destruction was no longer viable. While the popular rationale for nuclear weapons had always been that they were deployed in order not to be used, military planners were understandably more inclined to consider — and plan for — their use. Through his defense secretary, Caspar Weinberger, Reagan set out to build a strategic nuclear force that could not only "deter" war but also function within a nuclear war environment — in other words, that could fight a nuclear war. Speaking in defence of the MX missile, General John Vessey, then Chairman of the Joint Chiefs of Staff, put it this way: "We have to look at the prospect of deterrence failing and actually having to fight a nuclear war. We want to tell you that the hard target kill capability of the MX has a usefulness there."[3] These views were first officially articulated by President Jimmy Carter in a secret "nuclear weapons employment policy," signed as Presidental Directive 59 and leaked to the press. Reagan later ratified the plan as National Security Decision Directive 13.[4]

Previously, U.S. strategists had emphasized Soviet population targets, and later economic targets. Now, PD-59 made military targets the top priority for U.S. nuclear weapons — especially shelters for key Soviet officials; strategic targets (including ICBM silos, command and control bunkers, nuclear storage sites and strategic air and naval facilities); other military targets (including airfields, military units, supply depots, critical transportation hubs, and power projection forces); and key factories. These requirements imposed major new demands on American nuclear weapons systems. Obviously the 1,400 Soviet missile silos would be targeted only if they could be attacked in a pre-emptive first strike. Hence the United States now needed highly accurate weapons, with a very short warning time, that could destroy a hardened target — in the jargon, weapons with a time-urgent, hard-target kill capability.

Besides imposing the requirement for a time-urgent hard-target kill capability, PD-59 greatly expanded the number of potential targets and therefore necessitated substantial increases in the American inventory of warheads. In addition to land-and sea-based ballistic missiles, other deliverable warheads are to be provided by the B-1 bomber and B-52 bombers carrying air-launched cruise missiles. The Centre for Defense Information in Washington estimated in 1984 that the U.S. would spend about US$450 billion during the rest of the decade preparing for nuclear war. The cruise missile in particular is deployed for purposes not only of assured destruction but also of attacking secondary military targets such as airfields, naval facilities, weapons storage depots, general supply depots and so on. Such targets, being immobile, do not require time-urgency, but they do require accuracy and lower-yield warheads to limit collateral damage (in a protracted war, attacks must be limited so as not to trigger a massive Soviet response — this of course imposes on the Soviets a capability for distinguishing between massive and limited attacks on them).

Above all, the weapons chosen must be able to survive during a prolonged nuclear war. That the U.S. should have the capacity to fight such a war, lasting months instead of days, was a second requirement of PD-59. This requirement means that the U.S. needs sensors that can detect and follow an incoming weapon and anticipate the place of impact, command centres capable of receiving and evaluating this data, decision-makers in command posts capable of making decisions about retaliatory weapons firings, and communications links capable of connecting the sensors to the command posts to the decision-makers and back to the weapons systems. All of these capabilities must be sustainable over periods of months in a nuclear war environment. An additional need is for intelligence capabilities to assess immediately the effects of one's own attack upon the adversary, indicate which targets have been destroyed, and then communicate this data, along with information about targets that are still standing, back to command posts. Thus, a broad range of command, control, communications and intelligence "improvements" are now being implemented by the Reagan administration, emphasizing endurance of these facilities through prolonged war and flexibility in communicating with and retargeting weapons systems.

Ottawa watched these developments with a certain unease. It stuck doggedly to its support for an undefined "nuclear deterrence" and to its pledge that "Canada will never abandon the pursuit of global security at greatly reduced levels of armament." The Reagan administration, meanwhile, was carrying on with its pursuit of security at greatly increased levels of armament. Nevertheless, Ottawa never wavered in its public support for the Reagan program — or in its efforts to get a larger piece of the accompanying industrial action. It did not seem to bother Canada that it was supporting lower levels of armaments on the one hand, and seeking increased industrial participation in the Reagan arms buildup and testing cruise missiles and other weapons on Canadian soil on the other.

While General Vessey and Defense Secretary Weinberger were asserting the need for a nuclear war-fighting capability and for weapons that could threaten pre-emptive attacks against Soviet strategic weapons systems, Ottawa persisted in proclaiming Washington's innocence: "A first strike attack, to disarm the other side by destroying its nuclear weapons before they could be launched, forms no part of NATO's strategy. NATO and the United States neither have nor seek the capability for it."[5] Ottawa, of course, argued that testing the cruise missile and producing its guidance system in Canada were respectively expressions of alliance loyalty and good business, and that neither could be construed as support for the nuclear arms race.

Various Canadian government officials, including the prime minister, steadfastly refused to acknowledge the changes in American nuclear doctrine that Weinberger was making explicit. In his annual report to the Congress for fiscal year 1984, Weinberger openly committed the United States to the acquisition of a nuclear war-fighting capacity and nuclear first-strike options. While by this time Weinberger had learned to scale down his rhetoric about fighting and winning nuclear wars, he nevertheless assigned the highest priority to a program "to increase the ability of our strategic force management systems not only to survive but to remain capable of performing their basic functions through a sustained sequence of Soviet attacks."

He said that the United States must have the "ability to operate beyond the initial stages of nuclear conflict," not, mind you, for the purposes of winning a nuclear war, but rather for the purposes of "denying enemy war aims" and then "restoring peace on favourable terms."[6] In separate meetings with church leaders just before Christmas 1983, both Prime Minister Trudeau and former Prime Minister Joe Clark argued that while the early Reagan rhetoric had been disquieting, it had since been toned down and was now consistent with traditional American support for deterrence.

In effect, PD-59 became Canada's "nuclear weapons employment policy." Inasmuch as the Canadian government subsidizes Canadian industry to produce components for the weapons called for under PD-59, and inasmuch as Canada's military industry base is committed to supplying — among others — weapons consistent with PD-59, it is hard to avoid the conclusion that the document, at least implicitly, has Ottawa's blessing. Canadian industry was and remains dedicated to the supply of material for the Reagan arsenal, while the Canadian government was and remains dedicated to avoiding responsibility for the military roles assigned to that arsenal.

That arsenal's purpose was changing, and it soon became clear to Washington if not to Ottawa that there was a widening gulf between Canadian rhetoric and Canadian action. In 1978 Prime Minister Trudeau had gone to the UN to talk of the dangers of the arms race and the need to suffocate it. Part of the act of suffocation, Trudeau suggested, would be to stop the flight testing of nuclear weapons delivery vehicles. It was an innovative idea, but before he could repeat it at the second UN special session on disarmament in 1982, news of Ottawa's willingness to test the cruise missile in Canada was leaked to the Washington press. Whether or not that was their intention, U.S. officials had guaranteed that the Canadian prime minister would not again go to the UN with pious declarations about stopping the awful arms race while Canadian companies enjoyed lucrative contracts to build parts for those very same arms. As it turned out, at his next trip to the UN in 1982, Trudeau had to focus more on Canada's rationale for allowing cruise missile tests than on proposals to stop those tests.

Canada's proclamation of innocence (Trudeau had in 1978 explained to the UN that Canada was the first country with a nuclear weapons capability to reject nuclear weapons) had lost the little lustre it might ever have had. PD-59 was not a Canadian document, but it, and the policies it blessed, had begun to speak for Canada.

The Reagan nuclear buildup is closely related to a second, and perhaps more urgent, objective of current military planning and deployment. The global reach of the superpowers — their ability to project force into any region of the world in which their global economic interests are deemed to be threatened — is directly linked to their nuclear arsenals. President Carter's secretary of defense, Harold Brown, attributed the need for a nuclear buildup to two developments: the expansion of Soviet forces and growing international turbulence. U.S. nuclear capabilities, he said, "provide the foundation on which our security rests. With them, our forces become meaningful instruments of military and political power."[7]

Canadian politicans and officials have been reluctant to comment on these developments in U.S. strategic and military doctrines. Canadian policy has followed the rather difficult path of simultaneously trying to benefit from the military spending windfall that they represent, issuing bland public statements in support of deterrence and alliance solidarity, and affirming Canada's commitment to peace and stability at lower levels of armament. While Canadian political leaders have tended not to endorse new U.S. deployments overtly (with the exception of nuclear deployments in Europe), Canadian industrial participation in U.S. nuclear weapons systems has perhaps been endorsement enough.

The Canadian government became directly involved in supporting the new MX missile when it approved a $120,000 loan to Boeing of Canada Limited in Winnipeg under the Defence Industry Productivity program to help the company retool its plant for the production of nose-cone material for the missile. While the company failed to win a production contract, Prime Minister Trudeau defended the government's support of the attempt on the grounds that such a contract would obviously create significant numbers of jobs in Winnipeg.[8] The sale of light armoured vehicles to the U.S. Marine Corps to help improve its rapid deployment capabilities represents direct involvement in the other major development in U.S. military strategy under President Reagan. Canada has participated industrially in a variety of U.S. strategic and conventional weapons systems, but Ottawa denies that there is any implication of specific political support in this participation.

The government has instead decided that it is not Canada's place to make distinctions among various U.S. weapons systems and deployments. The assumption is that Canada exercised its options when it decided whether or not to participate in formal defence production sharing arrangements. Having made the decision in favour of participation, Canada now has to go along with whatever the Americans decide to build. To draw distinctions between acceptable and unacceptable weapons systems from the Canadian point of view, it is argued, would represent uncalled-for second guessing and interference with the sovereign responsibility of the United States. After all, it is only the United

States that can decide the appropriateness of the weapons it wishes to deploy.

It is obviously true that Canada cannot decide which weapons systems the United States will or will not deploy. However, Canada can and must decide which U.S. military deployments this country will or will not directly support. Under current policy, Canada does not make judgements on the basis of the military or political effects of particular weapons systems, but prefers to make no judgements at all and leave the question of Canadian involvement up to the marketplace. If we can get a piece of the action, we're happy to participate. As it turns out Canada does not have a prominent piece of the American strategic nuclear action, but it is involved in a number of areas — for example, Canadian aluminum is part of the fuel base for strategic ballistic missiles, while Canadian industry, as noted earlier, makes the guidance system for the cruise missile and manufactures receiver sets for the NAVSTAR system that will improve the accuracy of sea-based strategic weapons (see appendix 2).

Challenges to Shared Defence Production

Canadian industry and government officials faced the Reagan boom in military spending with a high degree of optimism. The *Financial Post* put it this way in 1981: "With U.S. defense spending heading for one of its greatest binges in peacetime, Canada faces a rare opportunity to boost its fortunes with the U.S. on the military, industrial, trade and technology fronts."[9] The Reagan administration's goal of rapid military expansion was not the only reason for optimism. Even in 1981, well before the election of the Tories and the sharp escalation of Reaganesque rhetoric in Ottawa, the newspaper could point to a number of recent expressions of Canadian goodwill: some major equipment purchases in the U.S., the NORAD renewal, and the continuing DPSA. All these combined to raise hopes "that more of the expanded U.S. military pie can be made in Canada by Canadians." The *Financial Post* did acknowledge, however, that this was not a sure thing. It listed some of the impediments to greater Canadian access to the U.S. military market:

- U.S. "socioeconomic" legislation to preserve certain elements of the military market for U.S. minorities, small businesses, etc.;
- "Buy America" provisions which, despite the DPSA, still give preference to U.S. suppliers of products such as textiles and ship components;

- Classified information and technology to which Canadian firms are denied access;
- the Pentagon's continued resistance to the purchase of major pieces of equipment offshore.

Beyond that, even after all these limitations have been dealt with, there are no guarantees. Neither the DPSA nor offset arrangements relieve Canadian firms of the requirement that they must enter competitive bids, and contracts must still be won. Canadian trade officials indicate that "the U.S. attitude is that they're giving us a duty-free market, so it's up to us to be competitive."[10] And despite the Reagan purchasing boom, Canada still has a defence trade deficit with the United States. Furthermore, Canadian industry and government officials alike continue to admit that Canadian purchases in the U.S. are at the high end of the technological continuum, while U.S. purchases in Canada tend to involve lower levels of technology and build-to-print arrangements that produce few long-term benefits for the Canadian economy.

As noted in chapter 3, much of the history of Canada-U.S. defence production sharing is the history of Canadian efforts to overcome American congressional resistance to U.S. military imports from Canada. The offset arrangements, negotiated as parts of aircraft purchase deals, were an attempt to take advantage of goodwill generated by significant export orders for U.S. firms. As far as Congress was concerned, however, that goodwill was rather quickly consumed. In 1983 alone, no fewer than thirty protectionist bills, every one of them representing a threat to Canadian business interests in one form or another, were presented in Congress.[11]

Congressional efforts to ban Pentagon purchases of equipment containing foreign specialty metals have already been mentioned (see chapter 3). These attempts continued in the 1980s. One such effort, in 1982, was defeated only after months of intense lobbying involving Industry Minister Herb Gray and protests to the White House and the Defense Department. The *Financial Post* noted at the time that Caspar Weinberger and senior Pentagon officials proved to be important allies in Canada's lobbying efforts.[12] Then, in late 1984, the waiver allowing Canada and several other NATO countries to sell military commodities with specialty metals to the U.S. was repealed without fanfare.[13] At the time, Canadian officials estimated that the measure could cost Canada $100 million a year in military sales to the U.S. However, another concentrated lobbying campaign by Canadian officials and their counterparts in the Reagan Administration succeeded in having the waiver reinstated roughly six months later.[14]

Even the Pentagon, which usually viewed international procurement programs as an element of alliance-building and was a consistent ally on the specialty metals issue, made its own bow to protectionism in 1983 with a suggestion that a five-year, $2 billion plan to "boost the cutting edge of defense technology" would be reserved for "domestic" firms and thus exclude Canada.[15]

For Canada this constituted a challenge to the spirit of defence production sharing, and was all the more disturbing since this time it came from the Pentagon, Canada's traditional defence production ally, rather than the Congress. The Pentagon's director of industrial resources told the House Subcommittee on Economic Stabilization that while "we consider Canada as part of the U.S. domestic industrial base," in this case the approach would be to help only U.S. manufacturers. The Ottawa *Citizen* quoted Pentagon officials as complaining about Canada's "free ride" on military expenditures, and noted that "concerns also have been expressed in Washington that Canadian participation in the new program could result in leakage of too many American secrets to the Soviets."[16]

With these sentiments apparently less and less restrained in Washington, it was no surprise that Canadian officials consumed a great deal of energy in ensuring that when Prime Minister Trudeau and President Reagan met in the American capital in May 1983, they would make a point of reaffirming the DPSA. In what the *Financial Post*'s Fred Harrison called a "seemingly bland assurance," Trudeau was presented with a Pentagon letter stating that the U.S. Defense Department had "made no changes to its long-standing policies regarding industrial preparedness planning with the Canadian government and Canadian industry."[17] Within the context of growing protectionist sentiments, the assurance was viewed as anything but bland, and revived the seemingly indestructible Canadian hope that the special Canada-U.S. defence industry relationship would yet yield windfall benefits for Canada.

Referring specifically to the technology development program, the letter said that while there were at the time no Canadian firms listed as candidates for development assistance, "this is not ruled out for the future."[18] A few weeks later, a CanAm Future Tech Conference in Ottawa, sponsored jointly by the Canadian Advanced Technology Assocation and the National Security Industrial Association of the United States, focused on promising new military technologies and the identification of areas in which Canadian industry might contribute. Canadian government representatives reported that U.S. defence officials were making special appeals to Canadian industry to become involved in the development of "emerging technologies to improve conventional defence."[19]

At the same time, U.S. concerns about the leakage of "sensitive" technology to the Soviet Union works against the promotion of Canadian participation in these developments — especially since the Americans apparently fear that Canada may be "a potentially easy conduit for passing U.S. technology on to the Soviet bloc."[20] The Reagan Administration has made something of a crusade out of blocking the transfer of technology with possible military applications to the Soviet Union or its allies.

Two issues were at stake. First, there was the question of "extra-territoriality" — the attempt by the U.S. to apply its laws in other jurisdictions. The second concern was the possibility that security classifications would exclude Canadian companies from bidding on various U.S. contracts. The *Financial Post* reported that Canadian contractors were complaining about U.S. security classifications that make it difficult to obtain the information needed to prepare a bid. As part of the crusade to withhold technology from the Soviet Union, these restrictions were extended.[21]

The focus of the restrictions is on military and space applications, and they include measures to limit work within sensitive technologies to contractors that are owned, controlled and operated by U.S. citizens or permanent resident aliens. Exceptions would be made only for contractors that agree to take appropriate measures to preclude access by foreign nationals to export-controlled data. Formal proposals routinely include exemptions for companies or countries with special project or infrastructure arrangements with the United States, but the fear in Ottawa is that an overall tightening of controls on technical information will have a cumulative effect of progressively denying Canadian firms the information on which competitive bidding can be based. In the context of considering Canadian access to work on the Strategic Defense Initiative, Canadian military analysts have estimated that such restrictions on technology transfers could bar Canadian manufacturers from about 70 per cent of the U.S. defence capital and research and development budget.[22]

Another impediment to Canadian sales is the difficulty encountered by some Canadian companies in sending people to the U.S. to service products which have been sold there. The general manager of the Aerospace Industries Association of Canada, Alex Bishop, told the Commons External Affairs and National Defence Committee in 1985: "We currently have a situation now where our technicians are not permitted entry into the United States to service products, for warranty and for quite a number of reasons. Now, if you can really look at this as a non-tariff barrier, the implications are incredible. Who would buy a product if it cannot be serviced by the seller?"[23]

At the same committee meeting, Clive Kingston, AIAC board chairman and chief executive officer of the Dowty North American Aerospace Division at Ajax, referred to a new interpretation of U.S. law by immigration officials as exacerbating a long-term problem: "My own company last week had a service rep stopped at the border and he was proceeding to comply with an FAA test requirement [imposed by yet another piece of U.S. legislation], and yet Immigration held him up at the border."[24] The industry idenitified this new policy as a serious problem with long-term ramifications for effective Canadian competition in the U.S. market.

While the "rough balance" provision was an impediment to Canada's access to the U.S. market in the early 1970s, some Canadian observers believe that in the present climate of high procurement by Canada in the United States, the provision will turn out to be to the advantage of Canadian companies. A case in point is the Low Level Air Defence (LLAD) and antitank system Canada is currently acquiring. The assumption is that this will create a new technology in Canada through which Canada will become competitive in the United States. With the cancellation of the DIVAD system in the U.S., the Canadian system will be in a particularly good position to compete for the U.S. contract. Canada was believed to have an added advantage by virtue of the Marine Corps's apparent satisfaction with the General Motors of Canada light armoured vehicle, a possible platform for an LLAD system. And with the U.S. enjoying a substantial surplus under the DPSA as a result of recent equipment purchases by Canada, LLAD production in Canada for the U.S. might contribute to redressing the imbalance.

But not everyone is convinced that the DPSA are a usable political tool in the current environment characterized by an enduring Canadian trade surplus with the United States. Tom Chell, then director of the Defence Programs Bureau, told the Commons External Affairs and National Defence Committee that even though there is a substantial defence trade balance in favour of the United States, it would not be wise at this time to try to use the DPSA as a lever by invoking the rough balance provision: "This is not the time to lever defence trade balances when Canada runs a trade surplus of some $10 billion to $20 billion a year. I just mention this to you because it has been suggested by U.S. officials that this is not the time to ask Congress to redress the defence

FIGURE 5
Cumulative Military Trade Balance Between Canada and the United States

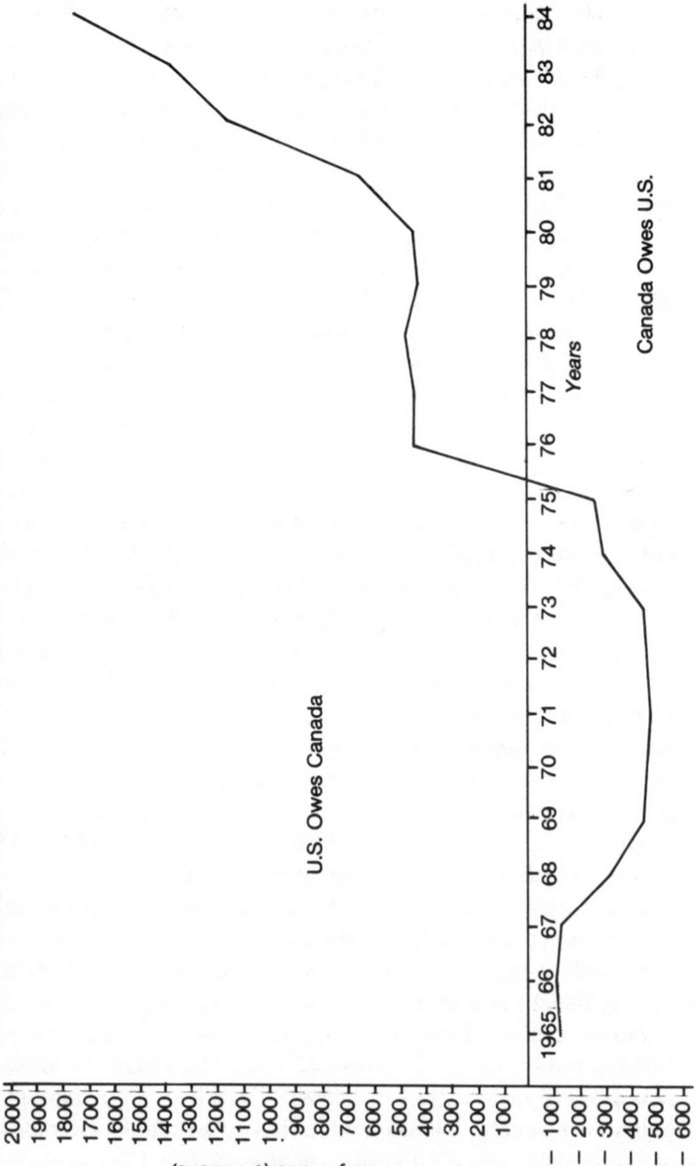

trade imbalance, because of the overall trade situation."[25]

But even so, hope springs eternal. Canadian officials still estimate that between 30 and 40 per cent of the U.S. procurement dollar is open to Canadian industry. This means a potential of $30 to $40 billion a year. As officials told the Commons committee, "there is a big market for our industry there, and our objective is to increase our share in that market in coming years."[26] While admitting that Canada ought not to look for a major reversal of the American military trade surplus in the context of an American civilian trade deficit, Canadian officials in the next breath allow as how they are determined to make major gains in Canadian military sales and to increase the proportion of the U.S. procurement budget that is spent in Canada. If even the DPSA cannot be appealed to, it is not clear how they will do this, nor is it clear, in the context of a major civilian trade imbalance, just how the DPSA provide any advantages to Canada.

Military Trade with Europe

When it comes to getting in on the European military market, it seems to be a matter of getting what you pay for. And lately, in Canada's case, that hasn't been much. Throughout the 1970s Europe received 22 per cent of all Canadian military exports. In 1985 it was down to 8 per cent, even though European countries account for one-third of NATO military spending. Canada's preoccupation with the U.S. market — in 1985 the U.S. received 85 per cent of all Canadian military exports — has turned out, according to some European officials, to be an impediment to doing military business with Europe.[27]

Actually, it is not the level of Canadian sales to the United States as such that is the problem, but rather the low level of Canadian purchases in Europe. If you want to get military exports to Europe, it seems you have to be prepared to import from Europe in return. At least that was the lesson Bombardier learned in its 1984 sale of 2,500 four-wheel-drive military vehicles to Belgium. Canada won the order, in competition with British and West German suppliers, but it took an offset agreement worth three times the value of the arms contract itself. As a result Canada will have to buy a substantial quantity of arms from Belgian producers and will give about the same amount of business to vehicle producers in Belgium. Additional purchases from other Belgian manufacturers were promised and, to top it all off, the vehicles were actually to be assembled in Belgium.[28]

According to the official testimony of the Defence Programs Bureau,

Canadian military trade with NATO "requires financial support within NATO." Europe is brimming with arms manufacturers, and the only way in which Canada will manage any sales on the continent will be as compensation either for Canadian purchases in Europe or for Canadian funding of NATO military equipment projects. Furthermore, for such military trade reciprocity to succeed there will have to be an overall political environment of strong Canadian support for NATO. The public musings of Prime Minister Trudeau in the late 1960s and early 1970s, together with subsequent freezes on Canadian military spending and the reduction of Canada's European troop strength, raised suspicions that Canada's support was something less than solid. Since then, however, Canada has been trying to behave itself, proclaiming its undying commitment to a peacetime military presence in Europe and upgrading its token military equipment assigned to Europe. Lately, the political environment has not been a particular problem.

In addition, Canada has been showing a willingness to contribute to joint military programs. Canada was the third largest contributor to the European airborne early warning and control system, funding almost 10 per cent of the $1.8 billion cost (in 1977 U.S. dollars). This participation promised to produce industrial benefits roughly equivalent to the contribution, and was considered a sign, as a Canadian official assigned to NATO noted, that Canada had "returned to the fold" and that we were recognized in Europe as "pulling our weight."[29]

The West German Connection

Canada has recently made a major effort to cultivate military ties with West Germany, covering both industry and training. Canada has purchased Leopard tanks from West Germany, in a deal that included industrial offset arrangements. In addition, West German aircraft and fliers train at Goose Bay, Labrador, and tanks carry out manoeuvres at Shilo, Man. The Iltis trucks that Bombardier supplied to the Canadian armed forces are built under licence from Volkswagen in West Germany, and Canadair Limited sold the West German armed forces six Challenger jets in 1984.

West Germany may be a likely candidate for Canadian military production sharing with Europe, since Bonn has made a particular practice of undertaking major procurements and development projects jointly. (This is due in no small measure to the legacy of World War II, which left Germany without a major military industry for many years and forced it to rely on leftover allied equipment.) One prominent cooperative project with Canada is a company-to-company contract between Canadair and the Friedrichshafen-based aerospace firm Dornier to develop the CL-289 surveillance drone (see chapter 4).[30]

CAE Industries Ltd of Toronto has set up a facility to manufacture flight simulators near Aachen and, in the process, has become a supplier for the West German air force.[31] At the same time, increased Canadian expenditures have attracted certain West German firms to Canada to compete for orders.[32]

This burgeoning relationship was tested somewhat when the West German firms Krauss Maffei and Euromissile were excluded from the short list of competitors for Canada's low-level air defence and antitank system. The exclusion produced what the *Financial Post* called "dramatic" fallout. In December 1985, the newspaper quoted a Canadian trade official as saying that "before that short list was announced, Krauss Maffei people were on the phone to me three or four times a week. They have not called once since, and that decision was made months ago. If you want to sell to Europe, you have to be in each other's major programs."[33]

Military procurement and military sales within the alliance are a highly political game — what the *Financial Post* described as "a game Canada is learning all over again after watching on the sidelines throughout much of the 1970s, when self-imposed budget freezes nearly forced it out of the defense equipment markets altogether."[34] Now, however, Canada's sharply increasing capital expenditures have created a new interest in Canada as an important market for European firms. In 1985, a dozen French, Dutch, British and West German firms set up shop in and around Ottawa to keep an eye on upcoming military projects.[35]

Thus, KUKA Wehrtechnik GmbH of Augsburg, which specializes in making and retrofitting armoured turrets, discovered that Canada is planning to update turrets on some of its older armoured vehicles and that the technology is not available here. The West German company now has an Ottawa-based subsidiary which it says will transfer the appropriate technology to Canada: "Our aim is to be number one in Canada in this field. And, insofar as it's possible, the components will be made by existing Canadian firms."[36] For the government, given its current orientation, this is good news. The Department of National Defence likes it because it expands Canadian industry's capacity to meet Canadian equipment needs — a matter of strategic significance during times of tension or actual hostilities. The job creators like it because they see it as giving Canada another leg up on a lucrative export market. And for the West German firm, labouring under the handicap of Europe's overall difficulty in cracking the American market, a Canadian subsidiary could serve as a foot in the American door.

Electronic Systems and Trucks

Another example of a European military firm active in Canada is MEL Defense Systems Ltd. near Ottawa. It is a subsidiary of Philips Canada Ltd. but operates under the Philips Defense Group of Britain. The company was established in 1982 in response to Canadian capital projects involving the company's specialty, electronic warfare. Two Canadian projects are CANEWS and RAMSES. CANEWS is the Canadian Naval Electronic Warfare System, which is an early warning system that allows a ship to detect and identify attackers — such as the Exocet missile that made history in the Falklands/Malvinas war — and provides it with sufficient information early enough to take evasive action. RAMSES is the Reprogrammable Advanced Multimode Shipboard Electronic Counter Measures System, which has the ability to jam the radar systems of incoming radar-guided missiles. These systems are being installed in Canadian destroyers, Tribal class, and in the new frigates Canada has purchased, giving the British-owned firm Canadian sales of $100 million or more.

But the company doesn't plan to serve only the Canadian market. Export markets are very much on its mind. "There's enough business here now to justify our growth," says a company official, "but our aim in the next five to ten years is to do 25 per cent to 50 per cent of our business in export markets."[37] The *Financial Post* noted — although without giving any particular basis for it — that "given the nature of the products, of course, offshore sales would be limited to NATO and a handful of countries deemed friendly and safe," adding that while the market for electronic warfare systems in airborne, land-based and sea-based weapons is growing, the competition is also getting tougher. In this more competitive environment, the definition of a "friendly and safe" country will tend to get a little loose and imprecise.

Europeans are also lined up to supply the Canadian Forces with new trucks. Two West German firms and one Swedish firm are currently in the running for the $150 million contract — which, as a result of budget delays, is not likely to be awarded until 1988. A dozen Canadian companies are being considered for the contract to build the trucks in Canada under licence from whichever firm is chosen in the final round of negotiations. DND has said that the trucks produced by all three of the European firms are acceptable, which means that the offsets package will be a prominent factor in the final decision.[38]

Equipment Standardization and Emerging Technologies

The fact that Canada has been stationing Canadian troops in Europe for decades without compensation is a matter of growing significance for this country. The proposal to transform the Goose Bay air base into a major NATO flight training facility is a direct response to the Canadian government's perceived need to repatriate Canadian dollars that have been going to Europe all these years.[39]

In an effort to facilitate long-term access to the European market, Canada has entered into a series of agreements with European governments "concerning cooperation in research, development and production of defence equipment."[40] The agreements cover a wide scope of activity, but are declarations of good intentions rather than substantive contracts. Canadian officials view them more as letters of introduction than as instruments on which actual transactions can be based. Each cooperative venture must be negotiated separately, but the declarations are intended to facilitate and encourage joint ventures and advance the NATO principle of equipment standardization.

The economic dimensions of NATO military cooperation — of which equipment standardization is part — are becoming progressively more important. Canadian military analyst Dan Middlemiss makes the point that economic considerations, in addition to political and military issues, are central to the main debates in the alliance, which he enumerates as "East-West relations, the relative emphasis on nuclear versus conventional deterrence and defence, the role of arms control, trade and technology transfers to the Soviet bloc, 'deep strike' doctrines, the role of 'emerging' weapons technology, and the perennial issue of burden-sharing."[41]

The goal of equipment standardization can be viewed either as identical equipment and doctrine throughout the alliance or as less comprehensive moves towards interoperability. In either case, standardization is based on both military and economic considerations, although national economic interests in domestic job creation may be as much an impediment to standardization as a reason for it. A Canadian weapons system that is common to four NATO members is the CL-89 Canadair drone, in service with France, West Germany, Italy and Britain (Canada did not purchase the system). Another example is a NATO 155-mm shell manufactured in various countries, including Canada where it is made by Canadian Arsenals Ltd. For NATO small arms there is now a standard 5.56-mm calibre for rifles and light machine guns. Diemaco is the Canadian manufacturer of the C7 rifle which makes use of this new ammunition.

In a sense, the premier economy drive within NATO has been the attempt to increase the bang for the buck in weapons systems. Nuclear weapons represent the clearest expression of this effort. From the early days of NATO, when painful recovery from the devastation of war placed severe limitations on military spending, the Western alliance has gone the cheap and dirty route. The reasoning was that the Soviet Union could be intimidated or deterred at much lower expense by relying on nuclear weapons. That worked until the Soviet Union also acquired the cheap and dirty. With the two nuclear powers now confronting each other across Churchill's Iron Curtain, it was clear that any hostilities would be plenty dirty, but the problem was that the weapons were no longer so cheap.

They have always, in relative terms, been much cheaper for the West, but in recent years both the economic and the political costs have been rising sharply. The political costs of nuclear weapons have led to a greater emphasis on conventional weapons, and NATO has now embarked on a strategy of getting more conventional bang for the buck through the application of "emerging technologies" (ET). The pursuit of more sophisticated technologies is not, however, guaranteed to be cheap since, as Middlemiss noted, "as NATO moves towards a 'high tech' conventional defence posture, as exemplified by the emphasis on ET munitions, costs are likely to rise correspondingly."[42]

Furthermore, these new technologies do not promise to be a whole lot cleaner. Indeed, part of the attraction of new conventional weapons is that they can muster a destructive power comparable to that of small nuclear weapons, and they are regarded as suitable for the "deep interdiction" roles now assigned to nuclear weapons. Fuel air explosives and clustered submunitions that can blanket large areas have blast powers comparable to nuclear weapons, and longer-range guided missiles loaded with smart submunitions will theoretically have the capacity to strike deep into an adversary's territory to select and destroy targets. While the U.S. Air Force has identified seventy emerging technologies meriting further study, an independent European program group has identified thirty for possible European cooperation. Six cooperative programs have already been established: aircraft identification, multifunction information terminal, Ada computer language support environment, autonomous 155-mm precision-guided munitions, air-

launched modular standoff weapons, and standoff airborne radar surveillance and target acquisition system.[43]

Canada is represented on the NATO Industrial Advisory Group sub-
group on Emerging Technologies, which has the responsibility of identifying new technologies that can be applied to defence, particularly
conventional defence. Nevertheless. the Canadian military industry
worries that Canada will not get a significant part of the action. At its
semiannual meeting in April 1986, the Aerospace Industries Association of Canada was told that "except for the NATO Emerging
Technologies activities and our own modest entry into the Eureka program, we [Canada] are being left out of most cooperative international
programs. The Europeans are strengthening their own competitive position to counter the perceived American technology threat, and Canada is almost universally being ignored." The AIAC recommended that
Canada do essentially what it is already doing: maintain the bilateral
relationship with the United States in research and development programs; seek out more opportunities for trans-Atlantic cooperation within
the NATO alliance; and establish individual industry-to-industry links
with foreign companies to pursue emerging technology opportunities
"for mutual benefit."

Current propaganda, therefore, seeks to take advantage of antinucle-
ar sentiment to develop support for increased spending on conventional weapons, arguing that this will not only advance nuclear disarmament but also yield major civilian economic advantages (see chapter 8).

North America: One Production Entity

Despite the apparent efforts to integrate overall NATO military production, the United States remains the obvious production leader and
supplier, and only Canada has been able to make significant inroads
into the U.S. military market. While the United States is a prominent
supplier to Europe, defence trade between Europe and the U.S. is not
reciprocal. In fiscal year 1983, European NATO collectively purchased
US$7 billion in military equipment from the United States, compared
with Canada's U.S. purchases of US$1.2 billion. In the same year, how-
ever, Europe's exports to the United States were US$1.03 billion, com-
pared with Canada's exports of US$995 million. In other words, all of
European NATO sold roughly as much to the U.S. as did Canada
alone.[44] These figures illustrate not only the fact that European NATO
has a major beef against the Americans regarding nonreciprocated military procurement, but also the extraordinary extent to which Canada,

compared with other major NATO partners, has become integrated with the United States. North America truly is a single military production entity.

Military and economic considerations alike clearly make defence industry ties to the United States and Europe the top Canadian military production priorities. However, it is in the Third World — where there is for the moment, little requirement for reciprocity in military trade — that Canada sees the greatest potential for growth in military exports. That is the subject of the next chapter.

7

Selling to the Third World

At least two-thirds of the world arms trade involves Third World customers. It is a large if somewhat unsteady market that continues to grow and continues to attract new suppliers. The competition is tough, but in other markets it's even tougher. Canada, by virtue of geography and history, has unique access to the U.S. market, but this is a privilege with definite limits. Canada-U.S. military trade reciprocity means that, in the long run, Canada must buy as much from the U.S. as it sells there. While a couple of major aircraft purchases in the U.S. have produced a military trade deficit for Canada, meaning that there is still export growth potential there, the level of Canadian military exports to the U.S. cannot be separated from the level of Canadian military spending. In the long run, the U.S. military market does not really function as an export market for Canada. The size of the U.S. market for Canada is determined by the size of Canada's defence capital budget.

Much the same applies to the European market. There are few prospects for Canada to expand its military sales to Europe beyond the level of Canada's own direct contribution to joint military development projects or joint NATO equipment acquisition programs.

That leaves the Third World market as the one offering the greatest potential. Furthermore, it is trade with the Third World that offers the greatest potential for a genuine contribution to a favourable Canadian trade balance. In this market there are no requirements that military exports be reciprocated, which means that Canadian sales here, unlike the American and European markets, can add to the trade surplus. And the Third World market has special attractions for Canada precisely because of the limitations on its other markets. Increased sales to the Third World, while not likely ever to replace sales to the U.S., might at least mitigate somewhat the heavy reliance on a single market.

In fact it hasn't turned out that way. Canada's interest in the Third World military market is not unique. So great is this interest, in fact, that it has become a buyers' market, offering Third World governments a stunning array of choices and bargaining opportunities. Canadian sales to the Third World have increased from an annual average of just over $50 million in the 1970s to $150 million per year in the 1980s, but a big breakthrough into the market has so far eluded Canada's arms sales forces. This is due less to an absence of skill and tenacity in Canadian sales efforts than it is to the kinds of military commodities that Canada can offer. By virtue of the integration of Canada's military industry with that of the United States, Canada (as already noted) is not a major supplier of complete weapons systems, so that few Third World countries look to Canada for such systems. Canada has, of course, been a consistent supplier of military transport aircraft, but apart from that, Canadian military sales to the Third World have consisted of the inter-mittent supply of subsystems and components. Canada has been trying to change that situation since the early 1970s, but the results have not been dramatic.

In the 1980s Canada is trying to add a new dimension to its Third World arms export capabilities. It hopes to increase its capacity to sup-ply major military systems or major subsystems by using its own pur-chases of military systems to develop production capabilities in Cana-da to manufacture the same systems for export to overseas customers. This policy's potential for running into direct conflict with other Cana-dian foreign policy objectives is enormous. While on the one hand the government pursues increased military exports by bolstering Canada's weapons-making capacity, on the other hand it also seeks to control weapons and develop more effective mechanisms for the peaceful set-tlement of international disputes. The main reason that this has not be-come a major conflict within the government is that, to date, the milita-ry export promotion effort has not been very successful. Nevertheless, arms control, the peaceful settlement of disputes, and greater respect for human rights represent three specific Canadian interests and policy ob-jectives that are undermined by an out-of-control world weapons trade. The Department of External Affairs thus finds itself with the task of si-multaneously finding ways to expand arms sales and to control them.

For Canada, arms sales represent an economic activity, not an instru-ment of foreign policy. It is not Canada's aim, through judicious arms sales, to influence the strategic environment. Strategic concerns, such as an appeal to the right of self-defence, may be invoked in support of arms sales, but Canadian arms sales clearly do not originate from strategic motives. Canada may argue that the sale of armoured vehicles to Saudi Arabia would enhance stability in the region, but that was not the basis of Canada's primary interest. There was no dispassionate assessment in External Affairs which led to the conclusion that what the Middle East peace process really needs is another set of Saudi armoured vehicles and that Canada must be willing to do its part. To the extent that arms sales are part of government planning, Canada starts from domestic economic interests. Hence, permission is granted to export armoured vehicles to Saudi Arabia out of the belief that this will advance Canada's economic interests and, to put the best face on it, contribute to the well-being of Canadians. The interests of the Saudis and the Middle East peace process may offer justifications, but not motives.

If the Middle East peace process, or respect for human rights, or regional stability, were the primary motives and objectives of arms sales, the arms export review and permit process would look rather different from the way it looks now. In its present form, the export permit system is there as a check or safeguard designed to unearth any compelling reasons why a proposed sale should not take place. The primary objective of arms sales is economic growth, but the export permit system is testimony to the recognition that the pursuit of this objective could be in conflict with other foreign policy objectives, such as the promotion of respect for human rights. The system is there not to advance human rights, but to ensure that human rights are not unduly damaged by a particular arms export. The opening bias is in favour of an arms sale, and the review process is a chance to indicate reasons why the opening bias should not prevail. If, on the other hand, the opening bias were against arms sales, the review process would then be the occasion to present evidence that a particular military sale could represent a positive gesture in pursuit of the primary objectives of Canadian foreign policy.

The Export Permit System

The export permit system is a safeguard system designed to screen out of arms exports those transactions which could damage Canadian security interests and which might unduly conflict with other Canadian foreign policy objectives. Canadian military sales are regulated through the Export and Import Permit Act, which requires permits for the export of strategic goods and technologies, including military and military-related goods. These goods are defined by an Export Control List (ECL) — with all goods on the list requiring permits for export, unless they are being exported to the United States. (There are some exceptions for which exports to the U.S. require permits, but none of these exceptions are for goods defined as military.) The Export Control List includes a wide range of commodities that are to be controlled — for example, endangered species, logs, various kinds of special machinery — in addition to military and strategic goods (the latter including commodities that are not military goods but could have a military application or advance the strategic interests of the importer).

Besides requiring permits for the export of goods on the Export Control List to any location other than the United States unless otherwise specified, the Act also requires permits for the shipment of all goods, whether appearing on the ECL or not, to countries mentioned on an Area Control List (ACL). Until recently the ACL included all Warsaw Pact countries plus a few others (Albania, Bulgaria, Czechoslovakia, East Germany, Hungary, Mongolia, North Korea, Vietnam, Poland, Romania, Soviet Union). In September 1986 a new export policy emphasized that trade in "peaceful goods," nonstrategic and nonmilitary, is encouraged with all countries and for that reason the Warsaw Pact countries, including the Soviet Union, would be removed from the ACL. As a result, export permits are no longer required for the export of goods that are not on the ECL to Warsaw Pact countries. The control of strategic and military exports to the Warsaw Pact countries is managed through the ECL.

The standards for the control of strategic and military goods are set by the international Coordinating Committee on Multilateral Strategic Export Controls (COCOM), which includes NATO countries and Japan. External Affairs describes COCOM as an informal arrangement to coordinate and "harmonize" the control of exports of strategic and military goods. Through COCOM Western countries agree to embargo all military and strategic goods to Warsaw Pact countries, and each country develops its own policies and guidelines for the control of these goods to other destinations.

The Canadian Export and Import Permit Act addresses itself directly only to security considerations, defining its objective as being "to ensure that arms, ammunition, implements or munitions of war, naval, army or air stores or any articles deemed capable of being converted thereinto or made useful in the production thereof or otherwise having a strategic nature or value will not be made available to any destination wherein their use might be detrimental to the security of Canada."[1] The act permits additional guidelines to be developed to regulate the granting of permits. In September 1986 External Affairs Minister Joe Clark restated the guidelines by which "the export of military goods and technology" would be "closely controlled." Such "close control" is to be applied to:

- "countries which pose a threat to Canada and its allies";
- "countries involved in or under imminent threat of hostilities";
- countries under United Nations Security Council sanctions;
- "countries whose governments have a persistent record of serious violations of the human rights of their citizens, unless it can be demonstrated that there is no reasonable risk that the goods might be used against the civilian population."[2]

External Affairs can divide the export permit applications it receives into essentially three categories. The first is applications for the export of military goods to countries on the Area Control List or to Warsaw Pact countries, which are automatically rejected. The second is applications to export military commodities to Canada's NATO allies or to other friendly countries such as Australia, New Zealand and Japan, and these are routinely, if not automatically, accepted. The third is applications to export military commodities to all other countries, and each application in this category is reviewed on a case-by-case basis. Under the new policy the department will maintain a confidential list of human rights violator countries. Applications for the export of military goods to a country on this list will result in closer scrutiny, although applications for exports to countries identified as human rights violators are not automatically rejected since the policy permits exports of military goods if there is "no reasonable risk" that they will be used against civilians.

Exporters are made aware of the need for export permits through a public education program. Application forms are usually obtained from an export broker, and then are completed and submitted along with documentation called for in the Notice to Exporters, a periodic information bulletin regarding regulations and procedures under the Export and Import Permits Act. The responsibility for monitoring compliance with export permit requirements rests with customs officials. Special officers are assigned at each of the departure points for Canadian goods. The RCMP also carries out investigations if it suspects that there are attempts to evade permit requirements.

These monitoring procedures, or lack of them, became the subject of greater interest in the wake of a 1978 episode in which Canadian long-range artillery technology was smuggled to South Africa by Space Research Corporation from a plant on the Quebec-Vermont border. More recently, President Reagan's campaign to stop the flow of strategic technology to the Soviet Union exposed Canada as something of a security sieve. Said David Adam of the Export Control Division: "For thirty years the controls were applied in a half-assed way, relying on the exporter to voluntarily disclose what he was shipping and where."[3] In 1985 Canada decided to crack down and monitor shipments more closely. Incidents have included attempts, some successful, to use Canada as a base to supply Pakistan with components for its nuclear weapons program, the Soviet Union with computer equipment, and Iran with helicopters and components for other aircraft.

Canadian interest in more effective control over the diversion of technology is based on Canada's economic interests as much as on security interests. "If we are to enjoy the benefits of unimpeded access to U.S. technology," David Adam says, "we must make sure it is denied to countries where the United States does not want it to go."[4]

Approximately 150 export permit applications are received daily; of these about a half-dozen are for the export of military commodities. All such applications go immediately to officers for review, and then information pertaining to each application is distributed for wider consultation. All applications for the export of military commodities, particularly to non-allies, go through this wider consultation process — those involved include the Defence Programs Bureau of the Department of External Affairs, the geographic desk in External Affairs relevant to the application, any other External Affairs branch that may be viewed as having an interest, and the Department of National Defence.

The consultation process operates on the basis of consensus, although unanimity is not technically required for an application to be approved. The director general of the Special Trade Relations Division, who approves and personally signs all permits, has the authority to approve an application against the advice of some of those consulted, but officials indicate that the system works through a strong commitment to consensus. If there are differences the issue is "talked through" until there is agreement one way or the other — it is said that the extended permit approval process resolves some contentious applications by simply grinding away in various consultations and reviews until the export opportunity has been lost.

The director general has the responsibility to decide whether or not to consult the minister, and the minister then decides whether or not the issue should go to cabinet. From time to time a routine application — either one that it is assumed will be accepted or one that it is assumed will be rejected — is put through to the minister to test his response and to see whether the basic operating assumptions are still valid. There is no formal appeal procedure for rejected applications, but if there is a change in circumstances an applicant is free to reapply.

End-Use Certificates

Permits for the export of military goods manufactured in Canada are granted on the basis of a specific destination, and it is the responsibility of the exporter to obtain assurances that the destination indicated is in fact the ultimate destination. The primary instruments for obtaining such assurances are Import Certificates or Licenses, Delivery Verification Certificates, and End-Use Certificates.

Members of COCOM have introduced a system of Import Certificates designed primarily to control the transshipment of restricted goods to Warsaw Pact countries. COCOM is actively encouraging other countries to join this system as a means of indicating that the importing country will be the final destination of the goods. Where Import Certificates or Licenses are not provided, the exporter is required to obtain an End-Use Certificate from the importer, certifying the ultimate destination of the commodity.[5]

Canadian authorities can only require that the Canadian exporter undertake to receive the certificate in good faith and complete the application form honestly. The applicant is required to include a certificate of the ultimate destination of the commodity as it is known at the time of the application, and a fine can be levied for submitting a false application, but there is no recourse in Canadian law if the importer fails to honour the End-Use Certificate. While there may be a nonlegal remedy inasmuch as the importer would risk not receiving further goods from the Canadian exporter, in a buyers' market this may not be a major risk. If an Import Certificate (as distinct from an End-Use Certificate) is not honoured, the importer has to answer to the home government from which the Import Certificate was received.

In Canadian regulations, transformation of a component through manufacturing means that Canadian end-use provisions no longer apply. The End-Use Certificate is intended to certify that the commodity will be used for the purpose indicated in the country indicated. In the case of components, the purpose indicated is manufacturing, following which there are no restrictions on the re-export of the "transformed" product. Given that Canada's military production is substantially oriented to the production of components, a great deal of Canadian military equipment has an ultimate destination beyond the initial importing country, but the End-Use Certificate system is ineffective in controlling the ultimate destination of this equipment.

In this, Canada differs from the United States, which claims the right to grant or withhold permission to re-export American equipment, even if — as in the case of aircraft engines, for example — it is transformed or incorporated into a major system built outside the United States. This point became embarrassingly clear to the Canadian government when it was disclosed in late 1986 that Pratt and Whitney had been sending aircraft engine parts to Iran. The parts did not need a Canadian export permit because they were designated as nonstrategic, but because the American content of the parts was at least 5 per cent, U.S. permission was required.

Ironically, while public controversy focused on Pratt and Whitney engine parts with possible military applications going to Iran, complete engines manufactured by Pratt and Whitney for unambiguously military helicopters and aircraft were going to both sides in the Iran-Iraq war. While Canadian regulations prohibit the sale of military goods to areas of conflict, these sales escaped control because they were sold to third parties in Switzerland, Italy and Brazil. In these countries the engines were "transformed" into aircraft subsequently sold to Iran and Iraq. Canadian End-Use Certificates made no claim on their ultimate destination.

This was not the first time the ineffectiveness of the system was clearly shown up. During the Vietnam War it was undermined by direct government collusion with exporters wanting to ship to Vietnam. As a country engaged in hostilities, Vietnam was not eligible to receive Canadian military commodities. The United States, while arguably also engaged in hostilities, was eminently eligible to receive Canadian military commodities, which can be exported to the U.S. without even the formality of an export permit. It was clear, however, that many of the goods destined for the United States during that period were in fact headed for Vietnam — sometimes without any manufacturing or transformation taking place in between. Documents obtained by the Toronto *Globe and Mail* in 1975 showed that, even though Canadian export permits are based on the "ultimate destination" of the exported commodity, the Canadian government cooperated with Canadian suppliers and U.S. defence officials and turned a blind eye to Canadian military goods going to the United States for direct transshipment to Southeast

Asia.[6] At the time Canadian officials argued that Canada had no say or control over how the United States used such military goods once they had been delivered and that the regulations pertained to the resale of military equipment, not the foreign use of it.

Wire Rope Industries of Canada was a particular beneficiary of Canadian government cooperation. A letter dated February 27, 1973, from the Department of Industry, Trade and Commerce to Wire Rope Industries showed uncommon understanding of the difficulties encountered by the company in selling equipment to the United States that was in fact destined for Southeast Asia. In cases where the U.S. wanted Canadian military goods shipped to Southeast Asia, the letter informed the company that alternative shipping instructions were available. Thus, the goods could be rerouted through the United States to the ultimate destination. The government asked to be advised of cases of this sort, and said that if such circumstances arose it would "endeavour to have the consignment point changed." Hence a delivery report shows Wire Rope Industries materials being shipped to Dover Air Force Base in Delaware, and "marked for" the "8 Tac Ftr Wg UBON Airfield Thailand."

The *Globe and Mail*'s Hugh Winsor reported that the external affairs minister at the time, Paul Martin, had maintained that "no one can obtain arms in Canada and ship them to any sensitive area." However, Martin also conceded that Canada had never asked the United States not to send military equipment of Canadian origin to Vietnam. To have done that, he said, would have wrecked the Defence Production Sharing Arrangements.[7]

In 1983 a similar situation arose when Geometrix Inc. of Toronto tried to supply parts for helicopters used by the armed forces of El Salvador. After a news story had indicated that the company was supplying these parts to the American manufacturers of Hughes and Sikorsky helicopters and that these companies were in turn selling them to El Salvador, the matter became the subject of correspondence between the Taskforce on the Churches and Corporate Responsibility and External Affairs Minister Allan MacEachen.

Under the regulations, Geometrix should have been obliged to determine whether the parts were being used by the importing U.S. companies to build helicopters or simply going to the U.S. companies in transit to El Salvador as spares for Hughes and Sikorsky helicopters already operating there. In the first case, since the act exempts military exports to the U.S. from export permit requirements, no permit would be required. The import certificate would simply identify the United

States as the ultimate destination, with the parts being used there for the purpose of manufacture. In the second case, however, the company would have had to apply for a permit to export the goods to El Salvador, even if the interim destination was the United States. Given the export guidelines, such a permit would presumably have been denied. In the event, MacEachen's response, like the fog on his beloved Cape Breton, served only to obscure the particulars. He simply reiterated that export permits were to be based on the ultimate destination and that there was no record of Geometrix having applied to export the goods in question to El Salvador.[8]

Canada's relaxed attitude towards the ultimate fate of the military commodities it exports is far from unique. In fact, Brazil has used the absence of End-Use Certificates as a competitive advantage in pursuing military exports. With a diversified industry capable of producing a variety of complete weapons systems, Brazil imposes no requirement that a recipient country seek authorization from the supplier company before selling Brazil-built commodities to third parties.[9]

On the other hand, the United States, as already noted, has not shied away from extraterritoriality — applying American laws in other jurisdictions — in controlling exports. The U.S. State Department's Regulations on the International Traffic in Arms require prior departmental approval of transfers of defence articles produced abroad with U.S.-origin technology. U.S. industry has opposed the regulations because, as a State Department official told the industry journal *Aviation Week and Space Technology*, "many in industry felt that foreign companies would refuse to sign onto some of these clauses which, for example, require end-use assurances from third parties, [and] periodic reports of what was sold to whom."

The department, however, defended the requirement on the grounds that "we require this information of American exporters, so there's no reason not to require it from producers of U.S. technology abroad. And if foreign companies don't like it, they're not forced to sign agreements for U.S. technology."[10] The *Globe and Mail* reported in March 1984 that "contrary to normal procedure, a U.S. customs officer, accompanied by a Royal Canadian Mounted Police officer, called on a Canadian company to discuss a possible breach of U.S. export control laws."[11] And in 1983 the Canadian subsidiary of Hewlett-Packard Co. of Palo Alto, Calif., wrote its dealers and customers, saying it was required to comply with U.S. export administration regulations in the sale of its goods and services in Canada.[12]

The Export Control Guidelines

Officials have for many years described Canada's military export policy as "restrictive." The External Affairs "Notice to Exporters" says that "exporters of military, military-related and strategic equipment are advised that Canadian policy with respect to the export of such goods is a restrictive one."[13] External Affairs Minister Clark puts the case more strongly when he says that "Canada maintains one of the most restrictive policies of any Western nation concerning exports of military goods."[14] The former minister of regional industrial expansion, Sinclair Stevens, described Canadian policy in similar terms: "Canada is not a major producer of defence products, and is by international standards, a very cautious exporter of military goods."[15]

The term "restrictive," as it has come to be applied to arms transfer policies, is widely used internationally and means rather less than it implies. According to the Stockholm International Peace Research Institute, which is acknowledged as the pre-eminent monitor of arms transfers, the primary criterion for a "restrictive" arms transfer policy is that it be aimed against supplying arms to a party to a conflict.[16] While some states with "restrictive" policies add other criteria, this is the one that is common to all and is central to the definition of a restrictive policy. The political principle embodied in the term is noninvolvement in conflicts. In some instances this is a legal requirement, while in others, such as Canada, it is simply a policy directive. Within current international practice, a "restrictive" policy does not always include prohibitions on arms sales to repressive regimes. A restrictive policy is best understood in contrast to a "directed" policy, where the operational principle is not noninvolvement but selective involvement. In other words, a "directed" policy is related to support for a particular party to a conflict.

At first glance Canada does appear to have a "restrictive" policy. The relevant directive in the current Canadian policy asserts the principle that military equipment should not be supplied "to countries involved in or under imminent threat of hostilities." External Affairs Minister Clark states it categorically: "In order to prevent the escalation of regional disputes, the Government does not issue permits for the export of military goods to countries that are engaged in or under imminent threat of hostilities."[17]

This in fact is not a correct statement of Canadian practice. Department officials themselves immediately qualify such an assertion. Neither the policy nor its implementation follows even the relatively narrow interpretation of "restrictive" operative in the international community. Of the more than $8 billion (current dollars) in military exports in the years 1980–85, for example, about 90 per cent went to destinations (the United States and European NATO) for which the policy against supplying arms to states in conflict is not applied. Obviously, there was no interruption of exports to Britain during the Falklands/Malvinas war (although permits to sell to Argentina during the war were not granted). Similarly, Canada continued to export arms to the United States both during the Vietnam War and during more recent conflicts of lesser magnitude and duration. In these instances the policy is more properly described as "directed" rather than restrictive. Despite Clark's statement, Canada does not deny permits for the export of military goods to countries that are engaged in conflict. Instead, Canada chooses the conflicts, and the side in each conflict, for which it is prepared to supply military commodities.

Even in the case of exports to the Third World, there is no prohibition on the export of military commodities to countries involved in hostilities. Table 6 indicates known or probable recipients of Canadian military commodities during the years 1980–84. Of the forty-five recipients, just over a third were involved in hostilities during the period under review. While this is an imprecise tabulation, chiefly because the government refuses to provide information on specific sales, it does raise the question of what defines a country as being "involved in hostilities" or as fulfilling the even less precise condition of being "under imminent threat of hostilities." Under the policy announced in September 1986 a list of such countries is to be maintained, but it too is to remain secret and no indication is given as to the criteria by which a country makes it onto, or off, the list.

Furthermore, External Affairs officials admit that the guidelines, in those instances where they are considered relevant (i.e. the Third World), are not in fact requirements but merely points to be considered, among many other considerations. Indonesia's involvement in hostilities in East Timor has not disqualified it as a recipient of Canadian military and military-related equipment, and in fact has not discouraged a Canadian government-led promotional push to increase military exports to Indonesia.

Another such case is Saudi Arabia, still in a formal state of war with Israel and an active supporter of the Palestine Liberation Organization — in other words, it would be hard to construe Saudi Arabia as not being a party to hostilities, real or imminent. Nevertheless, Canadian policy has been moving towards approval of direct military exports to Riyadh. While it may be that the current interest in military sales to

TABLE 6
Hostilities and Human Rights Violations among Third World Importers[1] of Canadian Military Commodities, 1980–1984

Country	Area of[2] Hostility	Human[3] Rights 1	Human[4] Rights 2
Algeria			
Argentina	x	x	x
Bahamas			
Barbados			
Brazil		x	
Burma	x	x	x
Bermuda			
Cameroon			
Chile		x	x
Colombia		x	
Costa Rica			
Ecuador			
Egypt		x	
Ethiopia	x	x	x
Guatemala	x	x	x
Honduras	x	x	
India	x	x	
Indonesia	x	x	x
Israel	x	x	
Ivory Coast			
Jamaica			
Kenya		x	
South Korea	x	x	x
Kuwait			
Liberia		x	
Malaysia	x	x	x
Mexico		x	
Nigeria			
Oman			
Pakistan	x	x	x

Paraguay		X	X
Peru	X	X	X
Phillippines	X	X	X
Qatar			
Saudi Arabia		X	
Senegal			
Singapore			
South Africa[5]	X	X	
Syria	X	X	
Tanzania			
Thailand	X	X	
Taiwan		X	
United Arab Emirates			
Venezuela		X	X
Zambia		X	

[1] This list of Third World importers of Canadian military commodities is constructed from sources which indicate a) that a direct sale has been made by Canada, or b) that Canada was willing to grant Canadian firms export permits for the sale of military commodities to the country listed. Owing to the government's refusal to disclose the details of Canadian military exports, it is not possible to determine in each case whether a sale has actually occurred. It is, however, the willingness to grant an export permit that is the more pertinent information in examining Canadian military export policy.

[2] Area of Hostility: Information on active military hostilities during the period is taken from surveys of world conflicts by the Center for Defense Information (*Defense Monitor*, no. 1, 1983), and the London *Times* (Toronto *Star*, February 5, 1984).

[3] Human Rights 1: This indicates countries cited for human rights violations during the years 1980–84 as compiled by Miles D. Wolpin, "Third World Repression: Parameters and Prospects," *Peace and Change* 11, no. 2 (1986). Countries are cited for "unexceptional state resort to one or more of the following during part or all of the period: execution, torture, disappearances, brutal treatment of dissidents or extremely harsh prison conditions." Sources include: Amnesty International; the U.S. Department of Commerce; *The Current History Encyclopedia of Developing Nations* (New York: McGraw Hill, 1982); the World Bank; the New York *Times* (various issues 1984); and Ruth Leger Sivard, *World Military and Social Expenditures 1983*

(Washington: World Priorities, 1983).

4   Human Rights 2: This indicates countries that have been cited for human rights violations by the UN Commission on Human Rights during the period (*Human Rights Quarterly*, Fall 1985.)

5   South Africa, under a United Nations arms embargo, does not legally receive Canadian military commodities. It is included in this list by virtue of being included in the Statistics Canada data as receiving "military weapons, ordnance and parts" in the amount of $9,000 in 1980 and $2,000 in 1981.

Sources:

Statistics Canada reports of sales of "military ordnance";

The Stockholm International Peace Research Institute Arms Transfer Registry;

The Project Ploughshares Military Industry Database, which includes information from the Canadian Commercial Corporation and various industry journals;

Letters from the Department of External Affairs to Project Ploughshares and the Taskforce on the Churches and Corporate Responsibility, January 24/83, June 5/84, August 20/84 and September 13/85;

Copies of Export Permits obtained by Nelson Riis, M.P., June 21/85.

Department of External Affairs acknowledgement of its military trade missions to various countries (the assumption being that sponsorship of a military trade mission reflects a willingness to grant an export permit for the sale of military commodities).

Saudi Arabia stems from the fact that Canada has only recently developed systems which are of interest to the Saudis, External Affairs provides a more nuanced, if not more convincing, rationale. Ottawa sees Saudi Arabia as an increasingly positive force in the Middle East: "There is a growing realization that Saudi Arabia is a stable, moderate power in the region that should be supported, including help for its defences."[18] This clearly represents an example of a "directed," rather than a "restrictive," policy.

Military commodities are sold to countries in either conflict or imminent conflict on the grounds that there are important strategic reasons for supporting them. The sale of LAVs to Saudi Arabia is further defended on the grounds that these vehicles are defensive rather than offensive, and that since they run on wheels (as opposed to tracks) they are unlikely to be used in a desert war against Israel. This is a curious line of argument, as the United States Marine Corps has acquired the same vehicles, specifically in aid of foreign military interventions, and has used them in desert manoeuvres, on the assumption that one potential use for the vehicles would be in Middle East desert conditions — in support, for example, of the Saudi royal family if its control were to falter.

When the German company Thyssen first broached the topic of opening a tank and armoured vehicle production facility in Cape Breton, Joe Clark was known to have strong reservations. In a letter to Project Ploughshares, Clark characterized Canada's traditional role as an arms exporter beyond the United States as minimal, adding that "the proposal by Thyssen AG would go beyond this traditional role for Canadian industry and as such would have an impact on Canadian foreign policy."[19] Two months later Clark's chief of staff, Jodi White, told the Toronto *Globe and Mail* that if Thyssen were to resubmit its proposal, this time without plans to build main battle tanks, considered by External Affairs to be offensive, "clearly the Cabinet will look at it."[20] The *Globe and Mail* suggested three reasons why Ottawa is now faced with the question of whether or not to sell military commodities to Saudi Arabia:

> First, Saudi Arabia had expressed serious disappointment with Canada. Five years ago, it terminated a joint economic commission that was supposed to build commercial ties between the two countries. Second, officials at External Affairs and in other economic departments have become increasingly concerned about losing out on lucrative arms sales to other countries that were increasingly prepared to supply Saudi Arabia. They point to the scale of recent U.S., British and French military sales to Riyadh. Third, there was the increased threat to Saudi Arabia from Iran.[21]

At the same time, Canada has also taken note of Washington's shift to a more positive stance towards Saudi Arabia.

Thus, economic or other considerations can override the criteria for a restrictive policy, insofar as the principle of conflict and imminent conflict is concerned. A variety of mitigating circumstances intrude to overrule the formal guidelines. These guidelines carry no legal obligation. The law says only that exporters must have permits, and the guidelines merely point to some of the factors that the director general will consider in coming to a decision on whether or not to grant a permit. The way in which the formal guidelines are published implies that they will be given a high priority, but the act does not require this, and in many instances, other guidelines that are not publicly specified carry greater weight than the specified guidelines do.

The department does not have an operational definition of conflict or imminent conflict. In general, internal conflicts and civil war are included, so that a country involved in actions against insurgent forces should not receive Canadian military commodities. But here too there are mitigating circumstances. At lower levels of conflict, for example, it may not be clear whether what is involved is merely an attempt to control criminal elements (as officials suggested might be the case in Peru or the Philippines), or whether it constitutes a genuine military/political conflict.

The guidelines are further mitigated by considerations involving both the nature of the importing country's relationship with Canada and the nature of the equipment. If the importing country has a strong, friendly relationship with Canada that includes significant economic relations, Canada would be much more reluctant to refuse to sell military commodities. If the equipment does not have a direct combat role, a permit would also be much more readily available.

Human Rights

On March 1, 1984, an amendment to the Notice to Exporters eliminated the one guideline that had explicitly called for consideration to be given to human rights questions in the issuing of export permits for military commodities. Until then the guidelines had included the notice that "military and military-related and strategic goods" destined for "military end-users . . . should not be supplied to regimes considered to be wholly repugnant to Canadian values and especially where such equipment could be used against civilians." Both Clark and officials in his department argued at the time that the removal of that particular guideline had not changed the practice within the department. They were probably right.

The guideline that military commodities should not go to regimes where they "could be used against civilians" was ambiguous. It implied a prohibition on certain kinds of equipment (repression technology), but in fact was not interpreted that way. The guideline was taken to mean that such equipment should not be exported to places where it was "likely to be" used against civilians (not merely *could* be used), and official statements indicate that there was even a requirement that the "probability," not simply the possibility, of such use be demonstrated before a permit would be denied. In January 1984 an official explained that "applications for permits to export defence equipment that might possibly be used against civilians are carefully scrutinized and would be rejected *if it appeared that such a use were probable*" (emphasis added).[22]

It is also clear that the term "wholly repugnant to Canadian values" was not one that could be easily defined or applied. Hence, it is not surprising that as long as this was a declared guideline, it was never invoked. In explaining that "it has not been necessary to designate any country with this characterization," the department went on to explain that, in particular, Chile had not been designated, and commented that Canada was "prepared to continue normal relations" with Chile.[23] This last comment implied that a guideline explicitly directed at military exports could not be invoked unless Canada was prepared to prohibit all exports. The point of the guideline's being related to military exports was, of course, that while one can find justification for continuing civilian trade relations with a country with values wholly repugnant to one's own, there can be no justification for providing such a country with military equipment. Military equipment carries a political, as well as a commercial, message — a message of support. Providing military commodities declares that in a conflict you will want the recipient of those commodities to win.

Despite the removal of the guideline, Clark insisted that the principle of not selling military commodities in cases where they might be used against civilians still applied: "When permit applications for military exports to countries with poor human rights records are being reviewed, the principal issue is whether there is a risk that the goods will be used against the civilian population."[24] Once again, however, the application of this principle was not straightforward.

During this time Canada did not maintain a list of human rights violator countries to which military sales were automatically prohibited. There were, in fact, many circumstances in which military sales to human rights violator countries would be acceptable. The assumed right of self-defence for all countries, whether violators of human rights or not, meant that in 1984, for example, a permit to export surveillance equipment to Chile was justified by "the need, indeed the right, of the recognized government of Chile to protect its borders and coastal waters from illegal penetration."[25] It was argued that such equipment was not related to the repressive practices of the Chilean government.

The type of equipment involved also makes a difference. Even in cases where the recipient country may have had a record of using weapons against civilians, it was still considered to be acceptable and within the guidelines to sell military equipment if it was clear that the particular equipment in question could not be so used. For example, it was permissible to sell sonobouys to the Chilean navy because it is clear that these would not be used against civilians. But, External Affairs said, "the issuance of a permit to export military rifle and howitzer repair parts to the Chilean army was refused in 1983 on the grounds that these goods could be used against the civilian population."[26] Equipment regarded as "repression technology," therefore, was to be more closely controlled.

Here too, however, the principle was narrowly applied. In the case of permits to export "body armour and flak suits" for bomb disposal units, a reasonable interpretation would be that this equipment would assist the Chilean military, not in its legitimate national defence commitments, but in its camapaign against insurgents and political dissidents. The department's interpretation, however, was that these were protective items that did not pose a threat to the civilian population. Technically, a shield may be protective and nonthreatening, but to the adversary the shield is offensive inasmuch as it permits the knight to go more bravely and aggressively into the fray.

In September 1986 the guidelines were restated in their present form, but by the government's own account, this involved few changes. Under the new policy there is to be a list of countries considered to "have a persistent record of serious violations of the human rights of their citizens." It is to be subject to regular review — all, however, to be done in secret. In fact, it is the secrecy that puts the policy, and the intent of the government, into question. Secrecy is defended on grounds of commercial confidentiality — disclosure could damage the commercial competitiveness of the firms involved — without any acknowldgement that secrecy also damages the unambiguous application of agreed-upon human rights standards.

In the new guidelines, the government claims that "strategic" goods, which can include computers, radios and the like, "are not by their nature used to abuse human rights," and therefore should not be subjected to "close control." Among military commodities themselves, a distinction is drawn between "offensive" and "defensive" equipment — it being considered acceptable to sell the latter to human rights violators. But there is no indication of how the department will decide whether a particular piece of equipment is likely to be used against civilians. A Twin Otter transport aircraft is not an instrument of torture and is not likely to be used to carry out summary executions, but if it hauls armed troops to their assignments, is it a part of the overall repressive capacity of the regime? Are photographic/surveillance equipment and microcomputers, which are used to identify and maintain records on persons marked for imprisonment or disappearance, part of the repressive apparatus? Clark's explanations suggest that these are not to be considered examples of equipment used to abuse human rights, and the extreme secrecy is designed to keep us from knowing for sure.

A second weakness of the guidelines is that there is no indication of criteria by which countries may or may not be defined as having "a persistent record of serious violations of the human rights of their citizens." For the period 1980–84, for example, Amnesty International and other groups have identified more than sixty countries in which there was "frequent" torture, brutal treatment of dissidents, disappearances and other human rights violations. At what point do "frequent" violations qualify as "persistent" violations and thus qualify a country for the secret Canadian list?

Asking this question raises a third concern — that there are no human rights violators to which the sale of all military commodities is prohibited. The restated policy insists that Canada is willing to export military equipment to human rights violators if it can be shown that these commodities will not be used against civilians. Apart from the lack of clarity in what is meant by "used against civilians," there is the question of whether the sale of a military commodity to a regime that is a persistent violator of human rights can be taken as a general statement of political and economic support for that regime in a way in which the sale of civilian commodities cannot. Is the sale of a paratrooper's parachute and a field commander's radio set a political act in a way in which the sale of a microwave oven is not? The government's answer to that question, as reflected in the present guidelines, is no; it takes the position that all states, even persistent human rights violators, are entitled to the means of self-defence and thus should be sold military equipment. Canada does not believe that there should be a general prohibition of military sales to regimes that are in the habit of attacking their citizens.

Even Canadian officials have questioned the assertion that an export permit granted by the government is not an expression of political support. To be sure, some officials say that a permit is not endorsement, period — sales are private company transactions and a permit is simply a government judgement that it has no objections to the sale. However, Tom Chell, then head of the Defence Programs Bureau, indicated the importance of government seals of approval. He said that an "export permit is generally granted by the Minister of External Affairs. In sensitive cases it is sent to Cabinet for the granting of that permit, so it is a conscious governmnent decision whether a defence export sale is to be made or not . . . It is not just officials who are saying they will sell . . . Government support has to be political."[27]

The Destinations of Canadian Military Commodities

Because of the disclosure practices of the Canadian government, it is not possible to identify precisely the destinations of Canadian military commodities. Some indicators, however, are available. Table 6 is an attempt to assemble some available evidence on the ultimate destinations of Canadian military commodities. The table indicates the countries for which Canadian firms have received export permits for military or military-related commodities during the period under study.

According to the evidence, there were forty-five countries that received Canadian military commodities or for which the Canadian government was prepared to grant military export permits. Of these, twenty-eight were cited by Amnesty International and other groups as carrying out, on a regular ("unexceptional") basis, torture, disappearances, brutal treatment of dissidents and other forms of human rights violations during the period. In other words, 60 per cent of all Third World recipients of Canadian military commodities were cited as regularly carrying out human rights violations. In that period a total of sixty-seven countries were cited for human rights infractions, so that of all countries so cited, 40 per cent received Canadian military commodities.

In the third column a more restricted definition of a human rights violator, based on actions by the UN Commission on Human Rights, is applied. In this case, 26 per cent of Third World recipients of Candian military commodities were cited as human rights violators, and 50 per cent of all UN-cited human rights violators received Canadian military commodities. Prominent human rights violator countries during the period — including Argentina, Chile, Guatemala, South Korea, Pakistan, Paraguay and the Philippines — were all looked on by the Canadian government as worthwhile recipients of Canadian military commodities.

It appears safe to conclude from this that Canada does not take extraordinary measures to avoid human rights violators in its military export dealings. It is true that not all countries cited, either by the UN or by Amnesty Intenational and other groups, are necessarily classified as "persistent" violators. Nor is there available evidence that the military commodities which Canada sold or was willing to sell to these countries would fit into the category of repression technology. Nevertheless, with more than half of Canada's customers on one human rights violator list, and almost a third on the other, the evidence does not argue for scrupulous avoidance. At the same time, however, there is no indication that Canada has made a point of seeking out human rights violators as prospective customers for military commodities — as might have been expected in a buyers' market, since there could be a tendency to focus more heavily on militarized societies as representing the best prospects for sales.

In general, there is little to indicate that the export guidelines are a significant factor in limiting Canadian military exports. Canadian military commodities go directly to human rights violators and countries involved in hostilities, apparently on a regular basis. The most effective constraints on Canadian arms sales are probably Third World recession and the relatively limited range of military wares available from Arms Canada.

8

Counting the Costs

Military spending, like virtue, is increasingly assumed to be its own reward. What the spending is actually for is secondary: the important thing is to be seen to be spending. Politicians and analysts earnestly inquire whether military spending should increase by 3 per cent or 4 per cent per year. Is 2 per cent of GNP an appropriate level, or should the defence budget be phased upwards to 2.5 per cent? And would a target of 3 per cent be realistic? Spending increases show commitment, while decreases show a lack of resolve or, in Canada, a shameless willingness to "take a free ride on defence."

If politicians were similarly to argue that health care spending should be pegged to the GNP, they would quite properly be dispatched to an extended care unit. Health spending is assumed to be a response to need that has no particular relationship to increases or decreases in the GNP. Since all sense of the rational has not yet been lost in the discussion of health care, criticisms and proposals still focus on program. Do we need more hospitals and fewer clinics? Or more clinics in the north and fewer teaching hospitals in the south? Or — there are any number of questions to which health policy is supposed to be responsive.

In defence policy, however, an analyst who calls for a doubling of defence spending is regarded as having said something significant. While defence policy professionals obviously address the details of policy and military commitment, there is nevertheless an assumption that national defence questions can be meaningfully addressed by talking about relative levels of defence spending. For the proponents of increased spending, it is an approach that can backfire. At the beginning of the 1970s the Trudeau government imposed a three-year freeze on defence spending, without any apparent notion of how Canada's defence needs might have changed to warrant such a freeze, or which commitments were to be eliminated and why.

The concept of a defence spending freeze and the linking of defence spending to GNP both betray an assumption that, unlike health spending, military spending is primarily a symbol. Health spending meets real and identifiable needs; military spending makes a statement. In fact, weighty deliberations on the pros and cons of percentage changes in military spending are undertaken with the explicit acknowledgment that Canadian military spending in many instances — in Europe for example — is of little or no military impact. Analysts, politicians and former deputy ministers of defence alike acknowledge that whether Canada operates fifty CF-18 fighter aircraft in Europe or none has no noticeable effect on Europe's "capacity to defend itself." But somehow, that is not taken to be the point. For admittedly inexplicable reasons, Europeans are declared to be enormously comforted by "a Canadian presence in Europe."

Analysts and generals are the first to agree that new strategic nuclear weapons are not "usable" and contribute no real military capacity to the state that acquires them. Soviet SS-18 or American MX missiles do nothing to create or correct military imbalances. That's not even their purpose. Their real function is to create or correct psychic imbalances. Weapons represent prudence or recklessness, determination or appeasement, comfort or threat.

Weapons, and the money it takes to build them, have become the grunts and gestures of a primal international language. And while generals and presidents harrumph at one another across their burgeoning arsenals, the rest of us, the objects and consumers of military "security," pay. It is little wonder then that consumer advocacy groups around the world have been asking whether consumers are getting good value for their security dollar. These concerned consumers of the public good called security — whom we more commonly refer to as the peace movement — have come to realize that price fluctuations (usually increases) have little to do with product reliability. Indeed, as expenditures and taxes mount, security seems all the more elusive. We have been so diligent in our purchase of military security that, for the first time in recorded human history, we face the daily possibility of annihilation at our own military hands.

The Competition for Public Resources

Not only is the discriminating consumer questioning the direct return on "military security" spending, but the indirect effects of this spending are also increasingly being recognized as deleterious. Military expenditures divert funds away from security spending of a different, nonmilitary sort. They undermine a country's capacity to acquire the nonmilitary goods and services that are central to a durable social security. The dollar that goes to weapons cannot be spent on health care, food subsidies, low cost housing or the arts. These are the "opportunity costs" of defence spending.

An inevitable and prominent focus of national political debate is the allocation of scarce public resources. At any particular time and in any political context there will be debate over the relative importance of social and military security measures, and as in any political debate, perceptions are crucial. When there is broad acceptance of existing levels of military spending as being essential to maintain national security, then that spending is likely to be considered worth its direct and opportunity costs. But when that consensus breaks down, when consumers begin to feel that their defence dollar is not delivering on security, then public support for military spending erodes.

When the security value of military spending is questioned, its nonsecurity — that is, economic — benefits are likely to be given their most vigorous workout. It is here that military spending ceases to be an economic burden, according to the testimony of its proponents, and becomes something more like a panacea. Whatever their impact on security, you the consumer should support military spending and production because they are part of what brings you the good life. If military spending doesn't make you noticeably more secure, at least it makes you more prosperous.

Of course, when politicians and industry representatives advance this argument, they do not concede the point that military spending produces insecurity. Rather, they simply de-emphasize the security implications of military spending and defend it on economic grounds. It is not unlike advocating increased expenditures on road construction without making any promise that passable highways will follow, on the grounds that just going through the motions of buying bulldozers and graders and bustling about on them is itself the benefit. It has become a commonplace for Canadian defence ministers to assert that new military procurement programs will invigorate the country's industry and help lift it out of the economic doldrums.

Prime Minister Mulroney used similar arguments in favour of increased military spending: "There can be a gradual affordable program for the re-equipment of our Armed Forces over a reasonable period of time that does not break the bank, but in fact constitutes a significant investment in jobs, economic development and the national security of our nation."[1] Robert Wenman, the parliamentary secretary to the minister of defence, went even further in his enthusiasm for the benefits of the "defence dollar," which, he said, "can be 'invested' in order to generate more wealth in Canada; can be 'invested' to increase economic activity and thus create more employment opportunities for Canadians."[2]

The most prominent image used for social spending is that of a "safety net," evoking a picture of helpless people being caught in a net supported by kindly social managers — but with the implied fear that as the net catches more and more of society's unfortunates it will become heavier and heavier and approach the point at which society can no longer bear the burden. In contrast, images invoked in support of military spending avoid all sense of burden, focusing instead on action and promise for the future. It apparently matters little that economic studies on employment, for example, actually indicate the opposite. Social spending generates more economic activity, leading to immediate job creation at two and three times the rate of spending on military equipment (see table 7).

This has become an important Canadian debate. Canadians are facing a period of accelerated military spending. While this acceleration includes plans for adding to the personnel of the forces, the current emphasis is on increased capital spending. Not surprisingly, this has generated considerable interest in the likely long-term economic effects of increased military procurement. Also not surprisingly, the government, charged with generating political support for these programs, is out to accentuate the positive.

In fact, by linking military spending with the pursuit of national economic objectives, as Royal Military College economist John M. Treddenick points out, several federal government bureaucracies develop mutual interests in increased military spending: "On the one hand, the military is able to use the argument of economic benefits to support funding of its programs; on the other, those bureaucracies concerned with trade, industry, technology and regional development are able to shape a large expenditure block in support of their own program interests."[3] If these mutual interests do not actually lead to active promotion of higher military spending, they are, at the very least, likely to mute opposition to military spending increases.

It is acknowledged that there are costs associated with military procurement, but to no one's great surprise, those with an immediate interest in Department of National Defence budget increases have identified military spending reductions as the real economic threat. We have no choice, the line goes, but to continue to increase military spending if we are to build technological sophistication into our indus-

TABLE 7
Jobs Created by One Billion Dollars Expenditure (1983$)

1983/84 National Defence Spending on Goods and Services	22,000
Road and Highway Construction	37,000
Residential Construction	38,000
Consumer Spending	39,000
Hospital Services	51,000
Education and Related Services	54,000
Radio and TV Broadcasting	55,000
Urban Transit Systems	87,000
Post Office	90,000

Sources: CUPE Facts, January-February 1986.

try and prevent unemployment from climbing even higher. In this perspective, it is really better to think of the costs as an investment in the future. Notably, it is argued that new military technologies acquired through Canadian military procurement will become marketable and that Canada will benefit from their export to the far corners of the globe.

It is clear that the injection of federal money into particular industries or regions of the country will produce some economic benefits for some people. These benefits have been well promoted and are now part of contemporary folklore: World War II got us out of the dirty thirties, hence military spending must be good for the economy. The mutual interests of powerful social groupings have given the "benefits" of military spending a prominent public profile. The military itself, the industry, and the industry and trade branches of the federal government all share an interest in military spending increases and have the resources to advance their interests publicly.

While special interests are inclined to devote near-exclusive attention to the positive effects of military spending, the more sober reality of course is that public expenditures of any kind, military or nonmilitary, represent a public burden to be borne, one way or another, by society as a whole. The task therefore is to understand more clearly the nature and implications of that burden, the better to weigh the benefits of the expenditures against the costs. While the budgetary costs of procuring military capital goods are there for all to see, there are also less obvious indirect economic and political costs that intrude by virtue of the means through which we arrange to acquire those capital goods. Some of these costs are inherent in military spending, and others are incurred by virtue of the particular structural arrangements under which Canada purchases major military equipment and produces military commodities for export.

The Economic Costs of Military Production

The publication in 1984 of a book by a senior business executive about the role of military spending in the economic decline of the United States marked the emergence into American mainstream economic and business thinking of a more critical understanding of the economic impact of military spending.[4] The book was *The Trimtab Factor,* and in it Harold Willens echoed the warnings that had been coming from academic and nongovernmental groups for two decades to the effect that military spending was a serious economic burden and an important factor in American economic decline.[5] Willens appealed to the U.S. business community to work to arrest this decline by working against President Reagan's accelerated military programs.

His point was that the economic and political consequences of military spending and production are part of the cost of military preparedness, and it is impossible to assess the true burden of national security policies without accounting for these costs as well. The tendency has been to underestimate the costs by ignoring the impact of military production and spending on industrial innovation, balance of payments, employment, inflation, and elements of foreign policy, among other areas. In this way, decisions become skewed. A bias in favour of military responses to political and social conflicts is likely to persist as long as there is a popular perception that military spending, whatever its value in relation to the settlement of disputes and national security, produces welcome economic effects.

Military R&D and Civilian Spinoffs

President Reagan's soaring military spending has added to the growing public skepticism about the benefits of military spending, and a growing number of economists now identify military spending as instrumental in U.S. economic decline. Singled out is the heavy focus on military research and development. Once widely claimed to be the source of industrial innovation beneficial to the civilian economy, it is now increasingly identified as the culprit, retarding innovation and productivity in the civilian sector. In 1984 Lewis Branscomb, an IBM vice-president and the company's chief scientist, told the U.S. Congress that "companies outside the defense sector generally discount the 'spinoff' of most defense and space research." He suggested that a more appropriate term would be "drip off," and warned that the huge military demand for scientists and engineers "may become an obstacle to economic progress."[6]

In fact, the Pentagon has become increasingly dependent on Japan for defence technologies. While the U.S. concentrated on the development of sophisticated weapons systems, Japan has emphasized the basic building blocks of technology.[7] In the meantime, as the Washington *Post* noted early in 1986, "largely through its strength in commercial electronics, Japan has rapidly become a strategic supplier of defense technologies to the Pentagon."[8] Thus, spinoffs in Japan, rather than working the way proponents of military spending claim they are supposed to, have gone in the opposite direction — military applications have spun off from commercial technology. The United States, despite its concentration on military research and development, now depends on imports for military subsystems and for 80 per cent of its military requirements for silicon chips.

Through an analysis of seventeen noncommunist industrialized countries over a period of two decades, the U.S. Council on Economic Priorities confirmed the observation that superior technological and industrial developments take place when the focus is on production for civilian use. Those economies with less emphasis on military production experienced faster growth and had a better job creation record. The Council also examined three key industrial sectors — aerospace, electronics and machine tools — to test the claim that commercial industries benefit from military research. If the spinoff theory were correct, there should have been evidence that firms and industries with substantial military production were expanding their overall market share. "In each case," the study showed, "the contrary proved true." Japanese and European firms have made major inroads into U.S. markets in all three sectors.[9] And as civilian production methods in the United States fail to keep up with those in Japan and elsewhere, relative production costs increase and the United States finds it more and more difficult to compete in international markets. As a result, inflation increases as higher labour and material costs not mitigated by increased productivity are passed on to the consumer, and unemployment increases as imports mount and exports decline.

In Canada, however, the spinoff argument persists. When he was associate minister of national defence, Harvie Andre described DND as having twin objectives in its equipment modernization program: "providing for Canada's defence needs and encouraging expansion of a Canadian defence industrial base."[10] Andre made the reasonable claim that the import of military technology would enhance Canada's military industry. That, however, is precisely the problem. Military technology and research enhance *military* production, not the civilian economy. A Fraser Institute review of research and development funding in Britain and the United States noted that in both countries, and especially in the United States, military R&D provided important commercial and trade advantages, but both countries were also "put at a disadvantage in world trade in those product groups in the non-military sphere where their technological effort was weak, such as in machinery, metal products and chemicals."[11]

That military research and development should produce innovation and competence in military production is not a surprise. However, Jean-Jacques Blais didn't leave it at that. As defence minister in the final months of the Trudeau government, Blais insisted that "any additional investment in the R&D field — particularly defence R&D — is good for the economy at large." He argued that companies that "develop military technology" are "in an advantageous position when this technology is later turned to commercial applications."[12] It is a persistent myth, and shows up again in a report on technology development prepared for the minister of state for science and technology: "It is no coincidence that some of this century's most awesome scientific achievements have been made in times of war."[13] The idea is that military requirements create a substantial and steady demand for scientific innovation, and war provides the urgency needed to produce the political will to fill those demands. If this argument is to have any relevance, short of hoping for an actual war to concentrate the national will, the extraordinary experience of war has to be universalized and applied to peacetime military spending. However, the vision of a frenzied war footing to spawn all manner of technological innovation needs to be tempered by the reality that a country not at war inevitably has more diffuse priorities.

The argument that technological spinoffs will benefit the Canadian economy in the long term has been a prominent Canadian rationale for initiating offsets as part of the package in which Canada purchases U.S. weapons systems. Industry representatives agree, however, that this has not worked out. Instead, offsets reinforce arrangements whereby the Canadian defence industry is geared to performing short-run tasks to meet specifications handed down by the Pentagon. While this may produce innovations, these innovations rarely lead to long-term mass production for civilian markets in Canada or abroad. In fact, industry officials have been complaining that federal defence industry subsidies are very narrowly focused on defence production without consideration for spinoff benefits for the civilian economy.[14]

The spinoffs argument has also been used to justify space research in Canada. Alex Curran, the former president of SED Systems and a member of the Space Policy Group of the Aerospace Industries Association of Canada, describes the Canadian space industry as "a leading edge industry which tackles difficult problems, finds solutions, and then makes those solutions available to others." As an example, he cites the space industry's search for exotic materials that combine high strength with low mass: "One typically Canadian spin-off is that some of the country's finest canoes are now manufactured not from birchbark, but from Kevlar, a material invented for space."[15]

As delightful as a Kevlar canoe may be, it is neither a necessary nor a sufficient justification for space research. The question that must be asked about any form of research is whether the direct objective of the research is worthy of economic and political support. Asking this question raises a fundamental distinction between Canadian space innovation in areas such as communications on the one hand and a program such as the U.S. Strategic Defense Initiative on the other. Space communications are worthwhile in their own right. They are worthy of public support because of the obvious and tangible benefits they provide to Canadians. The presence or absence of other commercial spinoffs is interesting, but not crucial.

With the Strategic Defense Initiative the opposite is the case. At the very least, the value of SDI in its own right is in dispute. Some (there must be some in addition to President Reagan) argue that it promises technological immunity to nuclear weapons, while others argue that it promises to destabilize the nuclear environment, undermine deterrence and make nuclear war more likely. It is in weighing the relative merits of these two arguments that the decision on Canada's response to SDI must be made. Some supporters of SDI in Canadian industry, however, profess not to know or to be concerned about the impact of strategic defence itself. They only know that participation in SDI would be worthwhile because SDI represents the concentration of an extraordinary bundle of research dollars, and any time you have such a concentration of research activity something good is bound to come out of it.

As an unrestrained advocate of greater military-industrial integration between Canada and the United States, the Aerospace Industries Association of Canada has made calling on "our U.S. ally to provide more business opportunity to Canadian defence industries" its institutional raison d'etre.[16] It has in particular sought "opportunities" related to SDI work. "Let us accept the fact," the AIAC told the Commons Committee on External Affairs and National Defence in 1985, "that computer technology is going to assist and in fact be the basis of future medical work as well as medical research." This established, the AIAC then shifted its attention to SDI, which "will use more computer capacity than the whole free world computer capacity which exists today." And since in addition "a lot of surgery in the future will relate to laser technology," and various forms of optics, photonics and light energy will be important in civilian life, it reminded the MPs that laser and other light technologies are central to SDI research. The organization then drew the conclusion that SDI would therefore "be good for Canada: it would be good for our universities and it would be good for the progress of humanity in medical fields and in other fields, in communications for instance."[17]

The most perplexing question all this raises is why the AIAC, given its concern for "the progress of humanity in medical fields," promotes weapons research rather than medical research. With its appeal to a moral obligation to do SDI work so that medicine can benefit from spinoffs, the AIAC is like a farmer who, anxious to fatten the chickens, increases the feed to the horses so that more of it spills over the edge of the trough, thus giving the chickens more scratchings for which to forage.

Throughout its argument before the parliamentary committee, the AIAC specifically did not defend SDI on its own merits. It did not say that SDI was important for national security or stability or disarmament, but defended SDI research only on grounds that it promised all manner of economic benefits and medical breakthroughs. So if there are no apparent merits intrinsic to SDI, why not promote those kinds of research in which there is intrinsic merit, such as medical research, and let the military benefit from spinoffs if that becomes necessary for security reasons? In theory, this approach should appeal to the AIAC, particularly since the organization approvingly quotes a statement by the science adviser to the president of the United States that "there is about 90 per cent commonality between" military and civilian research and development.[18] This should be an argument in favour of less military R&D, not more. If 90 per cent of R&D is common to both, the heavy emphasis on military funding of R&D is obviously not necessary.

Nevertheless, the president of a Canadian electronics/space firm, COMDEV Ltd., worries that because Canada will not be participating in SDI in a high-profile, government-involved way (including government funding for joint research activities that are based in Canada but related to SDI), "we could find that we are no longer at the leading edge of technology."[19] Is there no Canadian need sufficiently urgent to warrant R&D expenditures on it directly? Is Canada so lacking in ingenuity that its research and development funds must remain frozen as they wait for the initiatives of others? In no other activity would rational human beings argue that you should commit scarce resources to the pursuit of something which in itself is not considered valuable because, in the course of pursuing the useless, you may by accident find something useful.

The Impact on Jobs

Because of the "rough balance" provision of the Defence Production Sharing Arrangements and similar requirements for defence trade with Europe, the vast majority of the jobs created through Canadian military exports are the indirect result of Canadian government spending on military imports. Of course, when the government spends money, jobs are bound to be created. But if the issue is jobs, and not the quality of defence policy, then the real question is whether more or fewer jobs would be created if that money were spent in another way. And in such a comparison, military spending is the loser.

Almost any other kind of public spending will produce more jobs than will military equipment spending. A 1983 study by the Employment Research Associates in the United States examined the impact on employment of a $10 billion cut in U.S. military procurement. The study provided for the cut funds to be reinvested in four industries that were important to the U.S. national interest but had been experiencing shortages in capital — solar energy, gasohol production, railroad equipment and fishing vessel construction. It calculated that directly and indirectly, 346,000 jobs would be lost in military industries, while the reinvestment would produce 380,000 direct and indirect jobs. Thus, every $10 billion spent on military procurement, instead of in the four industries chosen, cost the United States 34,000 jobs.

Had the study called for the funds to be reinvested in service occupations, it would have ended up with a much larger number of jobs created. Indeed, the study also calculated that if every person directly affected by the $10 billion military procurement cut were laid off for one year, it would be possible to pay each of them 90 per cent of his or her salary (up to a maximum of $25,000), continue job-related benefits, and provide each with a $1,500 back-to-school grant — all for less than $3 billion.[20] The report's author, Marion Anderson, concluded that "a $10 billion transfer from military procurement to solar power, railroads, buses and fishing fleet construction would be a start in improving our national security." According to Anderson, expanding military capacity is not a way to increase employment, nor will it "run our cars, fuel our factories or heat our homes."

A similar study commissioned by the Canadian Union of Public Employees indicates that spending on military equipment is no more effective as a make-work program in Canada. The study used a Statistics Canada input-output model of the Canadian economy to indicate the number of jobs created by DND's 1983–84 spending on goods and services, and the number of jobs that would have been created had the same amount been added to consumer spending. It turned out that the military spending resulted in 146,641 jobs, while an equal amount of consumer spending would have created 257,844.[21] There is obviously no guarantee that a cut in military spending would result in an equivalent increase in consumer spending, but the study does suggest that a government with job creation as a top priority would be better advised to look to the promotion of consumer spending rather than increased military spending as a way of attaining that objective.

This is now a widely acknowledged reality. Having examined macroeconomic indicators in Canada, an economist for the Conference Board of Canada told a gathering of military strategists, planners and industry representatives: "If you are looking for an increase in defence expenditure for its macroeconomic impact on the economy, then everybody else can play the same game, and some can play it better than you can — they have a better claim in terms of getting the unemployment rate down. So you will have to look for different reasons."[22]

Jobs, however, remain a compelling political currency. In the debate over SDI research, for example, both Prime Minister Mulroney and External Affairs Minister Clark, while expressing reservations about Canadian participation in such research, also suggested that job creation might be its redeeming virtue. Both said they would have to look closely at Star Wars research if it meant jobs for Canadians, and Mulroney even advanced an off-the-cuff suggestion of 10,000 jobs.[23] Job creation is obviously not the primary objective of research funding, but since the prime minister raised the possibility of thousands of jobs from Star Wars, it is worth taking a closer look at this question.

As with military production, every job created by military research conducted in Canada, whether for DND or for the Pentagon, is directly or indirectly funded out of the Canadian public treasury. There are few precedents for research contracts to Canadian industry that do not inlude Canadian public funding, and aerospace industry officials have called, not only for Canadian endorsement of Star Wars, but also for Canadian funding of elements of Star Wars research.[24] In addition, the United States is not in the habit of contracting military production or research outside its borders without getting something in return. The Americans would happily accept part of the payoff in the form of more enthusiastic political support for Star Wars, but in the light of the huge U.S. trade deficit, it is likely to require economic reciprocation as well, especially since research contracts are included in the rough balance provisions of the Defence Development and Production Sharing Arrangements.

Thus, since money spent on Star Wars research in Canada would be public money, the real question is not whether it would create jobs — the expenditure of any research funds would do that — but whether it would create more jobs than the same funds applied to other job creation programs or even to tax cuts or deficit reduction. The job creation potential of funds applied to Star Wars research is uncertain, but a reasonable guide might be a recent $85 million research and development contract awarded to Spar Aerospace by the U.S. military.[25] This contract was said to promise 500 man-years of work. By comparison, if we were to estimate — generously — that direct government-to-government cooperation with the Americans in Star Wars research would yield $50 million a year in SDI contracts, it would be reasonable to expect that this might create about 300 jobs per year.

But what if that $50 million were spent elsewhere? Table 7 suggests that $50 million spent on urban transit systems could produce thousands of jobs. Obviously, spending public funds on Star Wars rather than urban transit represents the funding of unemployment. There are justifications for spending public funds on research, but immediate job creation is not among them. If Mulroney and Clark are unable to find defence and security reasons for supporting Star Wars, they engage in a high order of deception to suggest that job creation might be a sufficient justification.

Military research and development may well contribute to unemployment in other ways as well. American writers such as Seymour Melman increasingly relate economic decay in the United States to high levels of military spending.[26] The concentration of public research funds in the military retards civilian industries, makes them less competitive and results in lost markets. As already noted, the United States is losing ground even in the industries that are most closely related to military production and might be expected to benefit most directly from spinoffs. And the trend is towards a further undermining of civilian research and development by military R&D. In the past twenty years, military research in the United States has gone from 48 per cent to the current 70 per cent of federal R&D funding. The $7 billion increase in military research in 1986 was greater than the total increase in federal research funding, meaning that military research was directly crowding out civilian research in health and other fields.[27]

With science and engineering focused on military innovation, a retarded civilian sector finds it impossible to remain competitive in international markets. Lost exports and increased imports together add up to lost jobs. In addition, as noted earlier, they add up to inflationary pressure. Increased productivity has always been a primary means of compensating for increasing labour and material costs. The lack of research and development related to civilian production has meant relatively outdated production processes in the civilian economy and a reduced capacity to compensate for rising costs. Hence, the ultimate result of a heavy emphasis on military research and development is an unending spiral of inflation, reduced competitiveness, and unemployment.

Canada's Special Situation

While there are costs associated with military research and production in any context, there are also special factors that are felt with unusual force in Canada. As a result of the conditions under which Canada's military industry operates — especially the U.S.-Canada Defence Development and Production Sharing Arrangements and negotiated offsets — Canada does not enjoy in full measure even the normal range of benefits that countries derive from military production. These factors affect Canada's technological development, balance of payments, and employment.

Canada as a Third World Recipient

In both relative and absolute terms, the level of military spending in Canada is not comparable with the level in the United States. The political and strategic objectives of Canadian policy also have little in common with those of the United States. American military policy is premised on the military and strategic objectives of a superpower — including the maintenance and expansion of a global sphere of influence. The objective of Canadian military policy, besides trying to avoid being ignored or taken for granted by a superpower, is to do what we can to reduce the likelihood of a superpower-led nuclear war and to preserve the sovereignty and territorial integrity of Canada. Thus, in examining the economic and political consequences of the arrangements through which Canadian military goods are acquired, the United States may not be the most instructive analogy. In fact, Canada is more like a Third World importer of major weapons systems than a First World exporter of military goods.

Canada's military procurement policy has reflected its effort to avoid being ignored and its recognition that what it does militarily will not have a major impact on superpower behaviour. Ottawa has tried to acquire enough weapons to signal engagement but not enough to undermine other important social objectives. Trying to mitigate the costs of expensive imported weapons systems, it has sought to balance those imports with measures to generate economic returns through a unique set of production arrangements. While Canada tries to improve its situation by enhancing some of its own military production capabilities, it remains heavily dependent on imported capital and technology, as well as on foreign buyers, for the development of domestic military production. In the end, Canada still winds up with only limited indigenous technicial capabilities. In this, the parallels or analogies applicable to Canada may be found in semi-industrialized countries of the Third World. The economic and political impact of weapons transfers between industrialized suppliers and semi-industrialized recipients is the subject of an extensive literature.[28]

The more prominent suppliers of military equipment to the Third World see in weapons sales opportunities to establish and reinforce relations of economic and political dependence between themselves and the recipients of their weapons. Immediate economic return is obviously not to be ignored, but the major powers in particular consider weapons sales and military aid to be important instruments of foreign and economic policy, through which spheres of influence can be established, expanded and managed. Access to raw materials, to additional markets, and to strategic facilities such as military bases or protection of sea routes are all part of the economic/strategic objectives involved in the major powers' arms transfers.

For Third World importers, weapons systems and the infrastructure required to maintain and operate them (such as training, technical maintenance and spare parts) generally mean a long-term political and economic relationship with the supplier. Already scarce foreign currency is further depleted by the weapons and infrastructure imports, adding to pressures to accelerate raw materials exports, divert land into the production of cash crops for export, and welcome foreign investment and foreign loan capital. While from the perspective of the importer, these consequences are unwanted side-effects of weapons transfers, from the perspective of the exporter, they are among the objectives of those transfers — access to raw materials, places to invest. And attempts by the importer to mitigate the costs of imports through more indigenous military production can exacerbate, rather than alleviate, dependence. Even when you build your own weapons, you still need imported capital goods (the foreign technology needed to build the foreign designs), and the economic viability of the operation ultimately depends on an enduring export market.[29]

In the long run, the need for export markets is the most disturbing consequence, and it has global implications. Imports of weapons technology and capital equipment, on which a domestic production base can be established, can in the long run reduce industrial and military dependence, but the domestic market is unlikely to support an indigenous military industry on its own.[30] So while reduced dependence on the superpowers for military imports has economic, political and military advantages for Third World countries, their need to market their military wares to other states bodes ill for control of the world arms trade and for reducing the level of global violence.

While Canada is not a Third World country, it is directly affected by this dilemma. Relying on imports for most of its major weapons systems, dependent on exports for the viability of its military industry, able to carry out only a limited range of the functions normally identified with supporting a national defence capability, building to foreign designs, with foreign machine tools and subcomponents, and in many cases under foreign licence agreements, Canada acts as a regional supplier to a defence industrial base that is coordinated and managed in the United States. The result is that the much vaunted role of military production in industrial innovation is severely stunted in Canada. Instead of being a solution to Canada's industrial underdevelopment, military production may well be contributing to the problem.

Balance of Payments and Employment

Because of the rough balance provision worked out in 1963, the Defence Production Sharing Arrangements do not provide Canada with the possibility of earning either a balance of payments surplus or a net gain in jobs. With Canada reasonably assured, over the long term, of an export market up to the size of its military imports, but not a penny more, it cannot develop a long-term balance of payments surplus in military trade. Indeed, as long as Canada has a surplus in its overall trade with the U.S., successive U.S. administrations will view the commitment to balance military trade as what the Nixon White House called a "trade irritant."

For Canada, the maintenance of a rough balance in military trade may, in fact, represent a permanent trade deficit. Canadian production in fields such as aerospace and electronics depends upon imported subcomponents and machine tools. In the early years of some military production, foreign content can be very high; armoured vehicles exported to the United States, for example, included foreign material inputs of over 70 per cent. In some instances these imports of components and machine tools are calculated into the overall military trade volume, but in many cases this is not possible. Estimates are that these secondary imports account for as much as 20 cents of every dollar of Canadian production in these fields. In other words, every dollar of Canadian military exports generates a dollar of military imports by virtue of the rough balance provision of the DPSA, plus up to 20 cents worth of secondary imports.

A similar logic applies to employment. If military exports must, in the long run, be matched by military imports, then for every job that is created through exports, another job is lost by virtue of the reciprocal imports. Because a major part of Canada's capital defence budget is not spent in this country, Canadian military spending creates jobs in the United States, and to some extent in Europe, but not in Canada. Exports arranged through the DPSA or offsets simply compensate for this job loss. Military exports to the United States, therefore, do not create additional jobs in Canada in the way that civilian exports in the same industries do.

The DPSA, Offsets, and Technology

In an environment of competing priorities, the transfer of specialized military technology to civilian uses is less than a sure thing. This is especially so in Canada because of the development of Canada's military industry as an addendum to that of the United States. Leaders in the Canadian aerospace industry, which accounts for a major part of military production in Canada, have been insisting for some time that the DPSA have contributed to the technological impoverishment of industry in this country — not only civilian industry, but the military sector as well.

While arguing for still greater access to the U.S. military market, industry representatives regularly denounce the DPSA. "My experience is that the production-sharing agreement is largely a sham," says Douglas Reekie, president of CAE Industries Ltd. of Toronto. "The things available to Canadian industry are not generally worth going after or are not at the leading edge of technology." Alec Bishop, vice-president of the Aerospace Industries Association of Canada, agrees, noting that even if the trade in defence items between the two countries has been roughly in balance in dollar terms, Canadian imports have had a much greater technological component than have exports to the United States. While Canada purchases complete fighter aircraft from the United States, for instance, exports have been primarily small components for larger systems. Says Bishop, "you can't knock [the availability of] the work, but the quality is not there."[31]

In much the same fashion, the special offset arrangements that have been negotiated to give Canadian companies a part of the work generated by DND's recent capital purchases have served to maintain even the military industry at a lower level of technology. The president of a leading Canadian military exporting firm, Canadian Marconi, told the Commons Committee on External Affairs and National Defence in 1984: "The trouble with off-set is that, if you are trying to provide work in Canada for a system like an aircraft that has already been developed elsewhere, all that the Canadian companies can get is the scraps, the very low technology work that can be quickly put in here to create the political illusion of jobs."[32] In 1986, he reiterated his argument that the Canadian government's policy of negotiating offsets as a means to enhancing Canadian defence technology would not work, this time to the semiannual meeting of the AIAC: "Build to print work is no substitute for having Canadian indigenous products and developing our industry based on these."[33]

A survey by *Aviation Week and Space Technology* confirmed the failure of offsets to win technology benefits for Canada. The survey indicated that many U.S. aerospace and electronics firms found that the ability to offer offset purchases could be an important factor in landing an export contract for a piece of major equipment, and added that "technology transfer is not a problem since such transfers rarely involve state of the art technology."[34] The AIAC has also been a persistent critic of offsets, and has particularly noted the absence of research and development opportunities: "For our industry, offsets simply have not worked . . . People guard their research and development and technology."[35]

Other Effects of Offsets

In addition to their deficiency as a means to greater technological sophistication, offsets are getting Canada into trouble on other counts, not the least of which is the resentment they produce in the United States. Despite findings from the *Aviation Week and Space Technology* survey, the predominant American attitude is one of opposition to offsets. Congressional hostility to offsets is reflected in persistent calls to study their effects, and when the called-for study fails to yield the desired results, another study is mounted. In February 1985 a U.S. interagency study concluded that offsets have little economic or competitive impact on U.S. industry.[36] But that study's methods were later challenged, and in June 1986 the administration agreed, under pressure from Congress, to undertake another study of whether the U.S. defence industrial base is being eroded by military imports related to offsets, especially in the aircraft and engines sector.[37] U.S. concerns about offsets are not confined to Canada, but this country is the main focus.

Another cost of offsets may be their influence on Canadian military procurement. The president of one Toronto-based defence contractor has argued that the emphasis on industrial "benefits" or offsets may be undermining the military effectiveness of the capital purchases of the Department of National Defence. The insistence that the "benefits" be spread all over the country, even though most of the expertise is located in Ontario and Quebec, shifts the focus from a careful analysis of Canadian security needs to alleged economic advantages. The Department of National Defence, in other words, "has to figure out what it wants — a top-notch piece of military equipment or an industrial program."[38]

And finally, once you've invented the offsets approach, others may use it to their advantage against you. As the inventor of offsets, Canada is not really in a very good position to complain when it becomes the victim. For example, the Stockholm International Peace Research Institute reports that when Bombardier Inc. sold 2,500 military vehicles to Belgium, it had to promise offsets amounting to three times the value of the contract itself.[39] In another case, Spar Aerospace of Toronto sold two communications satellites to Brazil in the early 1980s with part of the deal being an undertaking by Spar to generate an equivalent value of Brazilian exports, not necessarily to Canada. In an attempt to honour the agreement, Spar has been reported as flogging Brazilian products ranging from bananas to emeralds to textiles.[40]

Private and Public Risk

For a Canadian company that is just entering the field, doing business with the Pentagon or its suppliers is not necessarily an attractive proposition. Entering a major bid — one which if successful would require capital expansion — is a risky undertaking. The U.S. Defense Department will not guarantee continued work beyond the initial order, and the product for which the capital expenditure is undertaken is likely to have no market in Canada. A member of the eighteen-member U.S. defence procurement delegation that toured Canada in December 1984 told the Toronto *Globe and Mail* that "Canadian companies must make that decision on the basis of their own self-interest. Our budgets are on a year-to-year basis and unfortunately we can't guarantee too much" in the way of contract renewals.[41] In effect, it is the Canadian taxpayer who gets to take the risk through Defence Industry Productivity program funding for capital costs related to certain export contracts.

The Political Consequences of Shared Defence Production

In addition to the economic distortions enumerated above, Canada's current approach to military procurement also produces some serious political distortions.

The central political fact about Canadian military production is that its survival depends fully on the United States. If the U.S. market were suddenly to dry up, there would be major repercussions in Canada's military-related industries. Workers would be laid off, plants would be closed and Canadian engineers and scientists would leave in droves for the United States. As John Diefenbaker discovered at the time of the cancellation of the Avro Arrow, these are not happy circumstances for any government.

If it was a sudden outbreak of peace that caused the bottom to fall out of the U.S. military market, most Canadians would happily endure and try to share the hardship. The more immediate prospect, however, is for that market to dry up as a result of changing American perceptions of self-interest and changing political and economic relations between the two countries — which is another way of saying that Canada has developed a stake in maintaining current American perceptions and current Canada-U.S. relations.

The U.S. administration, of course, views the continental integration of the defence industry as part of overall continental defence policy integration, but members of the U.S. Congress, with a rather more direct concern for employment in their own constituencies, tend to view Canadian production of U.S. military commodities as the export of jobs. There has, as already noted, been some attention paid in Congress to restricting Canada's pursuit of offset sales and in general to limiting the flow of Canadian-made military components into the U.S.

The White House and the Pentagon have resisted such moves. This should not be taken as altruism or concern on the administration's part for Canadian producers; rather, such action is based on the assumption of Canadian-American "cooperation" in support of a single, continental defence policy. If Ottawa were to signal explicit non-cooperation in some significant element of that policy — say by refusing to test the cruise missile on Canadian territory — the U.S. administration would, to no one's surprise, soon run out of enthusiasm for its role as protector of Canadian military-industrial interests in the United States. Canadian dependence on the U.S. market, in other words, provides the United States with a direct lever with which to influence Canadian foreign and defence policy decisions.

Procurement Decisions

Through the Defence Production Sharing Arrangements, Canada gave up much of its freedom to make independent military procurement decisions. The DPSA built in a requirement to purchase major equipment from the United States. In April 1963, Defence Production Minister Bud Drury explained Canada's plans to buy the U.S. Hercules transport aircraft, rather than a more expensive Canadian-built aircraft, by noting that the purchase in the U.S. would make it easier for Canadair to produce components for the American-built TFX aircraft being ordered by the U.S. Air Force: "If the position of the Canadian government should be that we are going to produce all our own military equipment, even on an uneconomic basis, then the willingness of the United States to have us share in the production of their military equipment, notably the TFX, I think would be seriously prejudiced."[42]

Canada's purchase of military equipment cannot simply be a careful response to Canadian defence needs. A major function of the capital spending of the Department of National Defence must, within Canada's current defence industry arrangements, be the purchase of military exports to the United States. If an important role of DND capital spending is the nurture of the American market for Canadian-built military components, it should be no surprise that those who control our access to the U.S. market find opportunities to influence Canada's military capital purchases.

Canada's purchase of maritime surveillance aircraft in the mid-1970s illustrates the point. That decision, the first major purchase following the lifting of the freeze on military spending of the early 1970s, was made in the context of some significant changes in Canada's security environment. Canada had just come through a major reassessment of its role in Europe. It was clear from the public debate that there were deep cracks in the national consensus in support of a continued Canadian military presence on the European continent. This was reflected in a reduction in Canadian commitments to Europe and, as called for in a government White Paper on defence policy at the time, an upgraded emphasis on a military role in the protection of Canada's sovereignty in North America.

Also in the early 1970s, there was a widespread debate concerning nuclear strategy. The debate over anti–ballistic missile (ABM) systems engaged the fundamental questions of nuclear deterrence and the basis of nuclear stability, and the ABM Treaty that emerged is testimony to the fact that the prevailing mood was in support of the preservation of strategic stability through mutually assured destruction. Basic to this strategy was the maintenance of an invulnerable second-strike capability by each side in the superpower nuclear contest. In that context, Prime Minister Trudeau questioned the wisdom of strategic antisubmarine warfare (ASW) activity: "Should we be having the kind of naval force which is prepared to destroy the Soviet nuclear-armed submarines, which are a deterrent for them as the Polaris is a deterrent for the United States?"[43] With the nuclear balance of terror dependent on invulnerable second-strike forces, Trudeau was questioning whether Canada should be engaged in a policy that could be seen as threatening the Soviet second-strike capacity.

Another significant element of the context in which the maritime surveillance aircraft decision was made was a depressed aerospace industry in Canada. At the conclusion of direct American involvement in the Vietnam War, a combination of sharply reduced military demand and severe American balance of payments problems led to a steep drop in U.S. purchases in Canada. The industry was in danger of collapse and Ottawa responded on several levels. The government purchased the two main aircraft companies operating in Canada, Canadair and de Havilland, to keep them from being closed by their parent firms and to rationalize aerospace production in Canada. It also embarked on major funding programs to develop additional short takeoff and landing (STOL) aircraft and a commercial business jet. At the same time, it was busy trying to restore Canada's access to the American market through diplomatic activity.

Maintaining access to that market, still viewed as the key to the long-term health of the aersopace industry in Canada, was not so simple. The Vietnam-induced trade balance was sharply in Canada's favour, and this was a situation the Americans were not keen on, given their own balance of payments problems (see figure 5). When Ottawa said to them that they ought to increase their purchases in Canada significantly in order to preserve the Canadian region of the North American defence industrial base, the Americans in effect reminded Canadians that they had given an undertaking to buy as much in the United States as the U.S. bought in Canada. So, before the Americans could resume high levels of military purchases in Canada, Canada would have to undertake some major purchases in the U.S.

This was obviously a matter of some importance when it came time for Canada to buy a new maritime patrol aircraft. The options were limited. Canada could not seriously consider buying a Canadian-built aircraft — such as the newly developed de Havilland Dash-7, a four-engine turboprop that could be modified for long-range patrol operations — because it was not simply buying a plane: it was buying a military market for its aerospace and electronics industries. In fact, the United States took an active role in advising the Canadians on just what airplane they should buy and even from whom they should buy it.

In the end, the long-range patrol aircraft Canada purchased was not suitable for sovereignty patrol, which had been identified as the first priority of Canadian policy. Instead, it was an aircraft designed for ASW activity within American ASW exercises — a role that had been publicly questioned by Prime Minister Trudeau because of its potential destabilizing aspects. A variety of factors led to the purchase, but not the least of them was Washington's wish to have Canada stay in the ASW role and, even more pertinently, to have it buy an aircraft from the troubled Lockheed Corporation. And Washington had the means at its disposal to make sure that its wish was fulfilled by exerting special influence over Canadian policy — an influence made possible by the dependence of the Canadian industry on the U.S. market and by the rough balance provision of the DPSA.

Perception of Threat

Through the Defence Production Sharing Arrangements, Canada has given a foreign power inordinate influence over Canadian military equipment decisions. And by handing a foreign power direct influence, if not control, over important equipment acquisitions, we are to some extent handing that power the means to influence our very view of the world. Weapons systems embody military strategies and roles and approaches to military power, and the domination of Canadian security arrangements by American military technology moves the Canadian defence establishment towards uncritical acceptance of U.S. descriptions of the strategic environment. In other words, when we import U.S. military technology, we are also importing a view of the world and of how to deal with international conflict.

The long-range patrol aircraft is a good example of this as well. The LRPA has no major role outside of the U.S. infrastructure it relates to. When hunting for Soviet submarines, an LRPA is a cog in a very big American wheel. Information on the general location of these submarines comes from U.S. underwater sound surveillance systems via U.S. communication satellites. The Canadian LRPA then sets out, using sonobuoys, to determine the location of the Soviet subs more precisely. It passes this information on to American killer subs or aircraft that can attack the Soviet subs with nuclear depth charges. Take away the American infrastructure, and all you have left is a $10 million aircraft with $50 million worth of more or less useless gadgetry on board from which the pilot and copilot might be able to spot a stray fishing trawler or two on a clear day. The military value of the LRPA is tied fully to its integration with American forces.

This has several pernicious consequences. A weapons system is a response to a particular perception of threat. The built-in world view that comes with the LRPA is of a world dominated by East-West rivalries in which the most urgent function is the location of Soviet weapons. In Ottawa, where weapons systems are justified and rationalized, the presence of the LRPA in the Canadian arsenal encourages the propagation of that world view. The purchase may not have been the first choice of military planners, but now it's there and itself becomes the generator of strategic interpretations. The central conflict in the world is the American conflict with the Soviet Union; the most imminent threat is the one we have just paid the major part of the DND capital budget to deal with. As a consumer of U.S. weapons systems, we are also consumers of the U.S. perception of the Soviet threat.

This perception also affects the Canadian Armed Forces and their view of what constitutes a significant military role. Political scientist Michael Tucker has suggested that there is a developing sense that to reach the pinnacle of professional soldiering, you have to be playing in the big game. A soldier's sense of professionalism is related to being involved the globe's main military action. If being a true professional means performing roles and duties within the main event, then there is likely to be a rather low level of enthusiasm for strictly Canadian roles such as sovereignty patrol or even peacekeeping operations. The combination of these factors serves to reinforce a political culture in which Canadian significance is viewed as being directly related to Canada's relationship with the United States.

To develop popular political support for significant levels of military spending and for the development of weapons systems that are increasingly recognized as threatening to the country that deploys them as well as to its adversaries, there must be an overriding perception of sustained threat. Under any circumstances, this obviously has direct effects on social planning, the identification of economic priorities and the political process. In Canada the political and social consequences of this phenomenon may be even more extensive by virtue of the fact that, as a consumer of U.S. weapons systems, Canada has also become a consumer of U.S. perceptions of the Soviet threat.

A Growing Stake in the Arms Trade

Current military production arrangements also affect Canadian foreign policy in several respects. One such consequence is the incentive these arrangements generate for Canada to increase its arms sales to the Third World (see chapter 7). Canada does not yet have a major stake in military exports to the Third World, but it is making determined efforts in that direction. When that stake reaches economically more significant proportions, a fundamental contradiction between significant Canadian foreign policy objectives will have been created — between the objective of increasing exports of Canadian high technology goods and the objective of making a constructive contribution to international peace and security, including the control of the international arms trade.

And, of course, the export of military commodities to the United States also develops for Canada a stake in particular weapons systems, nuclear and conventional. Through the sale of components (see appendix 2), Canada becomes implicated in the full range of American weapons systems and the military policies that they sustain. The fact that Canadian industry makes components for the F-111 long-range bomber obviously does not make Canada responsible for the U.S. raid on Libya, but the Canadian industry's extraordinary dependence on sales to the U.S. and identification as part of the U.S. defence industrial base does imply an overall endorsement and support of the general military policies of the United States. Canada has abdicated the responsibility of a sovereign state to carefully consider and formulate the military policies it advances. That careful consideration takes place in the United States — not in Canada.

The Loss of Canadian Independence

In 1969, when U.S. military intervention in Vietnam was in full flight, the Canadian philosopher George Grant reflected on the political situation of Canada on a continent dominated by a modern imperial power. Noting that "it is clear that in [Vietnam] the American empire has been demolishing a people, rather than allowing them to live outside the American orbit," Grant used Canadian ambivalence towards that intervention as an illustration of how Canada was thoroughly in the American empire, but still interested in being not entirely of it.[44] On the one hand, as Grant wrote, Canadians "are not yet so empty that they can take lightly the destruction of a people."[45] On the other hand, Canadian opposition to the war remained muted by the assumption that "the Canadian way of life" depended substantially upon Canada's maintaining a favoured place within the Western industrial empire centred in the United States.

Current Canadian reaction to the buildup of nuclear weapons contains the same ambivalence. One part of the reaction is the disturbing recognition that the major powers are poised to destroy civilization itself rather than permit the decimation of their respective empires. Having retained sufficient moral sensitivity to be disturbed by the destruction of a people in the late 1960s, Canadians now feel a similar moral unease at the potential destruction of civilization. At the same time, Canadians continue to assume — and perhaps none more so than the country's political leadership — that Canadian well-being is intimately linked to this country's essentially compliant place within an empire. Grant's words remain pertinent almost two decades later: "The very substance of our lives is bound up with the Western empire and its destiny, just at a time when that empire uses increasingly ferocious means to maintain its hegemony."[46]

Yet, despite national foreign and defence policies that actively devalue all sense of Canada as a separate and identifiable actor on the international stage, there remains a collective impulse to assert a Canadian attitude and response to the nuclear buildup that is distinguishable from at least the more crass enunciations of American nuclear doctrine. The broad public support for those modest public ventures that have become immodestly known as Canadian "peace initiatives" can be taken as evidence that there remains a sense of national calling or purpose which can be distinguished from continental destiny and to which Canadians can still appeal — at least in those moments when the two imperial blocs engage in overt military intervention and nuclear war planning, starkly revealing the ferocity of empire.

To the extent that Canadian independence encourages resistance to the ferocity of empire, it is a cause of genuine value. A more constructive Canadian contribution to international peace and security depends upon a sovereign and more independent Canada. Military technology and military industry, however, strengthen the impulse to acquiesce in domination. The present structure of military production in Canada facilitates external influences over Canadian foreign and defence policies. The continental integration of military planning and production has served to reinforce Canadians' perception of their country as being inextricably bound to American destiny and to American fortunes in the world at large, and as being unable to exercise choices and pursue significant independent options in the international community.

This loss of independence is to be lamented because it saps the strength and confidence of those Canadian initiatives which, in appealing to a not yet destroyed sense of Canadian identity and purpose, seek to impose political limits on the hegemonic ambitions and competitions of the superpowers. For the same reason, while Canadians working for a more peaceful and just world order are likely to reject nationalism as a cause of intrinsic value, they must make the recapture of a greater measure of Canadian independence a persistent theme.

The present culture of dependence is inevitably reflected in Canadian defence policy. To the extent that national sovereignty and independence can be measured by a capacity to deploy national defence forces, decide when and how the defence forces are to be mobilized, and produce the equipment those forces need, Canada must be judged to have forfeited a considerable measure of both independence and sovereignty.[47] Canada exercises little discretion over the strategies assumed by the Canadian Armed Forces. In North America, Canadian strategy is continentally-defined — read Washington-defined. Whether in antisubmarine warfare, northern surveillance or early warning, Canada has eschewed a national strategy in favour of selecting roles within U.S. strategy for the continent. In Europe, strategy is nominally alliance-defined, but again, in practice, Washington-defined. Canada, as the case of the cruise missile showed, busies itself more with demonstrations of alliance loyalty than with questions of strategy.

In the second test of sovereignty, national decision-making over troop mobilization, Canada would exercise little control during a war. Canada formally retains the prerogative of a sovereign nation to decide whether or not to commit troops to a conflict. However, its decision would have to be considered a foregone conclusion, meaning that Canada retains very little independence, as distinct from sovereignty, in this area. And after the initial decision was made, Canada would not have much say over the use of its troops in the context of NATO or NORAD.

In the third test, without any doubt, Canada does not have the capacity to supply its own forces. Canada's military manufacturing capability is responsive not to Canadian needs but to the needs of a foreign power; in consequence, Canada is fully import-dependent for the major military equipment which current policy defines as basic requirements.

Ironically, alliance membership and defence agreements are intended to safeguard formal sovereignty and mitigate the loss of independence. Canada preserves formal sovereignty, but independence is another matter. In effect, Canada is a military satellite. Canada's participation in NATO is intended to reduce its dependence on the United States by attaching Canada to a set of countervailing influences. At the formation of NATO, it was neither anticipated nor intended that the U.S. would remain the dominant force within the organization. As it has turned out, however, NATO has become at least as much an instrument of U.S. influence as a means of diffusing it. European states, committed to retaining American support for their collective defence, have managed to acquiesce in American leadership to the extent that the U.S. now holds virtual control over NATO policy.

The aim of American NATO strategy is ostensibly the defence of western Europe, but it has increasingly taken on elements of maintaining and managing America's global conflict with the Soviet Union. Gwynne Dyer has quoted a NATO diplomat as saying: "Don't you know why the Americans are really here? It is to prevent any agreement between Europe and the Soviet Union."[48] In Europe, in other words, Canada has attached its national policies to an alliance that has become substantially the instrument of one superpower for the purpose of managing its global conflict with another superpower. Conceived as a means of disciplining the West's superpower ally, NATO has now become the stick wielded by that superpower.

On the other hand, Canada participates in NORAD on the assumption that the United States will pursue its defence interests within Canadian territory in any event: a formal defence agreement will make it legal, and perhaps even give Canada some influence over how the U.S.

pursues those interests. Michael Tucker calls it a perplexing Canadian paradox.[49] If Canada did not participate in northern air defence, for example, that function would be carried out entirely by the Americans, with an obvious loss of Canadian sovereignty. By entering into formal joint air defence arrangements, Canada actually strengthens its sovereignty — which is not to say the same for its independence.

It is true that alliances between sovereign and independent states can be a means of pursuing autonomously defined national objectives, and as such they do not undermine independence. The case of Canada, unfortunately, is not so simple. So deeply have Canada's military-industrial arrangements undermined this country's capacity for autonomous definition of its own national objectives that even avowed Canadian nationalists seem reluctant to permit Canadian decision-making to produce results sharply at variance with the military attitudes or postures of the American-defined mainstream.

In his book *True North Not Strong and Free*, Peter C. Newman devotes an entire chapter to the proposition that Canada is unique in military matters. Not only are we a nonviolent people, Newman argues, apparently by virtue of both temperament and history, but our unusual geography and political makeup mean that military threats to our security are minimal and that in general our security needs are totally different from those of most other industrial countries. Newman then compares Canadian military expenditures with those of other industrial countries, summoning a show of great indignation about the fact that Canada's military forces and arsenals do not measure up to all others. Its not clear why, if Canada's military/security circumstances are unique, it is not permitted to have a unique approach to national defence.

There is by now a folklore attached to Canadian defence policy that characterizes Canada as militarily weak, bungling, and irresponsible. The mass media habitually portray Canada as being in a neck-and-neck race with Luxembourg for military irrelevance. But if the Canadian Armed Forces have assumed militarily irrelevant roles, it is not because Canada is a minor military spender. By global standards, Canada is no such thing: it is within the top 10 per cent of military spenders in absolute terms and within the top 20 per cent in per capita terms.[50] Even among northern industrialized countries, Canada is within the top third in absolute military spending. (In 1984, only seven out of a list of thirty European and North American countries — Britain, France, East and West Germany, Italy, the Soviet Union, and the United States — exceeded Canada in military spending.[51]) Canada's position as a major military spender should be a sobering truth for people who propose that Canada increase its military spending in order to enhance its diplomatic and political influence. If military budgets bought political influence, Canada's enhanced political influence should have been evident by now.

Obviously, it is not the level of military spending but its nature that counts. Symbolic military gestures in support of the military policies and roles of a superpower do not buy influence; they only demonstrate solidarity. An increase of 1, 2 or 10 per cent will not alter that. Canada's military irrelevance is due to its policy, not to its spending. And that policy cannot be separated from Canada's military production arrangements. The real indictment that can be brought against Canada's arms industry is not that it consciously subverts the policy-making process but that it unconsciously reinforces conventional wisdom about defence and the sources of peace and security.

The maintenance of a defence industry geared to exports — to the supply of foreign defence establishments — leads necessarily towards preference for the familiar and the predictable. If you are serving the American market, for example, you have an interest in being able to predict decisions that affect that market and to avoid surprises. Hence the desire to avoid radical changes and to support familiar policies and equipment requirements. A commitment to the status quo, however, does not build confidence in the future. It is the status quo that has brought us to the contemplation of self-imposed annihilation and to the experience of a daily holocaust of war and famine over large areas of the earth. It is not, to understate the matter, a foundation on which to build the future.

At the same time, when industry and government representatives discuss the development of a more viable and broadly-based military industry in Canada, they conspicuously avoid reference to the international arms race and arms trade. They acknowledge that military exports are pursued in a highly competitive environment, but this is regarded merely as an economic obstacle to overcome, not as evidence that perhaps there is a surfeit of military production on this planet and that we all might be better off if the capacity to build weapons of destruction were underdeveloped rather than overdeveloped. There is also some acknowledgement that any attempt to push Canadian exports of major weapons systems more aggressively might meet with political resistance, but this too is portrayed as a peculiar Canadian eccentricity that needs to be overcome in some way. Sadly, there is little recognition that political opposition to weapons sales might just be based on the perception that what the world needs is not increased weapons production capacity but an increased capacity to meet human needs. It is the desire for that latter capacity that should urgently impel us on the search for new and more promising approaches to peace and security.

9

Exploring the Alternatives: Military Production for a Permanent Canadian Peace Initiative

Military production cannot be justified on economic grounds, but only on military grounds. To the extent that sovereign governments identify military requirements for maintaining national security and contributing to international peace and security, there is a justification for states to pursue military production. But peace and security are the only permissible objectives: no state should encourage or even tolerate military production for economic reasons. Military production and exports obviously have economic consequences, but they cannot legitimately have economic motives. Because they have economic consequences, it is proper that military production, carried out in response to carefully defined military needs, be managed in an economically responsible way. But it is improper for military commodities to be produced in pursuit of economic objectives.

In the late 1980s the international arms trade has become thoroughly commercialized, and the distinction between military and commercial industries is becoming increasingly blurred. Through such features as industrial offset provisions and the production of dual-use technology, arms deals often include strictly civilian dimensions. The widespread use of arms deals to serve economic objectives and the growing integration of weapons production into civilian industry and its needs have made the arms trade more, rather than less, difficult to control. As researchers with the Stockholm International Peace Research Institute have concluded, "commercialisation and privatisation are detrimental to arms control, since control is by definition the responsibility of governments."[1] Since there has so far been no effective control of the arms trade, it is clear that governments have been acting irresponsibly indeed, and central to this irresponsibility is their attempt to use weapons production to address economic, rather than military, problems.

For Canada, a country that for the last two decades has been unsure of its military requirements and roles, military deployments have become largely symbolic, while military production has become simply one of the elements of economic and industrial management. If Canadian irresponsibility in this regard has not yet become wanton, it is not for lack of trying. Canada now consciously pursues military production as an instrument of economic policy, in violation of what should be a fundamental principle: that all military production should grow out of military needs, and all Canadian military production should grow out of Canadian-defined military needs.

Observers concerned with military industrial preparedness — the industry's capacity to meet emergency military mobilization requirements — have made the same point, criticizing the Canadian industry for being insufficiently geared to military needs. As retired General William J. Yost has noted, "the main thrust in developing a Canadian armaments industry by the federal government has been led by the civil departments, not National Defence."[2] Yost argues that the Defence Industry Productivity program is aimed at the development of an industry capable of capturing a larger share of the international market. The focus is not on developing a Canadian defence industrial base in support of Canadian defence requirements because "the primary aim has been to enhance economic growth."[3]

Military production in peacetime should be managed according to the same principles that apply in wartime. In war, the sole purpose of the defence industry is to supply the needs of the national armed forces, and to some extent allied forces, in support of national objectives. Other considerations are disregarded. There is no attempt to produce military goods for which there is no national use, and only a chance of exports, for the purpose of developing an industrial strategy. The goal is to produce the kind of equipment that will meet national objectives in the war effort. Similarly, a peacetime military industry should be solely devoted to supplying the kind of equipment that will meet the national objective of contributing to international peace and security.

The principle that all Canadian military production should grow out of Canadian-defined military needs applies to production for export as much as it applies to production for the Canadian Armed Forces. In other words, Canadian military production cannot simply be allowed to respond to international economic demand. Canadian military commodities should not be exported except in response to a Canadian assessment that such an export represents a responsible contribution to Canada's peace and security objectives — objectives that include the prevention of war, the maintenance of international peace and stability, the peaceful settlement of disputes, and the pursuit of the welfare and security of all people through the promotion of human rights. Obviously, when Canada exports a military commodity, the military requirement for that commodity originates with the recipient. Canada, however, must be in a position to make an independent assessment of the expressed need and to decide whether, given Canadian objectives, production to meet that need represents an appropriate deployment of Canadian industrial resources and skills.

The equipment produced by an industry organized on these principles is likely to be more, rather than less, costly, but that may well be an advantage. According to analysts of the military-industrial-bureaucratic complexes of the superpowers, military policies have been perverted by the insertion of economic incentives, or ulterior motives, into the weapons manufacturing process. Weapons produced without economic incentives attached to them are not as likely to be needlessly acquired. Furthermore, if the wealthy countries have difficulty carrying the burden of their perceived military requirements, it hardly seems appropriate to attempt to transfer some of that cost to other countries through the global marketing of military equipment. This, of course, is not an argument in favour of cost maximization as a deterrent to militarization. Governments bent on military-led aggrandizement do not seem to be effectively deterred by cost. Nor is it an argument against frugality. When countries identify common military requirements through independent assessments, cooperation can lead to important cost savings. It is, however, a warning against the distortions that military exports for economic ends can involve. Perhaps if countries had to bear the full costs of military equipment, unmitigated by exports, they would more urgently pursue nonmilitary means of conflict resolution.

Military Production and Political Independence

Proposing that Canadian defence and foreign policy objectives be made the focus of Canadian military production obviously begs the question of what Canada's legitimate military needs are. In his classic study of Canada-U.S. relations, *Canada and the Reagan Challenge*, political scientist Stephen Clarkson suggests that this question will not be easily resolved:

> To suggest that Canada has to make equipment choices, and therefore strategic choices, implies that the Canadian military have a strategy-making capacity. The practice of the Department of National Defence has been to act as a junior member of the international alliance, initialling strategy documents produced by the Pentagon. While the Department of External Affairs may

not accept the Reagan administration's simplistic cold-warrior view of the Soviet threat, it is not clear whether the Department of National Defence is able to counter the new American line with strategy thinking of its own.[4]

But strategy thinking of our own is urgently required. In the context of the free trade debate, the central issue for Canadians has been defined as "Canada's room for political choice. If Canadians have any collective goals, the most fundamental objective must be to preserve enough autonomy to achieve them."[5] The point applies just as well to Canadian defence and defence production arrangements. Insofar as Canada has any distinguishable peace and security goals — and not only goals, but also distinct ideas on means of achieving those goals — it must retain, or recapture, the capacity for political choice.

It has become the conventional wisdom that "realism" requires the recognition that Canada has few political and economic choices. The prevalence of this form of "realism" is not so much a result of lack of courage as a cultural condition. Since the end of the golden age of Canadian diplomacy, which was symbolized and substantially animated by the late external affairs minister, prime minister and Nobel laureate, Lester Pearson, the rallying cry of this country's foreign policy has been that Canada is incapable of decisions or actions of significance in the international arena. Prime Minister Pierre Trudeau, who assumed Pearson's mantle with a well-publicized disdain for what he regarded as Pearsonian self-delusion about the importance of Canada's role on the world stage, at the end of his political life became a victim of that same disdain. After a decade and a half of attention to the "practical" economic and constitutional conditions of Canada, a foreign policy focused on Canadian trade and economic interests, and a defence policy of benign neglect, Trudeau's parting "peace initiative" proved that his earlier skepticism was well founded.

Trudeau's initiative came in the context of two of the most celebrated recent examples of Canadian submission to U.S. and alliance pressure — support for new intermediate-range nuclear deployments in Europe (pledged by the short-lived Clark government) and permission to test the cruise missile within Canadian borders. While noble in intent and strengthened by Trudeau's own considerable personal commitment, the initiative proved to be a flash in the pan. It was a welcome individual initiative sincerely pursued and a set of credible suggestions and urgings from a person in whom there is interntational interest, but it was not a diplomatic initiative from a country with credibility and influence in the international arena. What was needed was not a Trudeau peace initiative but a Canadian peace initiative — a long-term national strategy to commit this country's considerable resources to the pursuit of a more stable, just and peaceful international order.

There are no easy paths to such an international order, but there are options, and some of these have much greater political currency in countries less able than Canada to act on them. In both Europe and the United States there are advanced debates over security alternatives. A full discussion of these alternatives is inhibited — not prohibited, but nevertheless inhibited — in Canada by the dependent nature of Canada's military and military-industrial arrangements. Canadian defence policy and defence industry are inextricably linked, and the extensive integration of both into American military initiatives is an obstacle to change.

By contrast, a public debate focusing on both practical and visionary alternatives to current arrangements can be a catalyst to change. The question of the kind of defence industry Canada should have, which is our primary concern here, is first and foremost the question of the kind of defence policy Canada should have. And the question of the kind of defence policy Canada should have is the question of how Canada can best arrange for the welfare and security of its people and institutions and contribute to international peace and security. The task is to define positive initiatives through which Canada can work towards these goals.

In Defence of World Order

As noted earlier, there is some truth to the frequent complaint that Canada does not have a "defence industrial base." For while Canada has an industry capable of manufacturing military commodities, it does not have an industrial base to support an independent Canadian defence policy. If Canada continues to build up its capacity to produce military commodities without articulating such a policy, its ability to compete in the international arms trade will be increased, but its ability to act independently in support of a more just and secure world order will be even further diminished.

Throughout the postwar period, it has been assumed that the defence of Canada is dependent on a world order that respects Canada's national boundaries and the right of Canadians to manage their own affairs. Canadian territory is not militarily defensible — not by Canada, and not even by the United States. Instead, Canada's defence rests on the existence of an international community that recognizes and respects the legitimacy of its borders and its right to exist as a sovereign nation. Accordingly, Canada's defence efforts should be directed, not towards the defence of its borders, but towards the strengthening of the just international order on which its existence as a nation depends.

Canada has a clear moral obligation to contribute to the building and nurturing of such a world order. This responsibility is primarily nonmilitary, and is manifested in such areas as disarmament and arms control diplomacy, equitable development, and the like. In the military sphere, in the absence of any direct military threats to Canada, this country's primary responsibility is to help prevent the disintegration of world order wherever it is threatened. In this context, the three foci of current Canadian military policy are Europe, North America and international peacekeeping.

It is Europe where the world's greatest military buildup has taken place, where any overt military engagement is most likely to lead to global nuclear war, and where the disintegration of order would hence be most threatening to the planet as a whole. As the zone between belligerent superpowers, North America is similarly central to the prevention of global nuclear war. And peacekeeping is premised on the dual proposition that regional conflicts can lead to escalation and ultimately to the engagement of the nuclear arsenals of the superpowers or of lesser powers, and that the world's survival ultimately depends on its capacity to develop peaceful means of settling disputes.

It is necessary to examine each of these areas in turn to see whether Canada is using its military instruments effectively, whether these instruments are still part of the solution or have become part of the problem, and whether it is time for radically new approaches. Answering these questions is central to any strategy for the production of military commodities in support of defence needs rather than economic needs.

Sustaining World Order in Europe

Since World War II, Canadians have assumed that what happens in Europe has immediate ramifications for Canadian security. If order disintegrates in Europe, there will be little stability in the rest of the world on which to rely. So Canada has quite properly accepted the responsibility of thinking about and contributing to an enduring peace in Europe. Sooner or later, therefore, Canadian strategists will have to face the increasingly obvious fact that the NATO and Warsaw Pact strategies of piling on more and more destructive power no longer represent a reassurance to the people of Europe and are certainly not a means of resolving conflict on the European continent.

Nuclear weapons, it need hardly be said, cannot sustain a society: they can only destroy it. The two sides to the East-West nuclear confrontation in Europe can clearly see that each has the capacity to destroy the other — that is an objective, observable reality. What is not observable, however, is how much destructive power each side needs to deter the other from using that capacity. There is no level of force that can be objectively defined as sufficient for deterrence. Thus, the European security problem is political — and even psychological — rather than military. It becomes necessary for political leaders to demonstrate that they have the political will to use nuclear weapons if their bluff is called. Since they obviously can't do this directly, they must resort to symbolic gestures. And since weapons are thought to demonstrate resolve, the favoured symbolic gesture is the deployment of still more nuclear weapons. But there being no point of sufficiency, the spiral continues. In the end, the doubts about deterrence remain, and the sense of danger and insecurity escalates.

Conventional wisdom thus proposes conventional weapons as the solution. As the argument goes, if the West had more conventional weapons — at a minimum, parity with the Warsaw Pact — it would no longer need to rely on nuclear weapons, or at the very least could adopt a nuclear no-first-use policy.[6] But even if there were agreed-upon conventional parity, both sides would still claim the need to retain nuclear weapons in the event of a stalemate. In this event, each side would face a choice between abandoning its objectives and reaching for nuclear options. A conventional buildup could theoretically delay the use of nuclear weapons, but only nuclear disarmament can eliminate ultimate reliance on them. Furthermore, it is doubtful that all-out conventional war with today's conventional weapons of mass destruction would be much of an improvement over nuclear war. Says the former U.S. diplomat and arms control specialist George Kennan, "such is now the destructive power of even non-nuclear weapons that a war fought with them, particularly a defensive war presumably conducted largely on our own territory, promises nothing but a degree of devastation that makes a mockery of the very idea of military victory."[7]

Obviously, what is to be defended — that is, protected and preserved — in Europe cannot be defended by the technology of mass destruction. Thus, if Canada is serious about making a genuine contribution to European security, it must surely promote and participate in the search for security arrangements that are capable of protecting and preserving. Taking his lead from the European peace movment's call for a nuclear-free Europe "from Poland to Portugal," the German political scientist

Ulrich Albrecht has suggested a compelling direction the pursuit of such a solution might take, and he has developed this suggestion in some detail.[8] Albrecht explores the idea of a nonnuclear security zone in central Europe — a concept that should be of special interest to Canada inasmuch as this country too is strategically placed on the frontier of the East-West conflict, the only difference being that we host a north-south manifestation of it. Albrecht looks to the Nordic region as a model for central Europe. The Nordic arrangements are based on nonnuclear "differentiated" zones between the two opposing blocs:

> Finland, as the Soviet Union's closest Scandinavian neighbor, serves as a glacis [a medieval term referring to a gentle, even slippery, slope leading from a castle or fortification to open country — in other words, an open area from which enemy forces cannot build up and launch an attack] for the Soviet Union; a neutralist Sweden feathers Finland against undue Soviet pressures while signalling both East and West that any violation of its neutral status will not be acceptable; a third layer of countries, including Denmark and Norway, remains within the Atlantic alliance, and provides the same kind of glacis for the West as Finland provides for the East.[9]

While constituting a threat to no one, these states represent an area of growing economic cooperation and political stability. Their defence obligations do not involve marshalling sufficient force to stop the opposing alliance at the frontier single-handed. But each state does have the obligation to ensure that neither side can use its territory for the purpose of threatening or attacking the rival alliance.

In central Europe, the model would be applied by "Swedenizing" West Germany and "Finlandizing" East Germany. "A differentiated security zone in Central Europe," Albrecht writes, "would provide a glacis for both East and West that would answer to their security needs in a way that current politics cannot. Even though under this scheme a central area of Europe would become neutral, it would nonetheless maintain a defense sufficiently strong to ensure that its territory could not be used for aggressive purposes by either side."[10] Such a task would be made manageable if the neighbouring alliance members on both sides of the neutral zone were denuclearized and largely demilitarized. These countries could not then be used as staging areas by either side, and the neutral countries would be protected from immediate military pressures.

While there is no simple formula available to solve the European security problem, there are directions in which to head in search of the solution. The alliances to date have chosen a dangerous and futile direction, and the most desperate need in Europe is to look in new places. As George Kennan writes:

> It might just be that in a world where the devices of long-range military destruction have proliferated beyond all reason, the greatest security any country can hope to have, imperfect as it is, will be found to lie primarily in its confidence in itself, in its readiness to leave other people alone and to go its own way, in its willingness to accept the sort of social discipline that a civilian-based defence implies — in a stance, in other words, that offers minimal incentive to foreign military intrusion but promises to make things difficult, painful, and unprofitable for any power that decides, nevertheless, to intrude.[11]

Canada, to understate the point, has not been in the forefront of the search for creative alternatives. Its deficiency in this regard is due in no small measure to the Canadian view that this country can make no significant contribution of a military — or any other — nature. The attitude is that because Canada's contribution will never make a decisive difference, Canada need concern itself only with symbolic gestures. As analyst Joel Sokolsky puts it in the context of North American defence, "the prevalent view [in Ottawa] is that Canada cannot make a significant contribution to collective defence, given Canada's small population in comparison with the United States. This view neatly dovetails into the perception that Canada, in order to secure its interests, need only make a symbolic contribution."[12]

It is true that Canada cannot play a decisive role, but in influencing the political environment in which alternatives are sought, Canada could make an important contribution to critical and independent assessments of threat, which are currently dominated by the United States. Superpowers thrive on the assumption of imminent danger — it makes weaker states want to lean more heavily on them and makes it possible to maintain domestic political support for high levels of military spending. Canada, like NATO countries in Europe itself, will make its most enduring contribution to European security by contributing an independent assessment of the Soviet threat, understood within the pursuit of peaceful coexistence with the Soviet Union. A diminished "sense of apprehension" and a more realistic assessment of threat are essential to the creation of an environment more conducive to disarmament and the demilitarization of the European conflict.

The pursuit of these objectives — the relaxation of military tension and the exploration of radical security alternatives — is not aided by Canada's symbolic military gestures in Europe. The idea of withdrawing Canadian forces from Europe is once again working its way into Canadian defence thinking. Such a move must, in fact, be considered inevitable. It makes little sense that a country with a vast territory and a small population should supply troops and equipment in peacetime to a heavily populated continent that is the wealthiest and technologically most advanced region of the world. The idea of withdrawing Canadian troops is generally characterized as highly controversial and potentially devastating to Canadian-European relations. Yet most NATO countries do not station their troops on foreign soil: their troops are deployed at home as a contribution to the collective defence effort. Canada's foreign basing of troops is a holdover from the early years of the alliance when the European partners were in an economically and militarily weakened position. That is obviously no longer the case.

A corollary to withdrawing Canadian troops from Europe and concentrating them in North America should be the exploration of alternatives. The pursuit of genuine alternatives to the present practice of heaping up the means of mass destruction will become a central element of the political debate in Europe over the coming years. As the Manchester *Guardian* suggested, "the issues of neutralism, or a quite new European defence community, will be the issues hammering at the electoral door every time a politician rises to his feet, and nervously clears his throat."[13] Canada should welcome and encourage this debate.

European military strategy must change, and the change will inevitably be towards greater European self-sufficiency. Canadian military production, with or without direct Canadian military involvement in Europe, has nothing to contribute to European military capabilities. The technology needed for European defence, whether in support of NATO's current misguided strategy of amassing the means of destruction or in support of new and more rational alternatives, is readily available in Europe. Canada's contribution is not required. Canadian policy and military production should instead be focused on special requirements related to Canadian territory.

World Order and Canadian Territory

The idea that central Europe could provide a glacis for both East and West has relevance for Canada. Canada brings to the pursuit of global peace and security — that is, the desire and right of people the world over to live in peace in just and participatory societies and to ensure that these conditions are sustainable over time — an extraordinary wealth of resources. Geography has given Canada a place of strategic

,ce as the proverbial ham in the sandwich between conflicting /ers. Natural and industrial resources have produced an ex- ti   iary degree of material wealth. And the people of Canada possess education and skills that are also well above average. These are all resources that Canada can mobilize in support of a just and lasting peace.

Changes in the political and strategic environment are investing Canadian territory with new and perhaps somewhat daunting significance. Canada's territory — notably its air space — and the outer space above it constitute a potential corridor of attack, and as such Canadian territory is also of increasing interest as a place from which to respond to attack. This means that what happens within Canadian territory is likely to have increasing strategic significance. It is Canada's job to see that activity and installations within its borders serve to stabilize the international order. In a climate of superpower nuclear confrontation, Canada must ensure that its territory, resources and skills are used first to ensure that the nuclear weapons that already exist will not be be detonated, and second to advance conditions that will be conducive to the reduction and eventual elimination of these weapons.

Just before World War II, Prime Minister Mackenzie King assured President Roosevelt that Canada would not allow the United States to be attacked via Canada. The by now well-known idea of "defence against help" makes this same point: the United States cannot but view what happens in Canada as vital to its own security, and Canada has a responsibility to ensure that direct military threats to the United States are not either launched from Canadian territory or made possible by virtue of Canadian neglect.

The interests of a more stable world order require that Canadian policy extend this principle so that Canadian territory, resources and skills will not be used to issue threats not only against the U.S. but against any other state as well. International peace and stability are not served by making Canadian territory available to the United States for it to pose direct military threats to the Soviet Union. Canada has acknowledged this principle to some degree and so does not permit the stationing of U.S. (or any other) nuclear weapons in Canadian territory. Instead, Canadian policy towards strategic nuclear weapons has rightly emphasized the importance of using Canadian territory for early warning and thereby for reducing incentives to attack. Canadian territory, resources and skills are nevertheless still used to provide various elements of the infrastructure on which the operation of U.S. strategic nuclear weapons systems depends.

In order to maintain and expand the operations of their nuclear weapons systems, the superpowers have been given access to the territories of other states, and in order to maintain political support for those systems, they actively court their respective allies. It is not an appropriate role for Canada either to provide a physical infrastructure for or to confer political legitimacy on strategic nuclear arsenals. Canadian resources should be used not to add to the burdensome inventory of weapons and to new weapons technology but rather to advance the means of reducing and eliminating those weapons. To do this, Canadians must take charge of their own territory to assure both of this country's neighbours, north and south, that neither is surreptitiously using Canadian territory as a platform from which to threaten the other.

Canada cannot possibly give such an assurance to the satisfaction of either neighbour if it has no demonstrable capacity to carry out the necessary air and sea surveillance. There is no requirement that Canada be able to fend off all intruders in war single-handed. In a Soviet-American war, no military force that Canada would ever be capable of mounting could prevent either country from using Canadian territory if it suited that country's purposes. The crucial question is how Canadian territory is used in peacetime. Do events within Canadian territory build stability and confidence, or instability and edginess? The requirement for policing the use of Canadian territory in peacetime has been referred to as a coast guard–style operation, in the air and at sea. Such an operation can serve the need for peacetime surveillance to ensure that Canadian territory is being used neither to advance nor to undermine the military interests of either of the world's pre-eminent belligerents. For example, Larry Clarke, the head of Spar Aerospace, has proposed a Canadian military satellite to serve the three-ocean frontier: "I think in the year 2000, we must be capable, independent of our allies, of knowing what is going on with respect to our territories, land, airspace over these territories and the adjacent waters."[14]

Reliable air and sea surveillance can preserve Canada as a neutral glacis. This is not a proposal designed to reduce Canadian military expenditures. Surveillance and reconnaissance activity (that is, the capacity to identify and then investigate activities within Canadian territory) requires a broad range of equipment, and such equipment should be the focus of Canadian military production.

Keeping the Peace

The third area of clear Canadian responsibility is in contributing to the control of conflicts in other parts of the world — most urgently where there is danger of such conflicts involving the major powers and escalating into direct confrontation. Peacekeeping is an international institution that has had strong Canadian support. The ability of independent, multilateral forces to intervene constructively in local conflicts, as an alternative to military intervention by major powers in support of their interests, is essential to the maintenance of a more just and stable international environment. Effective peacekeeping can become a form of peacemaking. Local belligerents can be given opportunities to enter into negotiations and pursue other means of conflict management and resolution when they have confidence in international forces to police and monitor ceasefires and temporary stalemates.

However, resources available for Canadian peacekeeping forces are severely limited. Steven Baranyi, a former researcher with the Canadian Institute for International Peace and Security, notes that External Affairs officials are apprehensive about future peacekeeping requests because of the fear that they would lead to shortages in other areas within the Armed Forces.[15] Canada has frequently been called on to provide technical and specialist support for international peacekeeping forces, and this support must come from units and individuals that have been earmarked for other elements of the Canadian Forces. And since replacements are not provided in their absence, peacekeeping operations in fact impose limitations on forces specializing in such areas as communications at bases in Canada.[16] Circumstances are thus not conducive to an interest in and openness to peacekeeping, unless major new resources are directly allocated to a standing peacekeeping force. Peacekeeping operations depend in particular on communications, surveillance and transport equipment, all worthy objects of Canadian military spending and production.

Patrolling and controlling Canadian territory in support of a more stable strategic environment and contributing to the world's ability to peacefully settle its disputes represent two elements of a permanent Canadian peace initiative. Canadian industry should be mobilized to these ends.

Reorganizing the Canadian Arms Industry

There is little doubt that the status quo in the Canadian arms industry cannot last. As currently structured, Canadian military production arrangements have managed the considerable accomplishment of satisfying no one. The Canadian industry complains that the technological and economic benefits of the Defence Production Sharing Arrangements are not what they should be. The government complains that Canada does not have enough indigenous systems capabilities to meet its growing military requirements. Critics claim that the industry is commercially motivated and under insufficient control in its dealings with the United States and other foreign governments. And the U.S. Congress complains that the Canadian industry's privileged access to the U.S. market threatens the interests of American producers.

The last complaint is probably the most pertinent one in that it is the one most likely to erode the status quo. U.S. protectionism represents the most direct threat to the one market on which the Canadian industry most depends. Even more sobering is the fact that in the long run Canadians won't have much say in the matter. Canadians have the capacity to reject defence production sharing with the United States, but they do not have the capacity to keep it going. That is entirely in the hands of the United States. If the Americans believe that it is in their interest, for strategic reasons, to maintain a decentralized North American defence industrial base, they will continue the Defence Production Sharing Arrangements. If they decide they don't need Canada's contribution to that industrial base, they will abandon the DPSA and Canada's preferred access to the U.S. market will end. Since the Reagan arms boom will not go on forever, perhaps Canadians should expect the latter contingency, welcome it, and begin to plan for it. As Gwynne Dyer has put it, "great powers don't have friends, they only have interests, and we're one of America's interests."[17] That means we are also expendable.

The conflict between the Canadian interest in access to the U.S. market and the interests of the U.S. military industry will very soon become sharper. This is not to say that the Pentagon's interests are the same as the industry's or that the administration would easily yield to such protectionist pressure. The Pentagon, as we have noted, takes rather a longer view of the arrangements. With perhaps a growing interest in Canadian territory for air and space strategic defence planning, the Pentagon is concerned with maintaining close Canada-U.S. cooperation, and will continue to see the integration of the defence industry as a means towards policy integration. But as U.S. military expenditures slow down, and as the U.S. industry develops a more noticeable surplus capacity, the Pentagon's protection of the Canadian industry will become more and more difficult. The political price for this privilege granted to Canadian industry is likely to rise in direct proportion to the perceived economic cost of the DPSA to the United States. So unless Canada is prepared to abandon all claim to military independence, some change is inevitable.

The most popular alternative to the present DPSA is an arrangement promoted by Barney Danson when he was minister of national defence in the late 1970s. In this plan, the industry would still be based on exports but the emphasis would be placed on major systems. In 1977 Danson outlined his proposal in the following terms:

> It would make economic sense if Canada were able to develop and build certain of the equipment needed jointly by the two countries. If the United States would agree to purchase Canadian-made equipment to fill all its needs for a particular item, Canada would be in a position to buy large defence items off-the-shelf from U.S. plants and not to have to insist on specific off-setting contracts as a precondition. There would be less duplication of research and development, no added costs for Canada in setting up production lines for its own short-run needs, a North American standardization of military products and Canada would have an assured market for a limited range of high technology goods.[18]

The Senate Committee on Foreign Affairs, which was studying Canada-U.S. relations at the time, agreed in principle with Danson's approach, but was "not optimistic regarding its potential as a solution to the growing problem."[19] The committee was justified in its lack of optimism. The attempt to build major weapons systems on the strength of the U.S. market was the strategy of the Avro Arrow. The Americans were not then prepared to buy major weapons systems from a foreign supplier, and they would not be prepared to do so now — unless of course Canada was willing to give up sufficient independence so that it would not be considered a foreign supplier.

More recently, John Sheppard, former chairman of the Science Council of Canada and now chairman of Leigh Instruments Ltd., has promoted a similar solution. Sheppard charges that Canada's engineering competence was "traded away in the Canada-U.S. DPSA in return for the right to bid on components of systems developed" in the U.S. He rejects a "go-it-alone" approach as impractical, and calls for a renegotiated DPSA under which "each country would develop systems for the other's markets."[20] Says Sheppard: "Canada, for example, would buy F-18s from the United States without investing in unproductive offset deals. In return, the United States would agree to buy systems Canadians would develop for their own use and for U.S. requirements."

It is not clear what makes this a "practical" option, given traditional American refusal to import major systems. Sheppard also repeats one of the great articles of faith of Canadian high tech promoters: "The defence link is a critical first step toward regaining the advantage we once held in the STOL/utility aircraft market and preserving the slim lead Canadair enjoys with the Challenger and military drones."[21] This is quintessential blind faith. It is obvious why sales of military surveillance drones depend on a defence link, but there is no reason why the same reasoning should apply to commercial business jet sales.

Another popular solution that has been advocated is "world product mandating." The idea is for a foreign parent firm to grant a subsidiary the world rights to a particular product or technology, along with full autonomy to develop its own products. Whatever their merit in general, world product mandates (WPMs) are a particularly undesirable model for the production of military commodities. WPMs rely on a worldwide export market. Subsidiaries that have been granted WPMs cannot afford to be politically selective and thus forgo sales: no transnational parent company would tolerate that kind of selectivity. The subsidiary would have to try to serve the world market, without political interference (implying that there would be pressure to relax military export guidelines), or else risk losing the mandate.

All of these "solutions" are based not on Canadian military requirements but on an enduring international military market — that is, an enduring arms trade. The world doesn't need a Canadian military industry to supply the arms race. The world does need responsible Canadian peace initiaitves, and Canada needs an industrial base to support them.

New Guidelines for Exports

The mobilization of Canadian industry in support of a "permanent Canadian peace initiaitve" does not settle the question of whether there should be any exports of military commodities. Exports of military commodities are, as noted earlier, traditionally justified on three primary grounds: economic benefits to the exporting country; the strategic interests of the exporting country; and the right of all countries to self-defence, which means that countries without domestic production capabilities must have access to weapons from other sources.

The economic argument can be rejected out of hand. Prosperity is not an adequate reason for the export of weapons of war. The profit motive may be a sufficient justification for selling jewellery, but it won't do for military goods. The second rationale, the strategic interests of the supplier, is really the economic argument dressed up. In its most elaborate costume, however, the strategic argument also claims that arms sales are a means of maintaining legitimate governments in power. It is argued, for example, that human rights and democracy are advanced by expanding the sphere of influence of the democratic West. With this assumption in hand, it is easy to rationalize policies of military aid to Third World states as a means of reinforcing political and economic relationships with Western democracies, led by the United States.

The evidence, however, points in another direction. Military state force is more typically associated with a decline in respect for human rights and democratic participation and with an increase in repression. Democratic values are not served by extending the military reach of the major powers or by enhancing the military strength of domestic governments. In fact, both foreign military intervention and increased diversion of resources to domestic military and paramilitary institutions tend to contribute to repression, not undermine it. On the basis of contemporary research, Miles Wolpin concludes that repression is more likely to be undermined by ending foreign military intervention, reducing the flow of resources to military and paramilitary institutions, restructuring external debt obligations to lessen the financial burden and reduce austerity in Third World countries, encouraging reforms that promote greater social equality in these countries, and strengthening the effectiveness of civilian control over military establishments.[22]

The only genuine argument in support of military exports is the right of self-defence. This right can be addressed through joint production arrangements that preserve the requirement that all Canadian military production grow out of Canadian-defined military needs — that is, military needs defined by responsible Canadian civilian authorities who are held accountable through the Canadian political process. In joint production, two governments consider common needs and take full responsibility for the ultimate destination and use of their military goods.

Since Canada has legitimate military equipment requirements, and since there are also likely to be other countries with similar requirements, there is little doubt that the burden of acquiring such equipment could be reduced through joint ventures. If two countries come to similar conclusions about requirements for a particular piece of equipment, both can save money through longer production runs and the elimination of costly duplication in production facilities. Two coastal states, for example, are likely to share requirements for maritime surveillance aircraft and ships. Reducing the burden of these requirements would serve the interests of all concerned. But joint production still requires the transfer of military commodities from one state to another, and the conditions under which such transfers can be undertaken still must be defined.

The following suggestions are intended to restrict Canadian military exports severely while acknowledging the need for an industry to supply Canada's legitimate military equipment needs. Rejecting the current practice of marketing the weapons of war as an entreprenuerial venture, they point to criteria according to which military commodity transfers from one country to another through joint production arrangements should be controlled and regulated.

1. The first, and most fundamental, requirement is that *military production and sales should not be pursued as a commercial enterprise.* Military production must be a publicly-controlled industrial activity confined to responding to publicly-defined military needs. Military industries should not have the freedom to respond to market conditions. No person or company has a "right" to manufacture and sell weapons, any more than there is a fundamental "right" to manufacture and sell other forms of contraband.

In special circumstances, publicly controlled and defined, there is a need for products that are not allowed to be traded under normal market conditions, and so arrangements must be made for their manufacture and distribution. The production and sale of the weapons of war is obviously a defensible human endeavour only in such special circumstances. In the absence of international laws and institutions to maintain order and equitable relations, nationally-based defence forces are granted legitimacy. This legitimacy is not intrinsic; it derives only from the particular context. The international transfer of arms thus requires controls that would be unacceptable if applied to trade in most commercial goods. To reinforce this distinction, Canada should not permit privately initiated military production and exports.

2. In keeping with the noncommercial nature of military production, *military transfers from Canada to another country should be permitted only within a government-to-government arrangement.* As argued above, military production in Canada, whether for domestic or foreign purposes, should grow exclusively out of publicly-defined Canadian requirements. In undertaking a joint venture with another country, the Canadian government would have to assess the military and strategic need for any military commodities that would involve Canadian resources. Only when responsible Canadian authorities, subject to public scruti-

ny, were satisfied that a genuine military requirement existed in the other country should Canada enter into joint arrangements for the supply of the military commodities in question. And the supply of those commodities should be governed by strict guidelines, as sketched below.

3. *Canada's military transfer policy should be "directed" rather than "restrictive."* Current export control guidelines call for "close control" of the export of military goods and technology to "countries involved in or under imminent threat of hositlities."[23] Premised on the principle of not getting involved in someone else's conflict, this guideline articulates what is referred to as a "restrictive" export policy. However, as noted in chapter 7, the evidence suggests that the policy is less than rigorously observed. When other factors such as economic interests come into play — notably in the case of Indonesia — the fact of the country's involvement in conflict is overridden. Canadian military commodities are then shipped to countries in conflict, but the Canadian government, which has approved the transfers, takes no reponsibility for introducing new military capability into those conflicts.

The responsible course is to acknowledge that weapons of war in fact end up on battlefields and that the suppliers of those weapons bear responsibility for them. It is hardly logical to be in the business of supplying weapons of war and then to insist that they can't go to countries at war. It is, after all, the purpose of weapons to be used in war, and to say that you sell weapons only to countries not at war is self-delusion on a grand scale. The manufacturer of weapons has a responsibility to assess the political and military causes and purposes those weapons will support and hence to decide in which wars and on which side they are to be used. It is a matter of putting your political money where your economic mouth is.

The principle underlying a "directed" arms transfer policy is the same one that joint production endeavours seek to address: that weapons transfers are to be deliberate government acts in support of articulated defence and foreign policy objectives. Weapons transfers should not be private acts for which there is no public accountability and for which public authorities do not take political reponsibility. If you are going to sell a weapon, you had better find the courage to defend that weapon's use. If you are unsure of its ultimate use and uncertain that you could support it, then don't sell the weapon. In this light, a directed policy means that the transfer of a weapon should be the result of a conscious government initiative subject to public scrutiny, with the supplier accepting full reponsibility for its ultimate destination and use.

Adopting a directed arms transfer policy creates the need to decide in what specific situations Canada should become a supplier of military commodities to countries in conflict. In particular, it raises the question of whether Canada should supply arms to a Third World country threatened by the overt or covert military actions of its neighbours and their big-power sponsors. A plausible argument could be advanced, for instance, in support of Canada's providing military equipment to equip Mozambique to deal more effectively with South African-supported destabilization efforts. How should Canada respond to such a proposition?

In general, Canadian industry should not be mobilized in response to the defence needs of other states. It has never been Canada's vocation to be an international supplier of arms in a kind of global strategic management exercise, and it is not a vocation that Canada should pursue, no matter how noble the cause. Canada could not begin to supply Mozambique or any other country with the range of combat equipment that might be required to achieve a military victory over its adversaries. Even to try to acquire such a capability, Canada would have to amass a military production capacity far out of proportion to Canadian needs. This industry could be sustained and kept in readiness to respond to whatever circumstances might arise only through the large-scale manufacture of combat equipment for the international market. And to sell these products in a highly competitive environment, Canada would have to relax export controls to the extent of being willing to sell simply to the highest — or more likely, in today's market, the lowest — bidder.

The circumstances under which the export of military commodities should be considered legitimate are highly selective. In the case of Mozambique — assuming that the other main criterion, that of human rights, is satisfied — Canada could and should export a military commodity if both countries identify a need for that commodity. Canadian military production, responding first to Canadian military needs, can quite properly be part of joint procurement arrangements with another country under such conditions, provided that the other conditions of a Canadian arms transfer policy suggested here are honoured.

4. In order to take full responsibility for the weapons it manufactures, *Canada should control the ultimate destination of military commodities produced in this country*. The current policy requires the importer of a Canadian military commodity to provide assurances about the end use of that commodity. Under this requirement, the importer assures Canada that the commodity will be used within the recipient country for the

purpose for which it has been imported, and that it will not be shipped on to another country in violation of Canadian export guidelines. It sounds good, but in practice it leaves a hole through which you could drive, if not a tank, then an awful lot of microcircuits, shock absorbers and assorted components. As appendix 1 indicates, the guideline represents something less than meticulous control. A large proportion of Canadian exports are components that are used for the purpose of manufacturing weapons systems. Once the component has been used for the purpose of manufacturing, Canadian control over its ultimate destination ends.

The government defends this policy on the grounds that it opposes the practice of extraterritoriality — that is, the application of one country's laws within another country's jurisdiction. In fact, however, Canada does practise extraterritoriality. If a Canadian helicopter engine is sold to a firm in Italy, the Italian firm, which now owns the engine, is not permitted to sell that engine to another country without Canadian permission — a clear instance of the extraterritorial application of Canadian law. It is only if the Italian firm builds the engine into an aircraft that Canada no longer exercises control over its ultimate destination. But engines are made to be used in aircraft, so it is not clear why Canada should exercise control over their ultimate destination only so long as they are not actually used for their real purpose. It makes no sense for Canada to refuse to sell a military helicopter engine directly to Iraq, but to permit the sale of that engine to Iraq if it first goes to Italy to become part of a military helicopter.

A serious criticism of close control over components is that it is impractical: how can you possibly keep track of every little piece that may somewhere end up in a weapon? In fact, however, such detailed accounting already takes place, not for the purpose of controlling the destination of components but for the purpose of tabulating military exports. Products are included under the provisions of the Canada-U.S. Defence Production Sharing Arrangements if they are linked to a specific military contract. Thus, every microcircuit or shock absorber must be linked to a military contract to be included under the DPSA for statistical purposes and to be permitted to cross the border duty free. Detailed accounting is possible: if it is carried out for statistical purposes, presumably it could also be carried out for export control purposes.

5. Under all circumstances, *Canada should refuse to transfer any military commodities to states known to be regular and persistent violators of human rights.* The current policy does not prohibit, or even require "close control" over, the sale of military commodities to human rights

violators if "it can be demonstrated that there is no reasonable risk that the goods might be used against the civilian population."[24] Weapons that are not likely to be used against civilians, such as maritime patrol aircraft, can be supplied to human rights violators.

This policy is based on the assumption that the supply of military commodities to a regime does not express overall approval of that regime and its policies, and is supported by the argument that it is perfectly legitimate to trade with a country with whose policies one disagrees. It is not clear, however, that this basic principle should apply to commodities that contribute to the overall strength and capability of the very institution, the military, that is frequently most directly responsible for or supportive of the human rights violations.

According to its most recent policy statement on the matter, the Department of External Affairs now maintains a list of human rights violators to whom the export of equipment that is likely to be used against civilians is to be "closely controlled."[25] However, not only is the list secret, but there is also no public accounting for the criteria or the information according to which states are added to or removed from the list. Updating the list should be an annual public exercise. In a joint submission to External Affairs Minister Clark during the department's internal review of export control policy, the Taskforce on the Churches and Corporate Responsibility and Project Ploughshares called for an annual public review of the observance of human rights in countries of particular interest to Canada. Because the human rights records of countries change, annual reviews by Parliament would be the best means of determining whether any adjustments in Canada's dealings with these countries were warranted.

Any review of the human rights performance of a country must include an examination both of human rights violations perpetrated by the government of that country and of violations tolerated by it. Annual hearings should bring together relevant information gathered by the Department of External Affairs and include testimony from national and international organizations concerned with human rights. And the Canadian government should place before the public the sources of the data it uses when it makes judgements about violations of internationally accepted human rights.[26]

6. In order to regain control over its own affairs, *the Canadian government should withdraw from the Canada-U.S. Defence Production Sharing Arrangements and deal with military exports to the United States, as with other military sales, through joint production and the export permit system.* Under the current arrangements, export permits are not required for the

sale of military commodities to the United States, regardless of whether they go directly to the Department of Defense or to private defence contractors. This means that the bulk of Canadian military production operates outside direct government scrutiny. Military production in Canada for the United States — which, as we have seen, represents well over half of all Canadian military production — does not grow out of Canadian-defined needs or policies and is not subject to Canadian decision-making. Placing military exports to the United States under the export permit system would ensure that Canada's declared export control policy applies to all Canadian-built military commodities.

In this way, the Canadian government would be able to make judgements about the appropriateness of the military commodities Canada produces. Under such a policy Canada would, for example, have to deal with the inconsistencies in its current policies relating to nuclear weapons. While claiming to be a non–nuclear-weapons state, Canada currently places no restrictions on the production of components for nuclear weapons systems. Canadian policy prohibits the sale of fissionable materials for weapons purposes, at least in theory (there are some genuine concerns about how effectively the policy is applied), but there is no prohibition on industrial participation in nuclear weapons systems. At the very least, it is incumbent on Canada, even in the context of its current policy which supports nuclear alliances, to indicate which nuclear weapons it finds stabilizing and acceptable and which it finds destabilizing and therefore unacceptable. At the moment, Canada says to the United States: you decide, and we'll help build whatever the market sends our way.

It would be consistent with Canada's policy prohibiting the possession of nuclear weapons and the export of fissionable materials for weapons purposes to extend that prohibition to industrial materials destined for nuclear weapons systems. Such a prohibition would be faithful not only to Canada's nonproliferation policy but also to its declared opposition to the export of military commodities likely to be used against civilians, nuclear weapons by definition being designed to be used primarily against civilians.

7. For purposes of implementing control measures, *the Canadian government should define a military commodity as a commodity purchased by a military force or agency*. For statistical purposes the Department of External Affairs already uses this definition (with the obvious exceptions of commodities such as foodstuffs and building materials for housing). In its policy announced in September 1986, however, the government

introduced a distinction between military and nonmilitary commodities purchased by military forces, with trucks and communications equipment among the examples of nonmilitary goods. The purpose of the distinction is to lessen the control over certain types of commodities. But the distinction is deceptive, ignoring the nature of modern military forces, and the argument the government uses in its support is specious. "We see no reasons," says the government statement, "for Canadian companies not to supply non-military goods, since these goods can be supplied by many countries, yet they add nothing to the offensive or belligerent capacity of the military or para-military organization."[27]

The relevance of the fact that others can supply such equipment is not immediately obvious. Many people are capable of supplying heroin on the street, but that fact would not provide a very effective defence for an accused dope pedlar. And to suggest that communications equipment and trucks do not contribute to an offensive or belligerent capacity is just plain wrong. For weapons to be used effectively in battle — whether in international war, civil war or repression — military forces clearly require much more than that which goes bang. Trucks haul troops to their assignments, communications facilities indicate targets, and so on.

All equipment purchased by a military institution improves that institution's capacity to meet its objectives. Therefore, it must be regarded as military equipment and controlled accordingly. In addition, nonmilitary equipment sold to nonmilitary customers, which nevertheless has direct military applications, requires the same control. The Department of External Affairs has defined such military-related and strategic goods as "equipment and technologies of a commercial civilian nature and design that could have military application." It cites as examples of such commodities "computers, telecommunication systems, certain civilian aircraft and avionics equipment, sophisticated industrial machinery, etc."[28]

8. No system to control the transfer of military commodities is likely to work effectively or enjoy public confidence if it is carried out in secret. Therefore, *it is essential that there be full public disclosure of military and military-related exports and that these exports be subject to an annual public review.* The main objection to full disclosure of the transfer of Canadian military commodities is that it would violate the commercial confidentiality of such transactions and would adversely affect the competitiveness of companies engaged in the manufacture and sale of

these commodities. A second objection is that the recipient country frequently requires that military transfers be kept secret and disclosure would make many sales impossible.

Both concerns have some validity: disclosure would indeed inhibit competitiveness and make some sales impossible. For that very reason, however, both arguments also support the case for full disclosure — the whole point of disclosure being restraint. Military transactions are not like all other transactions: they are of a special character and require special government intervention and control. In order to assure that political and strategic considerations take precedence over commercial considerations, *access to information legislation should be amended to require that none of the exemptions under the act apply to disclosure of the export of military commodities from Canada.*

9. The control of the arms trade has become urgent and pressing, and *the Canadian government should undertake vigorous diplomatic initiatives to place the arms trade on the international arms control agenda.* The only thing that can be said with certainty about the control of the arms trade is that to date nothing has worked. As noted in chapter 1, there are many reasons for this, notably economic incentives for the supplier and the persistence of internal and international conflict. There are few prospects for substantive change in either of these conditions. Some countries will always find benefit in arms sales, and some countries will always find occasions to use the arms offered for sale. This is the unpromising environment in which arms transfers must be controlled.

But if the environment is hostile to arms transfer control, it is nevertheless amenable to political shaping. There are, after all, also many economic and military reasons to curb arms transfers. Pre-eminent among measures that would alter the political environment in which arms transfers take place would be open reporting on all production and transfers of weapons. As the Stockholm International Peace Research Institute has put it, "secrecy promotes suspicion."[29] At the same time, full disclosure would promote greater public awareness of the dimensions of the problem and more vigorous public debate.

External Affairs Minister Joe Clark, however, has rejected the recommendation of the joint Parliamentary Committee on Canada's International Relations that Canada seek international support for an "international system to register exports and imports of weapons and munitions as one means of controlling the expanded trade in conventional weapons." In rejecting the proposal, Clark argued that "there is little evidence that transparency inhibits either weapons exporters or importers."[30] However, Clark did not give any basis for this conclusion, and it seems a curious position for a government that maintains extreme secrecy over its own weapons dealings on the grounds that disclosure would impede Canada's ability to compete. Full public scrutiny and debate of the international arms trade requires full disclosure. There is no easy way to control arms transfers, but secrecy makes the job even more difficult. At a minimum the secrecy should be removed, but beyond that first step, Canada should encourage international attention to the issue.

Various proposals for international controls have been developed. These proposals are focused on both recipient and supplier states and involve such measures as controlling weapons sales to particular regions, controlling the introduction of new military technologies into particular regions, basing weapons transfers exclusively on security considerations and limiting purely commercial sales. There is now no forum in which specific proposals of this nature are being considered. It is time to put the arms trade on the arms control agenda, and Canada could be a catalyst.

10. Inasmuch as people believe that their economic well-being depends in part on arms sales, *it is the responsibility of governments to introduce measures to minimize economic reliance on military production and provide for an orderly transition away from commercial military production and sales.* As long as military production is characterized not as a burden but as an endeavour with positive economic effects, the effort to control commercial military production will be all the more difficult. It is here that the issue of industrial conversion can enter the debate. Industrial conversion is first and foremost a political strategy to demonstrate that we as a society need not be locked into permanent military spending increases and weapons sales in order to save our economic skins. The point of industrial conversion is to show that alternative paths in fact produce fewer costs and promise more effective means of enhancing the economic security of the people of Canada.

The exploration of conversion in the Canadian setting serves at least two basic objectives. First, assuming that Canada as an independent sovereign state has legitimate military requirements and obligations, it is necessary to develop industrial support for those requirements in a way that is least damaging to the welfare of Canadians. The present structural arrangements under which Canadian military equipment is produced impose unacceptable political and economic costs on Canada. Industrial conversion, therefore, can be an aid to altering the present damaging military production arrangements and developing production and procurement policies that better serve Canadian interests and responsibilities.

Second, whatever Canada's current military equipment requirements might be, military production must by definition be considered temporary. Military production is undertaken for specific military purposes, and is never to be undertaken for its own sake or in pursuit of economic objectives such as jobs and exports. All military production should be carried out on the assumption that when the particular equipment needs in question are met, the human and material resources devoted to military purposes will be redirected towards meeting human needs. Industrial conversion, therefore, should be an integral element of all military production; in this way, continued military production will not be perceived as essential to the survival of the affected industrial firms or to society's overall economic well-being. The aim of industrial conversion is to dismantle an institutionalized military industry that influences and distorts assessments of military needs and actually drives military procurement, depends for its survival on regularly repeated military contracts, and relies on foreign sales that undermine constructive national policies related to peace and justice.

Economic dependence on such a military industry can be reduced in two ways: by finding new nonmilitary markets for commodities that have civilian as well as military applications, and by developing new products to replace commodities whose applications are exclusively or primarily military. In Canada, an example of a company that could follow the first strategy is Pratt and Whitney Aircraft. Its engines, while produced primarily for civilian aircraft, can also be used for military aircraft. What is required in this case is not plant or industrial conversion but the rather more difficult task of finding sufficient civilian markets to make up for lost military sales. An example of a plant that would follow the second strategy is the General Motors facility in London, Ontario, that produces light armoured vehicles. The life of that plant now depends upon winning export orders for armoured vehicles, but the plant's technology and the skills of its workers are clearly applicable to a wide variety of civilian pursuits. Conversion, therfore, would involve developing proposals for new products that would employ those resources and — again the more difficult task — developing reliable markets for these new products in order to reduce reliance on military orders while preserving and even increasing jobs.

The development of reliable civilian markets, either for dual-purpose goods or for new commodities introduced to replace military production, could be encouraged by changes in federal policies related to military exports and subsidies for those exports. The government could, for example, drop its role as a sales and promotional agent for the military industry, eliminate military-oriented incentive grants (such as the Defence Industry Productivity program), bring in stricter guidelines for military exports, and concentrate its export promotion on civilian goods and markets.

Canadians are not without choices. On the one hand, this country has the technical and financial resources to become a strong competitor in the race to make the weapons of war widely available in an unrestrained global arms bazaar. On the other hand, it has the political and moral resources to resist dealing in weapons for the economic fun of it. Canadians currently face a choice between these two paths. Official policy is eager to move us towards increased involvement as an arms merchant, but Canadians know that the world already has an abundance of arms merchants. In shorter supply are countries committed to weapons restraint and control of the arms trade. Such a commitment would be a worthy vocation for Canada. Rejection of the arms-for-profit strategy of the many will be a crucial step towards energetic and unencumbered Canadian diplomatic initiatives in support of international arms trade control and towards the recapture of Canadian sovereignty and independence in military and defence affairs.

Appendix 1
Destination of Canadian Military Components[1]

Recipient Country	Weapon System	Supplier Country	Canadian Component
Algeria	C-130H-30 transport a/c	USA	-navigational instruments -aircraft landing gear components
Angola	PC-7 turbo-trainer a/c	Switzerland	-PWC PT6A-25A turboprop engines
Argentina	Bell model 212 (UH-IN) helicopter	USA	-PWC PT6T-3B turbo twin pacs engines
Bahrain	1. F-4 Phantom II fighter a/c	USA	-aircraft landing gear components -aircraft air conditioning/heating -relays and solenoids
	2. F-5E/F Tiger a/c	USA	-aircraft landing gear components
	3. MGM/BGM-71A TOW antitank missile	USA	-guided missile remote control
Brazil	1. UH-60A helicopter	USA	-transmission parts -engine instruments -ballasts & lampholders
	2. LVTP-7A1 armoured amphibious assault vehicles	USA	-rocket & pyrotechnics launchers

Recipient Country	Weapon System	Supplier Country	Canadian Components
Chad	C-130H Hercules transport a/c	USA	- navigational instruments - aircraft landing gear components
Chile	1. EMB-120 military transport a/c	Brazil	-PWC PW 118 turboprop engine
	2. King Air C-90 trainer a/c	USA	-two PWC PT6A-21 turboprop engines
	3. Westland Lynx helicopter	UK	-transmission gears
Colombia	C-130 H Hercules transport a/c	USA	-navigational instruments -aircraft landing gear components
Egypt	1. F-16 Fighting Falcon a/c	USA	-maintenance/repair of a/c components -aircraft air conditioning/heating -switches -misc. communications equipment -radar equipment -flight instruments
	2. M109 A2 155 mm self-propelled howitzer	USA	-guns over 150 mm through 200 mm
	3. M60 main battle tank	USA	-vehicle furniture and accessories
	4. M113-A2 armoured personnel carrier	USA	-vehicle furniture and accessories

Recipient Country	Weapon System	Supplier Country	Canadian Components
Egypt cont'd	5. EMB-312 Tucano trainer a/c	Brazil	-PWC PT6A-25C turboprop engines
	6. M1M-23B Hawk land-mobile surface-to-air missile	USA	-components
	7. M1M-72F Chaparral surface-to-air missile	USA	-hybrid microcircuits for guidance control system -launcher components
El Salvador	1. C-130H Hercules transport a/c	USA	-navigational instruments -aircraft landing gear components
	2. UH-1 Iroquois (Bell model 205) helicopter	USA	-airframe structural components -gas turbines and jet engines
Guyana	EMB-111 maritime patrol a/c	Brazil	-PWC PT6A-34 turboprop engine
Honduras	1. C-130H Hercules transport a/c	USA	-navigational instruments -aircraft landing gear components
	2. EMB-312 Tucano trainer a/c	Brazil	-PWC PT6A-25C turboprop engine
	3. EMB-111 maritime patrol a/c	USA	-PWC PT6A-34 turboprop engine
Indonesia	1. UH-IN helicopter (Bell model 212)	USA	-PWC PT6T-3B turbo twin pacs engine

Recipient Country	Weapon System	Supplier Country	Canadian Components
Indonesia cont'd	2. T-34C-1 (Beech) trainer a/c	USA	-PWC PT6A-25 turboprop engines
	3. Model 412 helocopter (Bell Textron)	USA	-PWC PT6T-3B turboshaft engines
Iran	PC-7 turbo-trainer a/c	Switzerland	-PWC PT6A-25A turboprop engine
Iraq	1. EMB-312 Tucano trainer a/c	Brazil (via Egypt)	-PWC PT6A-25C turboprop engine
	2. AB-212 ASW helicopter	Italy	-PWC PT6T-6 engine
Jordan	1. AH-IS Cobra (model 209) helicopter	USA	-airframe structural components -research & development, aircraft engines -aircraft air conditioning/heating
	2. M60-A3 main battle tank	USA	-vehicle furniture and accessories
	3. M-109 155 mm self-propelled howitzer	USA	-guns over 150 mm through 200 mm
	4. MGM/BGM-71A TOW antitank missile	USA	-guided missile remote control
Korea, South	1. F-4 Phantom II fighter a/c	USA	-aircraft landing gear components -aircraft air conditioning/heating -relays and solenoids

Recipient Country	Weapon System	Supplier Country	Canadian Components
Korea, South cont'd	2. F-16 Fighting Falcon a/c	USA	-maintenance/repair of aircraft components -aircraft air conditioning/heating -switches -misc. communications equipment -radar equipment -flight instruments
	3. Model 412 helicopter (Bell Textron)	USA	-PWC PT6T-3B turboshaft engines
	4. LVTP-7A1 armoured amphibious assault vehicle	USA	-rocket & pyrotechnics launchers
	5. M1M-23B Hawk land-mobile surface-to-air missile	USA	-components
Kuwait	1. M-113 A2 armoured personnel carrier	USA	-vehicle furniture & accessories
	2. MGM/BGM-71A TOW anti-tank missile	USA	-guided missile remote control
Lebanon	1. M-113-A2 armoured personnel carrier	USA	-vehicle furniture & accessories
	2. M-248 main battle tank	USA	-engine fuel system components

Recipient Country	Weapon System	Supplier Country	Canadian Components
Lebanon cont'd	3. M-60 main battle tank	USA	-vehicle furniture and accessories
Lesotho	AB-412 Griffon helicopter	Italy	-PWC PT6T-3B engine
Liberia	1. IAI-201 Arava transport a/c	Israel	-PWC PT6A-34 turboprop engine
	2. IAI-202 Arava transport a/c	Israel	-PWC PT6A-36 turboprop engine
Libya	1. EMB-312 Tucano trainer a/c	Brazil	-PWC PT6A-25C turboprop engine
	2. EMB-111 maritime patrol a/c	Brazil	-PWC PT6A-34 turboprop engine
	3. EMB-121 Xingu transport a/c	Brazil	-PWC PT6A-135 turboprop engine
	4. Aeritalia G-222 transport a/c	Italy	-PMS-5 projected map display
Malaysia	1. PC-7 turbo trainer a/c	Switzerland	-PWC PT6A-25A turboprop engines
	2. F-5E/F Tiger 2 trainer a/c	USA	-aircraft landing gear components
	3. A-4E Skyhawk fighter/bomber	USA	-speed brakes and flags
Mexico	PC-7 turbo trainer a/c	Switzerland	-PWC PT6A-25A turboprop engines
Morocco	1. M-60 main battle tank	USA	-vehicle furniture & accessories
	2. C-130H Hercules transport a/c	USA	-navigational instruments -aircraft landing gear components

Recipient Country	Weapon System	Supplier Country	Canadian Component
Morocco cont'd	3. Super King air transport a/c	USA	-PWC PT6 turbo prop engines
Nigeria	1. C-130H-30 Hercules transport a/c	USA	-navigational instruments
	2. Aeritalia G-222 transport a/c	Italy	-PMS-5 projected map display
	3. Westland Lynx helicopter	UK	-transmission gears
	4. CH-47C Chinook helicopter	USA	-castings for retrofits -engine overhaul
Oman	C-130H Hercules transport a/c	USA	-navigational instruments -aircraft landing gear components
Pakistan	1. F-16A Fighting Falcon a/c	USA	-maintenance/repair of a/c components -aircraft air conditioning/heating -switches -misc. communications equipment -radar equipment -flight instruments
	2. AH-IS helicopter (model 209)	USA	-airframe structural components -research and development, aircraft engines -aircraft air conditioning/heating
	3. M-109 155 mm self-propelled howitzer	USA	-guns over 150 mm through 200mm

Recipient Country	Weapon System	Supplier Country	Canadian Component
Pakistan cont'd	4. M-110 8" self-propelled howitzer	USA	-guns over 150 mm
	5. MGM/BGM-71A TOW antitank missile	USA	-guided missile remote control
Papua New Guinea	IAI-201 Arava transport a/c	Israel	-PWC PT6A-34 turboprop engine
Paraguay	EMB-110 transport a/c	Brazil	-PWC PT6A-34 turboprop engine
Philippines	1. UH-60A Uttas Black Hawk helicopter	USA	-gas turbines & jet engines -airframe structural components
	2. Model 412 helicopter (Bell Textron)	USA	-PWC PT6T-3B turboshaft engines
	3. UH-IH Iroquóis helicopter (model 205)	USA	-airframe structural components -gas turbines & jet engines
	4. S-76 Sikorsky Spirit helicopter	USA	-PWC PT6B-36 turboshaft engine
	5. LVTP-7A1 armoured amphibious assault vehicle	USA	-rocket & pyrotechnics launchers
Saudi Arabia	1. F-5E/F Tiger-2 fighter a/c	USA	-aircraft landing gear components

Recipient Country	Weapon System	Supplier Country	Canadian Component
Saudi Arabia cont'd	2. F-15 Eagle fighter a/c	USA	-aircraft air conditioning/heating -aircraft landing gear components -pressure temperature humidity instruments -electric connectors -aircraft maintenance and repair shop equipment
	3. M-109-A2 155 mm self-propelled howitzer	USA	-guns over 150 mm through 200 mm
	4. M-113-A2 armoured personnel carrier	USA	-vehicle furniture and accessories
	5. M-60-A3 main battle tank	USA	-vehicle furniture and accessories
	6. KC-135 tanker/transport a/c	USA	-spares
	7. MGM/BGM-71A TOW antitank missile	USA	-guided missile remote control
	8. Panavia Tornado IDS fighter a/c	UK	-crash position indicators -flight data recorders -airborne microwave landing system receiver
	9. E-3A Sentry AWACS a/c	USA	-vertical stabilizer and rudder -communication equipment -misc. electronics

Recipient Country	Weapon System	Supplier Country	Canadian Component
Saudi Arabia cont'd	10. M-1 Abrams main battle tank	USA	-computing systems -fire control equipment
Singapore	1. F-16 fighter a/c	USA	-maintenance/repair of aircraft components -aircraft air conditioning/heating -switches -misc. communications equipment -radar equipment -flight instruments
	2. M1M-23B Hawk land-mobile surface-to-air missile	USA	-components
Sri Lanka	UH-IN helicopter (Bell model 212)	USA	-hybrid microcircuits for guidance control systems -launcher components
Sudan	1. F-5E Tiger 2 a/c	USA	-aircraft landing gear components
	2. C-130 H Hercules transport a/c	USA	-navigational instruments -aircraft landing gear components
	3. AB-212 helicopter	Italy	-PWC PT6T-3 engines
Syria	AB-212 ASW helicopter	Italy	-PWC PT6T-3 engines
Taiwan	1. C-130H Hercules transport a/c	USA	-navigational instruments -aircraft landing gear components

Recipient Country	Weapon System	Supplier Country	Canadian Component
Taiwan Cont'd	2. T-34C-1 (Beech) Trainer a/c	USA	-PWC PT6A-25 turboprop engines
	3. M-113-AC armoured personnel carrier	USA	-vehicle furniture and accessories
	4. F-5E/F Tiger 2 a/c	USA	-aircraft landing gear components
	5. M-109 155 mm self-propelled howitzer	USA	-guns over 150 mm through 200 mm
	6. M1M-72F Chaparral surface-to-surface	USA	-hybrid microcircuits for guidance control system
Thailand	1. Shorts 330-UTT transport a/c	UK	-PWC PT6A-45R turboprop a/c
	2. F-16A/B Fighting Falcon a/c	USA	-maintenance/repair of components -aircraft air conditioning/heating -switches -misc. communications equipment -radar equipment -flight instruments
	3. UH-IH Iroquois (Bell 205) helicopter	USA	-airframe structural components -gas turbine & jet engines
	4. UH-60A Uttas Black Hawk helicopter	USA	-gas turbines & jet engines -airframe structural components

Recipient Country	Weapon System	Supplier Country	Canadian Component
Thailand cont'd	5. C-130H-30 Hercules transport a/c	USA	-navigational instruments -aircraft landing gear components
	6. M-48-A5 main battle tank	USA	-engine fuel system component
	7. M-113-A2 armoured personnel carrier	USA	-vehicle furniture and accessories
	8. LVTP-7A1 amphibious assault vehicle	USA	-rocket & pyrotechnics launchers
	9. Super King air transport a/c	USA	-PWC PT6 turboprop engines
Tunisia	1. C-130H Hercules transport a/c	USA	-navigational instruments -aircraft landing gear components
	2. F-5E/F Tiger-2 fighter a/c	USA	-aircraft landing gear components
	3. M-109-A2 155 mm self-propelled howitzer	USA	-guns over 150 mm through 200 mm
	4. M-60-A3 main battle tank	USA	-vehicle furniture and accessories
United Arab Emirates	1. C-130H-30 Hercules transport a/c	USA	-navigational instruments -aircraft landing gear components
	2. MGM/BGM-71A TOW antitank missile	USA	-guided missile remote control

Recipient Country	Weapon System	Supplier Country	Canadian Component
United Arab Emirates cont'd	3. M1M-23B Hawk landing mobile surface-to-air missile	USA	-components
	4. A-129 Mongoose attack helicopter	Italy	-castings
Venezuela	1. C-130H-30 Hercules transport a/c	USA	-navigational instruments -aircraft landing gear components
	2. F-16 A/B fighter a/c	USA	-maintenance/repair of aircraft components -aircraft air conditioning/heating -switches -misc. communications equipment -radar equipment -flight instruments
	3. Aeritalia G-222 transport a/c	Italy	-PMS-5 projected map display
	4. IAI-201 Arava transport a/c	Israel	-PWC PT6A-34 turboprop engine
	5. Super King air transport a/c	USA	-PWC PT6A turboprop engines
Zimbabwe	AB-412 Griffon helicopter	Italy	-PWC PT6T-3B engines

¹Compiled by Ken Epps

Appendix 2

Canadian Production of Nuclear Weapons Components[1]

Canadians are well aware of the production by Litton Systems Canada in Rexdale, Ontario, of guidance systems for the Tomahawk and Air-Launched Cruise Missiles. Yet there are also other Canadian manufacturing companies playing a role in the nuclear arms race. This appendix, which lists Canadian components for nuclear weapon systems and for nuclear-capable weapon systems, demonstrates that Canadian companies produce, or have recently produced, a wide variety of parts for the U.S. nuclear arsenal. The tables distinguish between two types of nuclear-related weapons systems. "Nuclear weapon systems" we are systems designed primarily to carry nuclear weapons. Thus, MX missiles or Trident submarines are intended to carry nuclear warheads or missiles respectively — strategically they serve no other function. "Nuclear-capable weapon systems" are those that can carry nuclear weapons but can also, in a different configuration, serve other purposes. As an example, the F-18A Hornet aircraft can deliver B57 or B61 nuclear bombs but it can also (and, as the Canadian CF-18, can solely) be used as a jet fighter with conventional bombs and missiles. The available information indicates the systems for which components were provided but does not distinguish between nuclear-capable and non–nuclear-capable versions. The table was compiled from information contained in the Canadian Military Industry Database of Project Ploughshares and its background vertical files, with sources including company annual reports, trade journals, news periodicals and U.S. Department of Defense prime contract listings. It is worth noting that the appendix says nothing about Canadian participation in the U.S. Strategic Defense Initiative. One reason is that to date there have been no announcements by the SDI Office of Canadian companies receiving Star Wars prime contracts. Nor have there been announcements of Canadian subcontracts from U.S. prime contractors. Another reason is that the table lists Canadian components for nuclear weapons or nuclear weapon delivery systems only.

Appendix 2a
Canadian Components for Nuclear-Capable Weapon Systems Since 1982

System	Company	Components
Aircraft		
A-4D/E/M Skyhawk		
Capable of carrying one of B28, B43, B57, or B61 nuclear bombs	Fleet Industries Fort Erie, Ont.	Speed brakes and flaps
A-6E Intruder		
Capable of carrying three of B28, B43, B57, or B61 nuclear bombs	Fleet Industries Fort Erie, Ont.	Inboard and outboard flaps Bonded honeycomb assemblies
	West Heights Manufacturing Kitchener, Ont	Parts
A-7A/B/D/E Corsair II		
Reportedly capable of carrying four of B28, B43, B57 or B61 nuclear bombs	Canadian Commercial Corporation[2] Ottawa, Ont.	Maintenance-repair of components Flight instruments Maintenance-repair shop equipment Air conditioning/heating Navigational instruments
	Computing Devices Company Ottawa, Ont.	Spares
	Garrett Manufacturing Ltd. Rexdale, Ont.	Maintenance of shop equipment Aircraft equipment
AV-8B Harrier II		
Capable of carrying one B61 nuclear tactical bomb.	Canadian Marconi Co. Montreal, Que.	Misc communication equipment

System	Company	Components
AV-8B cont'd	Dowty Canada Limited Ajax, Ont.	Outrigger landing gear
	Lucas Industries Canada Ltd. Montreal, Que.	Hydromechanical parts for gas turbine starter control
	Rolls-Royce (Canada) Ltd. Lachine, Que.	Gas turbine jet engine parts
	West Heights Manufacturing Kitchener, Ont	Parts

F-4C/D/E Phantom II

Three pylons can carry nuclear weapons (B28RE, B43, B57, B61 or B83 nuclear bombs) weighing up to 2170 lb.	Canadian Commercial Corporation[2] Ottawa, Ont.	Electrical and electronics equipment Transmitter Equipment repair Air conditioning/heating Relays and solenoids Pressure/temperature/ humidity instruments Landing gear components Electronics
	Litton Systems Canada Ltd. Rexdale, Ont.	Light emitting diode data entry display

F-18A Hornet

Capable of carrying two of B57 or B61 nuclear bombs	Bendix Avelex Inc. Montreal, Que.	Fuel control components
	Canadair Ltd. Montreal, Que.	Nose barrel assemblies
	Canadian Commercial Corporation[2] Ottawa, Ont.	Misc communication equipment Air conditioning/heating Gas turbine/jet engine parts
	Cercast Inc. Montreal, Que.	Main heads up display housing

System	Company	Components
F-18A Hornet cont'd	Fleet Industries Fort Erie, Ont.	Radar racks Graphite composite gun-loader and avionics doors
	Garrett Manufacturing Ltd. Rexdale, Ont.	Temperature control systems Hybrid microcircuits
	Haley Industries Ltd. Haley, Ont.	Castings
	McDonnell Douglas Canada Ltd. Mississauga, Ont	Forward fuselage side panel Wing pylons
	Spar Aerospace Ltd. Toronto, Ont.	Automatic test equipment
	UDT Industries Inc. Montreal, Que.	Ribs and splice fittings
	West Heights Manufacturing Kitchener, Ont.	Launch bar power unit Side brace assembly
F-111A/D/E/F Can carry up to three of B43, B57, B61, or B83 nuclear bombs.	Canadair Ltd. Montreal, Que. Canadian Commercial Corporation[2] Ottawa, Ont.	Vertical fins Air conditioning/heating Pressure/temperature/humidity instuments Communications/electronic equipment repair and par Navigational instruments Maintenance-repair of components Hydraulic system Airborne radar equipment Unmounted antifriction bearings Screws Electronic microcircuits

System	Company	Components
F-111A/D/E/F cont'd		Communication equipment
		Repair equipment
	Canadian Marconi Co. Montreal, Que.	Radar equipment
	Garrett Manufacturing Ltd. Rexdale, Ont.	Temperature control systems
	Litton Systems Canada Ltd. Rexdale, Ont.	Hardware
	Magna Electronics Scarborough, Ont.	Heat exchangers and chassis
	West Heights Manufacturing Kitchener, Ont.	Parts
<ins>P-3A/B/C Orion</ins>		
Can carry two B57 nuclear depth charges	CAE Electronics Ltd. Montreal, Que.	Operational tactics trainer for Royal Netherland Navy AN/ASA-65(V) compensator
	Canadair Ltd. Montreal, Que.	Structural components
	Canadian Commercial Corporation[2] Ottawa, Ont.	Misc communications equipment
		Maintenance-repair of communication equipment
		Engine instruments
		Airborne radio navigation equipment
		Airframe structural components
		Misc electrical and electronic components
		AN/ASA-65(V) repair
	Fleet Industries Fort Erie, Ont.	Flight stations

System	Company	Components
P3A/B/C Orion cont'd	Leigh Instruments Ltd. Carleton Place, Ont.	Misc communications equipment
	Litton Systems Canada Ltd. Rexdale, Ont.	LTN-72R inertial/area navigation systems
	West Heights Manufacturing Kitchener, Ont.	Parts
	Garrett Manufacturing Ltd. Rexdale, Ont.	Relays and solenoids Temperature control systems
	Hawker Siddeley Mississauga, Ont.	Engine components
	Litton Systems Canada Ltd. Rexdale, Ont.	Hardware
	West Heights Manufacturing Kitchener, Ont.	Parts
F-15A/C/E Eagle Although not primarily for nuclear weapons use, the F-15 is nuclear certified. Can possibly carry the GENIE (W25) air-to-air missile.	Canadair Ltd. Montreal, Que.	Parts
	Canadian Commercial Corporation[2] Ottawa, Ont.	Measuring instruments Air conditioning/heating Pressure/temperature/ humidity instruments Electrical converters Maintenance-repair shop equipment Landing gear components
	Fleet Industries Fort Erie, Ont.	Rudder fairing structure
	Garrett Manufacturing Ltd. Rexdale, Ont.	Temperature control system Hybrid microcircuits

System	Company	Components
F-15A/C/E Eagle cont'd	Haley Industries Ltd. Haley, Ont.	Castings
	Rockwell International of Canada Ltd. Toronto, Ont.	Radio navigation equipment Airborne electronics equipment
	West Heights Manufacturing Kitchener, Ont.	Parts

F-16A/B/C/D/E Fighting Falcon

Capable of delivering up to five of B43 or B61 nuclear bombs. Standard weapons configuaration is one or two nuclear weapons.	Canadian Commercial Corporation[2] Ottawa, Ont.	Maintenance-repair of components Electronic parts Air conditioning/heating Flight instruments Switches Non-airborne radar equipment Misc communications equipment Accessories
	Garrett Manufacturing Ltd. Rexdale, Ont	Maintenance, repair and rebuilding Temperature control systems Hybrid microcircuits
	Haley Industries Ltd. Haley, Ont.	Gearbox castings
	Leigh Instruments Ltd. Ottawa/Carleton Place, Ont.	Parts
	Litton Systems Canada Ltd. Rexdale, Ont.	Light emitting diode data entry display

System	Company	Components

S-3A Viking

Capable of carrying one B57 nuclear depth charge.

	Canadian Commercial Corporation[2] Ottawa, Ont.	Switches Air conditioning/heating Spares
	Garrett Manufacturing Ltd. Rexdale, Ont.	Hybrid microcircuits

Tornado

Capable of carrying B28, B43, B57 and B61 nuclear bombs

	CAE Electronics Ltd. Montreal, Que.	Flight simulator Weapons procedure trainer
	Canadian Marconi Co. Montreal, Que.	Airborne microwave landing system receiver
	Haley Industries Ltd. Haley, Ont.	Castings
	Leigh Instruments Ltd. Ottawa, Ont.	Flight data recorder Crash position indicator

Helicopters

SH-3D Sea King

Capable of carrying one B57 nuclear depth bomb

	Canadian Commercial Corporation[2] Ottawa, Ont.	Hydraulic components Radar equipment Spares
	Indal Technologies Inc. Mississauga, Ont.	RAST hauldown system

SH-60 Seahawk

Capable of carrying B57 nuclear depth charge

	Canadian Commercial Corporation[2] Ottawa, Ont.	Aircraft arresting barrier Misc aircraft accessories Flight instruments Navigational instruments Airborne auto pilot mechanisms
	Canadian Marconi Co. Montreal, Que.	Miscellaneous accessories
	Fleet Industries Fort Erie, Ont.	Blade subassemblies

System	Company	Components
SH-60 Seahawk cont'd	Haley Industries Ltd. Haley, Ont.	Castings for T700 engine
	Indal Technologies Inc. Mississauga, Ont.	RAST hauldown system
	Spar Aerospace Ltd. Toronto, Ont.	Main transmission, intermediate and tail rotor gearboxes

Air Defense Systems

AEGIS anti-air defense system

Used on the Ticonderoga class cruiser. Primary weapon is the nuclear-capable Standard-2 missile system.	Fleet Industries Fort Erie, Ont.	Antenna
	Magna Electronics Scarborough, Ont.	Power divider

Missiles

Lance Missile (MGM-52G)

Nuclear-capable surface-to-surface ballistic missile	Canadian Commercial Corporation[2] Ottawa, Ont.	Launchers

Ships

Ticonderoga Class Cruiser (CG-47)

Capable of carrying nuclear anti-submarine rockets, Harpoon cruise missiles and Standard-2 missile system	Indal Technologies Inc. Mississauga, Ont.	Helicopter hauldown system

System	Company	Components
Spruance Class Destroyer (DD-963)		
Capable of carrying nuclear anti-submarine rockets, Harpoon cruise missiles and SH-3 helicopters equipped with B57 nuclear depth charges	Aircraft Appliance & Equipment Ltd. Bramalea, Ont.	Valves
	Indal Technologies Inc. Mississauga, Ont.	Helicopter hauldown system

Artillery

M-109 155mm Self-Propelled Gun		
Capable of firing W28 nuclear artillery projectile	Bata Industries Ltd. Batawa, Ont	Vehicular power transmiss
	Canadian Commercial Corporation[2] Ottawa, Ont.	Large calibre gun system Weapons

M-110 8-inch Self-Propelled Howitzer		
Capable of firing W33 nuclear projectile	Bata Industries Ltd. Batawa, Ont.	Parts
	Levy Industries Ltd. Toronto, Ont.	Fuel systems

Appendix 2b
Canadian Components for Nuclear Weapon Systems since 1982

System	Company	Components

Missiles

Air-Launched Cruise (ALCM)

System	Company	Components
Air-to-surface missile for B-52 and B-1 strategic bombers. Equipped with one W80-1 nuclear warhead in 200 kiloton range	Litton Systems Canada Ltd. Rexdale, Ont.	Inertial guidance system

MX

System	Company	Components
Four-stage intercontinental ballistic missile	Boeing of Canada Ltd. Winnipeg, Man.	Nose cone components
	Ebco Industries Ltd. Richmond, B.C.	Basing system Prototype component

Tomahawk Sea-Launched Cruise (SLCM)

System	Company	Components
Long-range missile capable of being deployed from a variety of air, surface ship, submarine and land platforms. Equipped with W-80-0 nuclear warhead in 200-250 kiloton range.	Litton Systems Canada Ltd. Rexdale, Ont. Canadian Commercial Corporation[2] Ottawa, Ont.	Inertial guidance system Guided missile components

System	Company	Components

Bombers

B-1B

| Strategic bomber carrying B28, B61 and B83 nuclear bombs, air-launched cruise missiles and short-range attack missiles | Haley Industies Ltd. Haley, Ont. | Castings |

B-52G/H Stratofortress

| Carrier of AGM-86 air-launched cruise missile | Gabriel of Canada Ltd. | Spares Toronto, Ont. |
| | Garrett Manufacturing Ltd. Rexdale, Ont. | Temperature control systems |

Ships

Trident Submarine

Nuclear powered submarine strategic weapons launcher. 24 missile tubes for Trident I C4 or Trident II D5 ballistic missiles. Each missile has eight or more nuclear warheads.	ATS Automation Tooling Systems Inc. Kitchener, Ont	Parts
	Canadian Marconi Co. Montreal, Que.	LN-66/SP surface search radar
	Versatile Vickers Inc. Montreal, Que.	Hull components Cylinders for torpedo tubes ICBM tube casings

[1]Compiled by Ken Epps and Bill Robinson
[2]Where the Canadian Commercial Corporation is identified as the supplier, it is actim for another company that actually makes the component. In these cases, the manufac er cannot be identified from the available data.

Notes

Government agencies are agencies of the government of Canada unless otherwise specified.

SCEAND is an abbreviation for Parliament, House of Commons, Standing Committee on External Affairs and National Defence, *Minutes of Proceedings and Evidence*.

Introduction: Making War for All the Right Reasons

[1]Manchester *Guardian*, March 16, 1986.
[2]A 1975 report quoted by the *New Internationalist*, September 1980.
[3]*SIPRI Yearbook* 1984, p. 197.
[4]James Kelleher, speech to Hi Tech '86 Conference, March 12, 1986.
[5]Toronto *Globe and Mail*, April 10, 1986.
[6]Toronto *Star*, December 4, 1975.
[7]Michael T. Klare, *American Arms Supermarket* (Austin: University of Texas Press, 1985), p. 27.
[8]W.N. Russell, "France's Self-Supporting Armament Industry," *Canadian Defence Quarterly*, Summer 1985.
[9]Sinclair Stevens, letter, February 5, 1985.
[10]Allan MacEachen, memorandum to Cabinet, March 29, 1984.
[11]Ruth Leger Sivard, *World Military and Social Expenditures 1985* (Washington: World Priorities, 1985), p. 5.
[12]Seymour Melman, speech to Fate of the Earth Conference, Ottawa, June 7, 1986.
[13]John M. Treddenick, "The Arms Race and Military Keynesianism," *Canadian Public Policy*, March 1985.

Chapter 1: Canada at the Global Arms Bazaar

[1]This account of equipment used in the invasion is drawn from press reports — each reference to Canadian components is based on information from the Project Ploughshares Canadian Military Industry

Database on components that are regularly supplied for the weapons systems indicated. In most cases the Canadian company is not the exclusive supplier of the particular components, which means that, while Canadian firms regularly supply the components referred to, it is not possible to verify that the Canadian components were present in each particular case.

[2]Department of External Affairs, "Notice to Exporters" no. 12, July 6, 1982.

[3]Ottawa *Citizen*, February 17, 1986.

[4]Compiled from records of Canadian component manufacturing and sales in the Project Ploughshares Canadian Military Industry Database, and from arms trade data compiled by the Stockholm International Peace Research Institute. Canadian government refusal to disclose Canadian military exports means that appendix 1 provides only a partial list of such sales. It is not possible to be certain that each of the weapons systems transferred actually includes a Canadian component, but only that a Canadian company is a supplier of parts for that weapons system.

[5]Quantifying the world arms trade poses a myriad of problems. The following are some of the difficulties:

a) Since arms transfers are politically sensitive and involve security issues, the trade is characterized by an unusual level of secrecy. Both suppliers and recipients are frequently reluctant to disclose transactions and in many instances nondisclosure is a condition of sale.

b) Some trade in weapons is illegal and thus difficult or impossible to identify.

c) The trade in components is difficult to quantify since many components — along with some major systems such as transport aircraft — can be used for both military and civilian purposes.

d) Small arms are difficult to identify and the Stockholm International Peace Research Institute (SIPRI), for example, does not include them in arms trade statistics.

e) Currency valuations make quantification difficult — how do you compare the cost or value of a Soviet tank with that of an American tank?

f) Military sales contracts vary in that some include only equipment costs, in others the costs are affected by offset arrangements, while in still other cases concessions such as technology transfers affect the price.

g) Statistics are gathered in various ways. In Canada, for example, three different agencies use three different bases for tabulation. The

Defence Programs Bureau bases its figures on orders, Statistics Canada uses shipments, and the Canadian Commercial Corporation bases its records on invoices. A single transaction could be recorded in three different years by the three agencies.

There are three main primary sources for arms trade statistics: SIPRI, the International Institute for Strategic Studies, and the United States Arms Control and Disarmament Agency. Prominent secondary and interpretive sources include the writings of Michael T. Klare, notably *American Arms Supermarket* (Austin: University of Texas Press, 1985); Ruth Leger Sivard's annual *World Military and Social Expenditures* (Washington: World Priorities); and SIPRI's annual *World Armaments and Disarmament: SIPRI Yearbook* (London: Taylor and Francis).

[6]Klare, *American Arms Supermarket*, p. 7.

[7]Michael Klare, "The Transformation of the International Arms Trade," *Ploughshares Monitor*, March 1985.

[8]*Jane's Defence Weekly*, May 24, 1986.

[9]Michael Brzoska and Thomas Ohlson, eds., *Arms Production in the Third World* (London: Taylor and Francis, 1986), p. 10.

[10]SIPRI, *World Armaments and Disarmament, 1985*, p. 351.

[11]Ibid., p. 448.

[12]James Everett Katz, *The Implications of Third World Military Industrialization* (Lexington, Mass.: Lexington Books, 1986), p. xvii.

[13]Klare, *American Arms Supermarket*, pp. 26–38.

[14]Tom Chell's testimony in *SCEAND*, October 2, 1985, p. 32:6.

[15]Lewis W. Snider, "Arms Exports for Oil Imports?", *Journal of Conflict Resolution* 28, no. 4 (December 1984): 665–700.

[16]Miles Wolpin, *Military Aid and Counterrevolution in the Third World* (Lexington, Mass.: Lexington Books, 1972).

[17]Sivard, *World Military and Social Expenditures 1985*, p. 25.

[18]Ibid., p. 6.

[19]Kitchener-Waterloo *Record*, April 29, 1986.

[20]Mary Kaldor, *The Baroque Arsenal* (New York: Hill and Wang, 1981), pp. 131–68.

[21]Canadian Council of Churches, "Brief to the Special Joint Committee on Canada's International Relations," pp. 34–35.

[22]Richard Falk, "Militarization and Human Rights in the Third World," in *Problems of Contemporary Militarism*, edited by A. Eide and M. Thee (London: Croom Helm, 1980).

[23]See International Peace Research Association, Study Group on Militarizatrion, "The Impact of Militarization on Development and Human Rights," *Bulletin of Peace Proposals* 9, no. 2 (1978).

[24]Canadian Council of Churches, "Brief to the Special Joint Committee."

[25]*Defence News*, February 10, 1986; Klare, *American Arms Supermarket*, p. 12.

[26]Deliveries reported in *Jane's All The World's Aircraft 1984–85*.

[27]Robert Coates, Minister of National Defence, "Notes for a Speech on the Occasion of the Arrival of the CF-18 at CFB Bagotville," December 13, 1984.

[28]Toronto *Globe and Mail*, March 25, 1985; Kitchener-Waterloo *Record*, July 27, 1985.

[29]C.G. Galligan, "The Impact of Canadian Defence Expenditures: FY 1983/84 Update," in Royal Military College of Canada, Centre for Studies in Defence Resources Management, *Report No. 7* (Kingston, 1985), p. 50.

[30]Peter Chapman, "Canadian Defence Spending," *Ploughshares Monitor*, June 1985.

[31]External Affairs Coordinator of Access to Information and Privacy, letter to the author, November 8, 1985.

[32]Parliament, House of Commons, *Debates*, November 24, 1975.

[33]Iran was "apparently" the single largest Third World customer because actual sales have not been disclosed. Unofficial sources, however, suggest that Iran was a major customer with purchases in the amount indicated.

[34]Department of Regional Industrial Expansion, *Administrative Directive for the Defence Industry Productivity Program*, September 1, 1983.

Chapter 2: Canadian Military Production from the Great War to the Permanent War

[1]"GM Goes Military," Kitchener-Waterloo *Record*, November 2, 1985.

[2]"GM Deal for Armored Vehicles Jeopardized by Falling Oil Prices," Toronto *Globe and Mail*, February 26, 1986.

[3]Ramon Lopez, "The U.S. Army's Future Light Infantry Division," *International Defense Review* 2 (1982), p. 186.

[4]William J. Yost, *Industrial Mobilization in Canada* (Ottawa: Conference of Defence Associations, 1983), p. 20.

[5]"Return to Defence Technology the Best Offence for Leigh," *Financial Post*, November 10, 1984.

[6]A reporter-artist in Cuba sent Hearst a message that, there being no war to report or draw, he wanted to return home. Hearst replied: "Please remain. You furnish the pictures and I'll furnish the war."

(Robert Leckie, *The Wars of America* [New York: Harper and Row, 1968], p. 544.)

[7]Desmond Morton, *Canada and War* (Toronto: Butterworths, 1981), p. 57.

[8]Quoted by R.T. Naylor, *The Canadian State, the Accumulation of Capital, and the Great War* (Montreal: McGill University, 1978), p. 17.

[9]Morton, *Canada and War*, p. 58.

[10]Naylor, *Canadian State*, p. 18.

[11]Ibid., p. 22.

[12]Edelgard E. Mahant and Graeme S. Mount, "Reciprocity and World War I," in *An Introduction to Canadian-American Relations* (Toronto: Methuen, 1984), pp. 100–101.

[13]R.D. Cuff and J.L. Granatstein, *Ties That Bind: Canadian/American Relations*, 2nd edition (Toronto: Samuel Stevens Hakkert, 1977), p.7.

[14]Morton, *Canada and War*, p. 59.

[15]Cuff and Granatstein, *Ties that Bind*, p. 37.

[16]Mahant and Mount, "Reciprocity and World War I," p. 110.

[17]Naylor, *Canadian State*, p. 52.

[18]Morton, *Canada and War*, pp. 94–95.

[19]Fred Gaffen, "Canada's Military Aircraft Industry: Its Birth, Growth and Fortunes," *Canadian Defence Quarterly*, Autumn 1985.

[20]Morton, *Canada and War*, p. 109.

[21]Cuff and Granatstein, *Ties That Bind*, p. 165.

[22]Morton, *Canada and War*, p. 112.

[23]W.N. Russell, "The Need for a Viable Canadian Defence Industrial Base," *Canadian Defence Quarterly*, Spring 1986.

[24]John W. Holmes, *The Shaping of Peace: Canada and the Search for World Order 1943–1957* (Toronto: University of Toronto Press, 1982).

[25]Morton, *Canada and War*, p. 153.

[26]Jerry Saunders, "Forty Years of Pax Americana: What Comes Next?", *World Policy Journal*, Summer 1984, p. 684.

[27]Holmes, *The Shaping of Peace*, p. 144.

[28]Holmes, *The Shaping of Peace*, p. 86.

[29]Michael Hart, *Some Thoughts on Canada–United States Sectoral Free Trade* (Montreal: Institute for Research on Public Policy, 1985), p. 9.

[30]R.D. Cuff and J.L. Granatstein, *American Dollars — Canadian Prosperity* (Toronto: Samuel Stevens, 1978), p. 175.

[31]*Industrial Canada*, November 1959; Holmes, *The Shaping of Peace*, p. 97.

[32]Holmes, *The Shaping of Peace*, p. 5.

[33]Quoted by Cuff and Granatstein, *American Dollars*, p. 165.

[34]Holmes, *The Shaping of Peace*, p. 29.

[35]See Department of External Affairs, *Competitiveness and Security: Directions for Canada's International Relations* (Ottawa, 1985).

[36]Richard Barnet, *The Lean Years* (New York: Simon and Schuster, 1980), p. 219.

[37]Ibid., p. 219.

[38]Ibid., p. 219.

[39]Quoted by Michael T. Klare, *World without End: American Planning for the Next Vietnams* (New York: Vintage, 1972), p. 8.

[40]Cuff and Granatstein, *American Dollars*, p. 230.

[41]William Willoughby, *The Joint Organizations of Canada and the United States* (Toronto: University of Toronto Press, 1979), p. 165.

[42]Ibid., p. 166.

[43]The "defence against help" theme has been most consistently expounded by Nils Orvik. See, for example, his "Defence Against Help — A Strategy for Small States," *Survival* 15, no. 5 (1973): 228.

[44]James Eayrs, *In Defence of Canada*, vol. 3, *Peacemaking and Deterrence* (Toronto: University of Toronto Press, 1972), pp. 336–44.

[45]James Fallow pointed out in 1982 that fighter aircraft costs had risen, in constant dollars, by a factor of 100 since World War II, and quoted a U.S. aerospace executive as saying that if this trend were to continue, "in the year 2054, the entire defense budget will purchase just one tactical aircraft . . . to be shared between the Air Force and the Navy, three and a half days each per week" ("The Conventional Weapons Fallacy," *Atlantic Monthly*, May 1981).

[46]James Eayrs, *In Defence of Canada*, vol. 4, *Growing Up Allied* (Toronto: University of Toronto Press, 1980), p. 192.

[47]By the 1973 Yom Kippur War even conventional warfare was consuming weapons at an extraordinary pace, with sophisticated fighter aircraft being destroyed at the rate of one every five minutes during the first few hours of that war (T.B. Winfields, "The Future of Mechanized Warfare: The Lessons of Yom Kippur," *Canadian Defence Quarterly*, Winter 1978).

[48]D.W. Middlemiss, "A Pattern of Co-operation: The Case of the Canadian-American Defence Production and Development Sharing Arrangements, 1958–1963," Ph.D. dissertation, University of Toronto, 1975, p. 2.

[49]Jon B. McLin, *Canada's Changing Defense Policy, 1957–1963* (Baltimore: Johns Hopkins University Press, 1967), p. 176.

Chapter 3: From the Arrow to Offsets: The Perils of Production Sharing

[1]For one account of the story of the Jetliner, as well as the Avro Arrow, see E.K. Shaw, *There Never Was An Arrow* (Ottawa: Steel Rail Educational Publishing, 1979).

[2]This and the following description of the Arrow's development program is taken, unless otherwise noted, from Jon B. McLin, *Canada's Changing Defense Policy, 1957–1963* (Baltimore: Johns Hopkins University Press, 1967), pp. 61ff.

[3]Lester Pearson, letter to Professor Peter Hughes, Victoria College, University of Toronto, February 21, 1967.

[4]John W. Holmes, *The Shaping of Peace: Canada and the Search for World Order 1943–1957* (Toronto: University of Toronto Press, 1982), p. 284.

[5]John Kirton, "The Consequences of Integration: The Case of the Defence Production Sharing Agreements," in Andrew Axline, ed., *Continental Community? Independence and Integration in North America* (Toronto: McClelland and Stewart, 1974), p. 123.

[6]Gideon Rosenbluth, *The Canadian Economy and Disarmament* (Toronto: Macmillan, 1967), pp. 36–37.

[7]Holmes, *The Shaping of Peace*, p. 282.

[8]U.S. National Security Council, Document #5822, December 12, 1958, quoted by David Cox, *Canada and NORAD, 1958–1978: A Cautionary Retrospective*, Aurora Papers 1 (Ottawa: Canadian Centre for Arms Control and Disarmament, 1985), p. 27.

[9]Kirton, "Consequences of Integration," p. 122.

[10]*SCEAND*, October 2, 1985.

[11]Kirton, "Consequences of Integration," p. 124.

[12]Ibid., p. 124.

[13]*SCEAND*, October 2, 1985.

[14]"That is done through a set of administrative arrangements where, as long as the Canadian company has identified a U.S. military contract number, the paper flow takes place" (*SCEAND*, October 2, 1985, p. 32:9).

[15]*Industrial Canada* (Ottawa: Department of Industry, Trade and Commerce), November 1979.

[16]Holmes, *The Shaping of Peace*, p. 285.

[17]See Gwynne Dyer's film *The Space Between*, from the series *Defence of Canada*, produced by the National Film Board of Canada, 1985.

[18]D.W. Middlemiss, "A Pattern of Co-operation: The Case of the Cana-

dian-American Defence Production and Development Sharing Arrangements, 1958–1963," Ph.D. dissertation, University of Toronto, 1975, p. 259.

[19]Ibid., p. 260.

[20]Ibid., p. 261.

[21]Ibid., p. 298.

[22]Ibid., p. 298.

[23]Ibid., p. 299.

[24]Ibid., p. 302.

[25]Ibid., p. 304.

[26]Ibid., p. 318.

[27]*Financial Times of Canada*, June 10, 1963, as quoted in Middlemiss, "Pattern of Co-operation," p. 320.

[28]Middlemiss, "Pattern of Co-operation," p. 334.

[29]William Willoughby, *The Joint Organizations of Canada and the United States* (Toronto: University of Toronto Press, 1979), p. 171. The reference to legislators is to a statement by U.S. Senator Stuart Symington (D — Missouri) in the Senate, June 13, 1961.

[30]Frank Jackman, "The Canada-U.S. Defence Production Sharing Arrangements," mimeo (Ottawa: Department of Industry, Trade and Commerce, Defence Programs Bureau, undated).

[31]Michael Tucker, *Canadian Foreign Policy; Contemporary Issues and Themes* (Toronto: McGraw-Hill/Ryerson, 1980), p. 81.

[32]Middlemiss, "Pattern of Co-operation," p. 369.

[33]Ottawa *Journal*, November 29, 1971; Toronto *Globe and Mail*, December 1, 1971.

[34]*Financial Post*, October 30, 1971.

[35]Parliament, Senate, Committee on Foreign Affairs, *Report on Canada-U.S. Relations*, vol. 2, *Canada's Trade with the U.S.*, 30th Parliament, 3rd Session, 1977–78.

[36]Parliament, Senate, Committee on Foreign Affairs, *Minutes of Proceedings and Evidence*, April 6, 1976, p. 30:20.

[37]*Financial Post*, April 16, 1977.

[38]Lester R. Brown, "Redefining National Security," *State of the World Atlas*, edited by Lester Brown et al. (New York: Norton, 1986), p. 200.

[39]*Financial Times of Canada*, May 1, 1978.

[40]*Financial Post*, August 12, 1978.

[41]*Financial Post*, May 12, 1979.

[42]*Financial Post*, December 26, 1981.

Chapter 4: Canadian Military Production for Export

[1]Both are claims made by the Aerospace Industries Association of Canada in testimony before the Commons Committee on External Affairs and National Defence (*SCEAND*, October 8, 1985).

[2]*Aerospace Canada International*, April 1985.

[3]See, for example, Seymour Melman, *The Permament War Economy* (New York: Simon and Schuster, 1975), and *Profits without Production* (New York: Alfred A. Knopf, 1985).

[4]*Financial Post*, December 1, 1984.

[5]These changes in strategy are outlined in W.N. Russell, "The Need for a Viable Canadian Defence Industrial Base," *Canadian Defence Quarterly*, Spring 1986.

[6]Ibid.

[7]Ibid.

[8]Ted Hallas, "Canada's Defence Industrial Base: Long-Term Planning is the Key to Developing a Systems Integration Capability," Special Report, *Aerospace Canada*, April 1985.

[9]Military exports are tabulated by the Department of External Affairs, while records of total exports are kept by Statistics Canada. The categories used by the two agencies do not precisely match. Furthermore, Statistics Canada figures are based on deliveries and External Affairs figures are based on orders, so that the two sets of figures are not directly comparable in any one year.

[10]*U.S. News and World Report*, June 16, 1986.

[11]D.W. Middlemiss, "The Political Economy of Defence: Dimensions of Government Involvement in the Canadian Aircraft Industry," a paper presented to the 50th annual meeting of the Canadian Political Science Association, London, Ontario, 1978, p. 2.

[12]Ibid., p. 37.

[13]The following description of the aerospace industry, unless othewise noted, is taken from *A Report by the Sector Task Force on the Canadian Aerospace Industry* (Ottawa: Department of Industry, Trade and Commerce, 1978), and *Memorandum of Understanding for Industry Development Planning* (Ottawa: Department of Regional Industrial Expansion, 1985).

[14]*Memorandum of Understanding*, Schedule A, p. 2.

[15]J.M. Treddenick and C.G. Galligan, *The National Industrial Aerospace Base Now and Tomorrow* (Kingston: Royal Military College of Canada, 1986), p. 6.

[16]Hallas, "Canada's Defence Industrial Base."

[17]Toronto *Star*, August 11, 1984.

[18]The following descriptions are taken from *International Defense Review*, 6/1986, and *Jane's All The World's Aircraft 1984–85,*

[19]Toronto *Globe and Mail*, July 6, 1986.

[20]*Financial Post*, April 19, 1986.

[21]*Aviation Week and Space Technology*, May 16, 1986.

[22]Deborah G. Meyer, "A Growing Canadian Defense Industry Pursues U.S. Military Market with Gusto," *Armed Forces Journal International*, November 1984.

[23]*Canadian Aviation*, August 1986, p. 4.

[24]*Armed Forces Journal*, November 1984.

[25]*Financial Post*, November 24, 1986.

[26]Department of External Affairs, Press Release no. 42, February 17, 1986.

[27]*Military Technology*, no. 1, 1984.

[28]Toronto *Globe and Mail*, May 22, 1984.

[29]Toronto *Globe and Mail*, June 17, 1986.

[30]*Canadian Defence Products Guide* (Ottawa: Department of External Affairs, Defence Programs Bureau, undated).

[31]*Armed Forces Journal International*, November 1984.

[32]Toronto *Globe and Mail*, July 21, 1986.

[33]*Financial Post*, July 26, 1986.

[34]*Defence Newsletter* 4/12 (Halifax: Dalhousie University, Centre for Foreign Policy Studies, undated).

[35]Toronto *Globe and Mail*, July 21, 1986.

[36]Alex Curran, "The State of Canada's Industry," in *Canada, the United States and Space*, edited by John Kirton (Toronto: Canadian Institute of International Affairs/New York: Columbia University, Canadian Studies Program, 1985), p. 40.

[37]Toronto *Globe and Mail*, September 20, 1984.

[38]Toronto *Globe and Mail*, August 8, 1984.

[39]*Armed Forces Journal International*, November 1984.

[40]Hallas, "Canada's Defence Industrial Base."

[41]*The Canadian Electronics Industry Sector Profile* (Ottawa: Department of Industry, Trade and Commerce, 1978).

[42]Toronto *Globe and Mail*, May 27, 1986.

[43]Gilbert R. Winham, *Canada-U.S. Sectoral Trade Study: The Impact of Free Trade* (Halifax: Dalhousie University, Centre for Foreign Policy Studies, 1986), pp. 227–30.

[44]Helmut Hoffman, speech, March 11, 1986.

[45]*SCEAND*, October 2, 1985.

[46]*Defence Newsletter* 5/3.

[47]Toronto *Globe and Mail*, August 10, 1984; Toronto *Globe and Mail*, August 9, 1985.

[48]*Armed Forces Journal International*, November 1984.

[49]*Financial Post*, December 28, 1985.

[50]*Armed Forces Journal International*, November 1984.

[51]*Military Technology*, no. 1, 1984.

[52]*Canadian Defence Products Guide.*

[53]*International Defense Review*, 6/1986.

[54]Ibid.

[55]*Military Technology*, no. 1, 1984.

[56]General Motors, *Annual Report 1983*, quoted in the London *Free Press*, October 21, 1985.

[57]*National Defense* (Journal of the American Defense Preparedness Association), May 1985.

[58]*International Defense Review*, 6/1986.

[59]*Jane's Defence Weekly*, July 5, 1986.

[60]Toronto *Globe and Mail*, July 29, 1986.

[61]*Financial Post*, June 21, 1986.

[62]Toronto *Globe and Mail*, May 13, 1986.

[63]Department of External Affairs, Press Release no. 71, February 6, 1986.

[64]*A Report by the Sector Task Force on the Canadian Shipbuilding and Repair Industry* (Ottawa: Department of Industry, Trade and Commerce, 1978); *Financial Post*, May 31, 1986.

[65]*Financial Post*, June 7, 1986.

[66]*Production Sharing Handbook* (Ottawa: Department of External Affairs, Defence Programs Bureau, undated).

[67]*Defence Newsletter* 5/1.

[68]*Defence Newsletter* 5/3.

[69]*Engineering Times*, March 19, 1984.

[70]*National Defense* (Journal of the American Defense Preparedness Association), May/June 1986.

[71]*Military Technology*, no. 1, 1984.

[72]*Financial Post*, December 14, 1985.

[73]*Aerospace Canada International*, January/February 1986; *Financial Post*, December 14, 1985.

[74]*International Defense Review*, 6/1986.

[75]Hallas, "Canada's Defence Industrial Base."

Chapter 5: Promoting the Industry

[1]*SCEAND*, October 2, 1985.
[2]Department of External Affairs, Defence Programs Bureau, "Defence Programs Bureau," mimeo, undated.
[3]Ibid.
[4]*SCEAND*, October 2, 1985.
[5]James Kelleher, speech to Hi Tech '86 Conference, March 12, 1986.
[6]*SCEAND*, October 2, 1985.
[7]Toronto *Star*, December 4, 1984.
[8]Ibid.
[9]Toronto *Star*, December 8, 1984.
[10]Col. Larry L. Smith, "Defense Contract Management in Canada," mimeo (Ottawa: Department of External Affairs, Defence Programs Bureau, undated).
[11]Tracy LeMay, "Low-Profile Crown Corporation," Toronto *Globe and Mail*, December 5, 1983.
[12]Smith, "Defense Contract Management in Canada".
[13]Toronto *Globe and Mail*, August 15, 1986.
[14]Toronto *Globe and Mail*, July 28, 1986.
[15]Toronto *Globe and Mail*, August 15, 1986.
[16]Science for Peace (Toronto), memo and attached documents to the Minister for Science and Technology, January 18, 1982.
[17]Patrick Luciani, "Export Financing: Determining Government's Role in the Financial Support of Aerospace Exports," *Aerospace Canada International*, March/April 1985.
[18]*Canada Commerce*, July/August 1984.
[19]*Aerospace Canada International*, May/June 1986.
[20]*Financial Post*, December 1, 1984.
[21]Toronto *Globe and Mail*, June 19, 1986.
[22]Aerospace Industries Association of Canada, press release concerning its Semi-Annual General Meeting in Ottawa, April 13–15, 1986.
[23]*Financial Post*, April 4, 1981.
[24]Ibid.

Chapter 6: Rough Riding on the Reagan Arms Boom

[01]Michael Hart, "Some Thoughts on Canada–United States Sectoral Free Trade" (Montreal: Institute for Research on Public Policy, 1985), p. 7.
[02]Jerry W. Sanders, "Security and Choice," *World Policy Journal*, Summer 1984.

[3]Department of External Affairs, Defence Programs Bureau, "Defence Programs Bureau," mimeo, undated.

[4]The description of PD-59 is taken from Jeffrey Richelson, "PD-59, NSDD13 and the Reagan Strategic Modernization Program," *Journal of Strategic Studies* 6, no. 2 (June 1983): 125–46.

[5]Department of External Affairs, Press Release 88/83, July 15, 1983; Department of National Defence, "Cruise Missile Testing in Canada: Background Notes," July 15, 1983.

[6]Quoted by Emma Rothschild, "The Delusions of Deterrence," *New York Review of Books*, April 14, 1983.

[7]Quoted in *Ploughshares Monitor*, September 1984.

[8]Winnipeg *Free Press*, November 30, 1982.

[9]*Financial Post*, October 24, 1981.

[10]*Financial Post*, December 1, 1984.

[11]*Financial Post*, February 26, 1986.

[12]*Financial Post*, September 4, 1982.

[13]Toronto *Globe and Mail*, December 21, 1984.

[14]Department of External Affairs official, interview with the author, November 13, 1986.

[15]Ottawa *Citizen*, April 23, 1983.

[16]Ibid.

[17]*Financial Post*, May 7, 1983.

[18]Ibid.

[19]Toronto *Globe and Mail*, May 18, 1983.

[20]Toronto *Globe and Mail*, March 15, 1984.

[21]*Financial Post*, March 17, 1984.

[22]Toronto *Globe and Mail*, March 28, 1985.

[23]*SCEAND*, October 8, 1985.

[24]Ibid.

[25]*SCEAND*, October 2, 1985, p. 32:15.

[26]Ibid., p. 32:14.

[27]"How West Germany Slices Defense Pie," *Financial Post*, December 7, 1985.

[28]John Turner and SIPRI, *Arms in the Eighties* (London: Taylor and Francis), p. 74.

[29]Quoted in *Aerospace Canada International*, October 1984.

[30]*Financial Post*, December 7, 1985.

[31]Ibid.

[32]*Financial Post*, December 5, 1985.

[33]Ibid.

[34]*Financial Post*, December 7, 1985.

[35]Ibid.

[36]Ibid.

[37]Ibid.

[38]Ibid.

[39]Department of External Affairs official, interview with the author, November 1986.

[40]Sample "memorandum of understanding" supplied to the author by the Department of External Affairs.

[41]Dan Middlemiss, "Nato: The Economics of Alliance Defence," paper presented to the conference on "NATO: Towards the Year 2000," Canadian Forces Maritime Warfare School, Halifax, May 28, 1986.

[42]Ibid., p. 9.

[43]Aerospace Industries Association of Canada, press release concerning its Semi-Annual General Meeting in Ottawa, April 13–15, 1986.

[44]*NATO's Sixteen Nations*, September/October 1984.

Chapter 7: Selling to the Third World

[1]Canada, "Export and Import Permits Act," Article 3.

[2]Department of External Affairs, "Export Controls Policy: Background Paper," attached to Press Statement no. 155, "Export Controls Policy," September 10, 1986.

[3]*Maclean's*, July 28, 1986.

[4]Ibid.

[5]Department of External Affairs, "Notice to Exporters" no. 21, July 18, 1984 (amended March 1, 1985).

[6]Toronto *Globe and Mail*, January 24, 1975.

[7]Ibid.

[8]Allan MacEachen, letter to the Taskforce on the Churches and Corporate Responsibility (TCCR), March 16, 1983.

[9]Toronto *Globe and Mail*, June 11, 1986.

[10]*Aviation Week and Space Technology*, December 17, 1984.

[11]Toronto *Globe and Mail*, March 15, 1984.

[12]Toronto *Globe and Mail*, March 30, 1984.

[13]Department of External Affairs, "Notice to Exporters" no. 21.

[14]Joe Clark, letter to Nelson Riis, June 19, 1985.

[15]Sinclair Stevens, letter, February 5, 1985.

[16]SIPRI, *The Arms Trade with the Third World*, Paul Elek: *SIPRI Yearbook 1971* (London: Taylor and Francis, 1971) , p. 35.

[17]Clark letter to Riis, June 19, 1985.

[18]Toronto *Globe and Mail*, June 19, 1986.

[19]Joe Clark, letter to Project Ploughshares, April 30, 1986.

[20]Toronto *Globe and Mail*, June 19, 1986.

[21]Ibid.

[22]Department of External Affairs, letter to TCCR, January 12, 1984.

[23]Department of External Affairs, letter to TCCR, June 5, 1984.

[24]Clark letter to Riis, June 19, 1985.

[25]Department of External Affairs, letter to TCCR, June 5, 1984.

[26]Department of External Affairs, letter to TCCR, December 5, 1984.

[27]*SCEAND*, October 2, 1985, p. 32:18.

Chapter 8: Counting the Costs

[1]Quoted by Robert Wenman, parliamentary secretary to the minister of defence, speech, November 28, 1984.

[2]Ibid.

[3]John M. Treddenick, "The Arms Race and Military Keynesianism," *Canadian Public Policy*, March 1985."

[4]Harold Willens, *The Trimtab Factor* (New York: William Morrow, 1984).

[5]See, for example, Robert W. DeGrasse, Jr., *Military Expansion, Economic Decline* (Washington: Council on Economic Priorities, 1983); L.J. Dumas, *The Overburdened Economy* (New York: Simon and Schuster, 1985); Seymour Melman, *The Permanent War Economy* (New York: Simon and Schuster, 1975), and *Profits without Production* (New York: Alfred A. Knopf, 1985); Project Ploughshares, *Peace, Employment and the Economics of Permanent War*, Working Paper 84-5 (Waterloo, 1985); Marion Anderson, Jeb Brugmann and George Erickeek, *Destructive Investment: Nuclear Weapons and Economic Decline* (Lansing, Mich.: Employment Research Associates, 1983).

[6]*Journal of Commerce*, April 11, 1984, p. 4.

[7]Toronto *Globe and Mail, Report on Business Magazine*, August 1986.

[8]Washington *Post*, March 11, 1986.

[9]Robert W. DeGrasse, Jr., "The Military: Shortchanging the Economy," *Bulletin of the Atomic Scientists*, May 1984.

[10]*Aerospace Canada International*, November/December 1985.

[11]Kristian S. Palda, *Industrial Innovation: Its Place in the Public Policy Agenda* (Vancouver: Fraser Institute, 1984), p. 124.

[12]Jean-Jacques Blais, speech to CANAM Future-Tech Conference, Ottawa, May 9, 1984.

[13]Task Force on Federal Policies and Program for Technology Development, July 1, 1984, cited by Peter Langille, "The Canadian Defence

Industry: An Overview," mimeo (Ottawa: Peace Resource Centre, 1984).

[14]Canadian Institute of Strategic Studies, spring 1984 conference proceedings, p. 131.

[15]Quoted in John Kirton, ed., *Canada, the United States and Space*, (Toronto: Canadian Institute of International Affairs/New York: Columbia University, Canadian Studies Program, 1985), p. 41.

[16]*SCEAND*, October 8, 1985.

[17]Ibid.

[18]Ibid.

[19]Toronto *Globe and Mail, Report on Business Magazine*, August 1986.

[20]Marion Anderson, *Converting the Work Force*, a report of the Employment Research Associates (Lansing, Mich., 1983).

[21]Toby Sanger, "Military Spending," *CUPE Facts*, January/February 1986.

[22]Canadian Institute of Strategic Studies, spring 1984 conference proceedings, p. 111.

[23]Toronto *Globe and Mail*, March 25, 1985.

[24]Lt.-Gen. (Ret'd) Kenneth E. Lewis, then president of the Aerospace Industries Association of Canada, commented in a 1985 CBC radio debate with the author that it was likely that any Star Wars research in Canada would require some direct funding by the Canadian government.

[25]Toronto *Globe and Mail*, August 8, 1984.

[26]See Melman, *The Permament War Economy* and *Profits without Production*.

[27]Janice R. Long and David H. Hanson, "Funds for R&D Up 13 Per Cent in Administration's Budget Proposal," *Chemical and Engineering News*, February 18, 1985.

[28]See, for example, Michael Brzoska and Thomas Ohlson, eds., *Arms Production in the Third World* (London: Taylor and Francis, 1986); James Everett Katz, *The Implications of Third World Military Industrialization: Sowing the Serpent's Teeth* (Lexington, Mass.: Lexington Books, 1986); Mary Kaldor and Asbjorn Eide, eds., *The World Military Order: The Impact of Military Technology on the Third World* (London: Macmillan, 1979); Mary Kaldor, *The Baroque Arsenal* (New York: Hill and Wang, 1981).

[29]Kaldor and Eide, eds., *The World Military Order*.

[30]Katz, *Implications of Third World Military Industrialization*.

[31]Toronto *Globe and Mail*, November 22, 1984.

[32]*SCEAND*, March 14, 1984.

[33]Aerospace Industries Association of Canada, press release concerning its Semi-Annual General Meeting in Ottawa, April 13–15, 1986.

[34]*Aviation Week and Space Technology*, May 7, 1984.

[35]*SCEAND*, October 8, 1985.

[36]*Aviation Week and Space Technology*, June 17, 1985.

[37]*Aviation Week and Space Technology*, June 23, 1986.

[38]*Financial Post*, April 27, 1985.

[39]SIPRI, *World Armaments and Disarmament: SIPRI Yearbook 1985* (London: Taylor and Francis, 1971). , p. 363.

[40]Toronto *Globe and Mail*, June 11, 1986.

[41]Toronto *Globe and Mail*, December 8, 1984.

[42]Quoted in D.W. Middlemiss, "A Pattern of Co-operation: The Case of the Canadian-American Defence Production and Development Sharing Arrangements, 1958–1963," Ph.D. dissertation, University of Toronto, 1975, p. 323.

[43]Quoted in Michael Tucker, *Canadian Foreign Policy: Contemporary Issues and Themes* (Toronto: McGraw-Hill/Ryerson, 1980), p. 145. Tucker also discusses U.S. actions to influence Canada's long-range patrol aircraft purchase, and the following account relies on his discussion.

[44]George Grant, *Technology and Empire: Perspectives on North America* (Toronto: Anansi, 1969), p. 63.

[45]Ibid., p. 64.

[46]Ibid., p. 65.

[47]Stephen Clarkson, *Canada and the Reagan Challenge* (Toronto: James Lorimer and Co./Canadian Institute for Economic Policy, 1982), p. 245.

[48]Kitchener-Waterloo *Record*, July 4, 1986.

[49]Tucker, *Canadian Foreign Policy*, pp. 149–50.

[50]Ruth Leger Sivard, *World Military and Social Expenditures 1986* (Washington: World Priorities, 1986), pp. 33–36.

[51]*The Military Balance: 1986–87* (London: International Institute for Strategic Studies, 1986), p. 212.

Chapter 9: Exploring the Alternatives: Military Production for a Permanent Canadian Peace Initiative

[1]Michael Brzoska and Thomas Ohlson, "A Buyers' Market: The Arms Trade in the 1980s," *ADIU Report* (Sussex, England: University of Sussex, Science Policy Research Unit, March-April 1986), p. 5.

[2]William J. Yost, *Industrial Mobilization in Canada* (Ottawa: Conference of Defence Associates, 1983), p. 5.

[3]Ibid., p. 5

[4]Stephen Clarkson, *Canada and the Reagan Challenge: Crisis in the Canadian-American Relationship* (Toronto: James Lorimer and Co./Canadian Institute for Economic Policy, 1982), p. 266.

[5]R.A. Young, "Free Trade: The Effect on Canada," Toronto *Globe and Mail*, May 9, 1985.

[6]Soviet conventional weapons superiority can be granted for the sake of argument, but there are those who doubt that it represents a militarily significant or usable superiority. See for example Tom Gervasi, *The Myth Of Soviet Military Superiority* (New York: Harper and Row, 1986), in particular the chapter on "The Balance of Ground Forces in Europe."

[7]George F. Kennan, "A New Philosophy of Defense," *New York Review of Books*, February 13, 1986.

[8]Ulrich Albrecht, "Alternative Designs of European Security: The Palme Commission Report and the Conventionalization of Forces," a paper presented to a 1985 conference at the University of Toronto on European Security Requirements and the Mutual Balanced Force Reduction Talks.

[9]Ibid.

[10]Ibid.

[11]Kennan, "New Philosophy of Defense."

[12]Joel J. Sokolsky and Joseph T. Jockel, "Canada: The Not So Faithful Ally," *Washington Quarterly*, Fall 1984.

[13]Quoted by Gwynne Dyer, Kitchener-Waterloo *Record*, July 4, 1986.

[14]Quoted by Val Sears, *Toronto Star*, May 24, 1986.

[15]Steven Baranyi, "Peacekeeping Updated," letter to the *Ploughshares Monitor*, September 1986.

[16]Lt.-Col. J.R. MacPherson, "A Canadian Initiative and Its Results: Active Peacekeeping after Thirty Years," *Canadian Defence Quarterly*, Summer 1986.

[17]Interview, *Peace Magazine*, June/July 1986.

[18]Parliament, Senate, Committee on Foreign Affairs, *Report on Canada-U.S. Relations*, vol. 2, *Canada's Trade with the U.S.*, 30th Parliament, 3rd Session, 1977–78.

[19]Ibid.

[20]Toronto *Globe and Mail*, September 14, 1984.

[21]Ibid.

[22]Miles D. Wolpin, "Third World Repression: Parameters and Prospects," *Peace and Change*, 11, no. 2 (1986): p. 119.

[23]Department of External Affairs, "Export Controls Policy," Press Release no. 155 and accompanying documents, September 10, 1986.

[24]Ibid.

[25]Ibid.

[26]Taskforce on the Churches and Corporate Responsibility and Project Ploughshares, joint letter to the Secretary of State for External Affairs, January 10, 1986.

[27]Department of External Affairs, "Export Control Policy."

[28]Secretary of State for External Affairs, letter to the Taskforce on the Churches and Corporate Responsibility, June 15, 1982.

[29]Brzoska and Ohlson, "A Buyers' Market."

[30]Rt. Hon. Joe Clark, Secretary of State for External Affairs, *Canada's International Relations: Response of the Government of Canada to the Report of the Special Joint Committee of the Senate and the House of Commons* (Ottawa, 1986), p. 48.

Index